Thomas Cadell, Richard Chandler, James Dodsley, George Robinson,
Peter Elmsley, Daniel Prince, James Robson

Travels in Greece

An Account of a Tour Made at the Expense of the Society of Dilettanti

Thomas Cadell, Richard Chandler, James Dodsley, George Robinson, Peter Elmsley, Daniel Prince, James Robson

Travels in Greece

An Account of a Tour Made at the Expense of the Society of Dilettanti

ISBN/EAN: 9783337345853

Printed in Europe, USA, Canada, Australia, Japan

Cover: Foto ©Andreas Hilbeck / pixelio.de

More available books at **www.hansebooks.com**

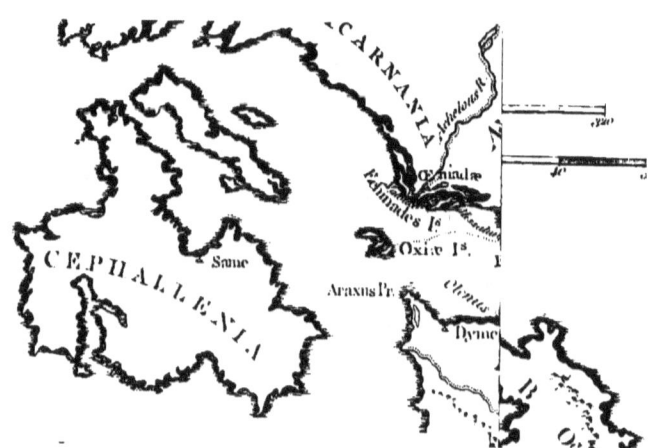

TRAVELS

IN

GREECE:

OR

AN ACCOUNT OF A TOUR

MADE AT THE EXPENSE

OF THE SOCIETY

OF

DILETTANTI.

By RICHARD CHANDLER, D.D.
FELLOW OF MAGDALEN COLLEGE,
AND OF THE SOCIETY OF ANTIQUARIES.

EST QUODAM PRODIRE TENUS, SI NON DATUR ULTRA.
HORAT.

OXFORD:
PRINTED AT THE CLARENDON PRESS.
M. DCC. LXX. VI.
Sold by J. DODSLEY, J. ROBSON, T. CADELL, P. ELMSLY, and
G. ROBINSON, LONDON; and by D. PRINCE, OXFORD.

THE PLATES.

To face p. 1. A Map of part of GREECE and of the PELOPONNESUS by KITCHIN.

p. 20. A Plan of Port PIRÆUS.

N. B. This and the following, the Plan of ATHENS excepted, may be found in a very valuable work entitled *Descripticn Géographique du Golfe de Venife et de la Morée. Par le Sieur Bellin, Ingénieur de la Marine, &c. Paris* 1771. Some alterations and additions are here made in the titles and in the names of places.

p. 25. A Plan of ATHENS, taken from *Atene Attica*, an account of that city when under the Venetians, publifhed in 1707 by *Fanelli*; improved and adapted to this Work.

p. 204. A Chart of the Bay of SALAMIS, with the Piræus, &c. given in Bellin as the road of Athens.

p. 210. A Plan of the Harbour of TROEZEN, and of the ifland of CALAUREA with the adjacent coaft.

p. 234. A Chart of the ISTHMUS of CORINTH, taken in 1697 by order of *Cornaro*, Captain-General of the troops of the republic of VENICE.

p. 282. A Chart of the Iflands of ST. MAURA, CEPHALLENIA, ZANTE, and the adjacent Coafts.

REFERENCES

TO THE

PLAN OF ATHENS.

A A   The Iliffus.
B   Muféum, and the monument of Philopappus.
C   Lycabettus.
D   Areopagus.
E   Temple of Thefeus.
F F F The town, with its walls.
G G   The Acropolis or Citadel.
H   The Propylea.
    a b The antient entrance.
    c   The right wing, or temple of Victory.
    d   The left wing.
I .   The Parthenon, or great temple of Minerva.
    e   The Mofque.
K   The Erectheum.

f The

f	The temple of Neptune.
g	The temple of Minerva Polias.
h	The portico of the temple of Minerva Polias.
L	The Pandroseum.
i	The cave of Pan, beneath the temple of Victory.
k	A fountain.
l	Pelasgicon.
m	Cavern.
M	The theatre of Bacchus.
n	Cave, and the choragic monument above the theatre.
N	The Odeum.
o o	The Ceramicus *within the city*.
p p	Cœle, or *The Hollow*.
O	Pnyx.
P	Gymnasium of Ptolemy.
Q	Prytanéum.
R	A Doric vestibule, or the portal of the new Agora or Market-place.
S	The tower of the Winds.
T	The choragic monument of Lysicrates.
U	Hadrian's Gate.
V	The temple of Jupiter Olympius.
W	Anchesinus.
q	Ionic columns.
r	A church.
X	The bridge over the Ilissus.
Y	The Stadium.
s	The private way.
Z	The Eleusinium, or temple of Ceres and Proserpine.
t	A rocky dell.
1	Mosques in the town.
2	A mosque, which served as a magazine.
3	A mosque, which was the Lutheran church.
4	A column then standing.
5	A church.
6	A church.
7	Temple of the Muses, according to *Fanelli*.
8	Sepulchres, stiled by *Fanelli* the prisons of Areopagus.

CONTENTS.

CHAPTER I.

OUR bark——We leave Smyrna——The sails and yards ——We put into a creek——The vintage begun—— Off Psyra—— A storm—— The night——We gain a port in Eubœa——Sail by Carystus——In a creek of Attica. Page 1

CHAP. II.

Set sail——Of Hydre——We pass the island Helene——In the port of Sunium—Of the town—The temple of Minerva Sunias—Hydriote vessels. 5

CHAP III.

Of the island Ægina—We sail by the island of Patroclus—Our mariners—We arrive at Ægina—View from mount Panhellenius—Story of Æacus—Temple of Jupiter—We set sail for the city of Ægina. 9

CHAP. IV.

Shoals and rocks——A phænomenon——We anchor in the mole of Ægina——Of the city——Of the barrow of Phocus—— Phreattys——Of Oea——The present town——The island. 13

CHAP.

ii   CONTENTS.

CHAP. V.

We arrive in the Piræus — Of the ports of Athens — Phalerum and Munychia — Remark on Phalerum — Piræus — The town — The long walls — Other fortifications — Their state under the Romans — Present state of Phalerum and Munychia — Of the Piræus — Inscriptions.   18

CHAP. VI.

We set out for Athens — Two roads described by Pausanias — The barrow of Euripides — The public cisterns — M. Lycabettus — We arrive at the French convent — Reception at Athens.   23

CHAP. VII.

The city of Cecrops ——— Athens burned by the Persians, &c. ——— Under the Macedonians ——— Receives a Roman garrison ——— Defaced by Sylla ——— State under the Roman emperors ——— Governed by a pro-consul ——— Kindness of Hadrian ——— The city-wall restored ——— Besieged and taken ——— Favoured by Constantine the great ——— In danger from the Goths ——— Sacked by Alaric ——— A chasm in its history ——— Under various masters after the twelfth century ——— Unknown in the sixteenth ——— Antient extent of the walls.   27

CHAP. VIII.

Of modern Athens ——— The antiquities ——— The citadel ——— Its antient and present state.   34

CHAP. IX.

Of Pericles ——— Of his buildings ——— Entrance of the acropolis ——— The propylæa ——— Story of the architect ——— The temple of Victory, or right wing of the propylæa ——— The left wing ——— Present state of the propylæa ——— Of the temple ——— Ignorance of the Turks and Greeks ——— Of the left wing ——— The propylæa when ruined ——— Inscription on a pedestal.   38

CHAP.

CONTENTS.

CHAP. X.

Of the parthenon——*Of the statue of Minerva*——*Of Phidias* ——*The statue remaining after Julian*——*When removed* ——*The temple when ruined*——*Described in 1676*—— *Present state*——*The pediments*——*Other sculptures*—— *Copied by Mr. Pars.* 44

CHAP. XI.

Of the Erectheum——*Temple of Neptune*——*Temple of Minerva Polias*——*Story of Pandrosos*——*Present state of the temples of Neptune and Minerva*——*Of the Pandroseum*—— *Business of the virgins called Canephori*——*Images of Minerva* ——*The treasury*——*Inscriptions.* 52

CHAP. XII.

Front of the hill of the acropolis——*The cave of Apollo and Pan*——*A fountain and statue*——*The pelasgicon and long rocks*——*An inscription*——*The theatre of Bacchus*—— *The Athenians fond of gladiators*——*A grotto and choragic monument*——*The Odéum of Pericles and Atticus Herodes.* 58

CHAP. XIII.

Of the areopagus——*The tribunal when extinct*——*The pnyx* ——*Account of pnyx.* 66

CHAP. XIV.

Story of Theseus——*A temple erected to him*——*The decorations* ——*Present state of the temple*——*The sculptures*—— *Gymnasium of Ptolemy.* 69

CONTENTS.

CHAP. XV.

A marble arch or gate-way——The temple of Jupiter Olympius —— Not finished before Hadrian——Number of statues, &c. ——The ruin——Of the water of Athens——An aquæduct ——Of the Eridanus and Ilissus——Remark——An antient bridge   73

CHAP. XVI.

The stadium——Rebuilt by Atticus Herodes——Present state ——A temple by the Ilissus——Once the Eleusinium——The lesser mysteries——Temple of Diana the huntress——The fountain Callirhoe or Enneacrunus——Scene of a dialogue of Plato——Changed.   80

CHAP. XVII.

The Museum——Monument of Philopappus——Sepulchres—— The Cimonian sepulchres——The eminence fronting the acropolis.   85

CHAP. XVIII.

Of the gate called Dipylon——Abstract of Pausanias——The Pompeium, &c.——Statues of Jupiter and Hadrian——Of Harmodius and Aristogiton——Paintings in Pœcile——The region called Melite——The Agora——The altar of Pity.   89

CHAP. XIX.

Abstract of Pausanias——Of the temple of the Dioscuri and of Agraulos——Columns of different kinds of marble——Of the Delphinium——Of the temple of Venus in the gardens.   94

CHAP.

CONTENTS.

CHAP XX.

Abstract of Pausanias——The Prytanéum——Of the street called The Tripods and a monument remaining——Inscriptions——The Dionysium——Other temples——Of Pandion and of the goddess Rome, &c. in the Acropolis——The fountain Empedo——Cessation of the magistracies at Athens——Of the Panathenæan procession. 96

CHAP. XXI.

Omissions in Pausanias——The tower of the Winds——Dance of the Dervishes——A Doric portal——Supposed the entrance of an Agora——The Athenians given to flattery——Pausanias illustrated. 103

CHAP. XXII.

Athens the seat of philosophy——The way to the Academy——Of the Academy——Of the Colonus Hippius——Gardens of Philosophers——The graves and sepulchres levelled——Site of the Academy——Colonus Hippius——The river Cephissus. 107

CHAP. XXIII.

The Lycéum——Cynosarges——Mention of them in Plato——The site. 111

CHAP. XXIV.

Of the University of Athens——The Professors——Degrees——Dresses——Manner of entrance——Character and extinction of the Philosophers——Ruin of the University. 113

CHAP. XXV.

Of the people of Athens——The Turkish government——The Turks——The Greeks——The Albanians——The Archbishop——Character of the Athenians. 117

CHAP.

CONTENTS.

CHAP. XXVI.

Care of the female sex at Athens— Dress of the Turkish women abroad—Of the Greek—Of the Albanian—Dress of the Greek at home—Manner of colouring the sockets of their eyes—Their education. 121

CHAP. XXVII.

Of the territory of Athens—The olive-groves—Bees—Provisions — Birds—Hare-calling—Wild beasts—The horned owl— A water-spout — Antient prognostics of weather — Sting of a scorpion. 125

CHAP. XXVIII.

We remove from the Convent—A Turk described—The Athenians civil to us—A Turkish foot-race and wrestling-match—Dance of the Arabian women—Greek dances—Marriages of the Turks—Of the Greeks—Of the Albanians—Funeral ceremonies—No learning—Credulity and superstition. 131

CHAP. XXIX.

We continue at Athens— Account of Lombardi—The archbishop forced to fly—Distress from want of corn—Intrigues of Lombardi. 138

CHAP. XXX.

Journey to mount Hymettus—An antient well—Vestiges of Alopece —Arrive at some bee-stands—Alarmed in the night—Turkish rigour—A well—The shaft of a mine—Dinner—At Dragonisi—A speckled owl—The monastery of St. Cyriani. 141

CHAP.

CONTENTS.

CHAP. XXXI.

Towns between Phalerum and Sunium——Capes and iſlands——Barrows by Alopece——Veſtiges of Æxone and Anagyrus——Entertained by a Greek Abbot——A Panéum or ſacred cave——Wheler's rout from Sunium to Athens——Remarks. 146

CHAP. XXXII.

Diſtinct provinces of the heathen gods——Their characters and places of worſhip——A Panéum or Nymphæum, with inſcriptions——Of Archidamus and the age when he lived——Of the Nymphs——Of Nympholepſy——Of ſacred caves——Of a cave in Ithaca——In Paphlagonia——Of the two entrances——The offerings——Deſign of the cave. 149

CHAP. XXXIII.

Towns on the eaſtern coaſt of Attica——Of Thoricus——Of Potamus——Of Praſiæ——Of the port of Praſiæ or port Raphti——The road to it from Athens——Extract from Wheler continued. 156

CHAP. XXXIV.

Road to Marathon——Of Cephiſia——An inſcription at Oxford brought from thence——Another inſcription——Journey continued——Of Brauron——Of Marathon——Funeral of Atticus Herodes——Paſs the night on Pentele. 159

CHAP. XXXV.

Of the plain of Marathon——Extract from Wheler——Of Rhamnus——The battle of Marathon——Deſcription from Pauſanias——The large barrow. 163

CHAP.

CONTENTS.

CHAP. XXXVI.
A cave and the goat-stand of Pan near Marathon——Story of the woman of Nonoï——Way to the cave——Account of it ——Remarks. 166

CHAP. XXXVII.
Ascend mount Pentele——The Quarries——Chapels, &c.——The Monastery of Pentele—— Return to Athens —— Numerous Churches, &c. 169

CHAP. XXXVIII.
The northern boundary of Attica——Wheler's rout from Marathon to Oropus—— Eleutheræ—— Deceleia——Phyle—— Harma——Wheler's rout from Thebes to Athens. 172

CHAP. XXXIX.
Excursions by sea——The straits of Salamis——Manner of fishing with a light——Mode of living——Arrive at Eleusis. 175

CHAP. XL.
Of the Eleusinian Mysteries——Of Eleusis——Of the mystic temple and the ministers——Of the secrecy observed by the initiated—An hypothesis concerning the design of the mysteries — Account of the ceremony of initiation — The foundation of the mysteries. 178

CHAP. XLI.
The procession of Iacchus from Athens—The sacred way to the mountains—The monastery of Daphne, &c.—The sacred way beyond, to Eleusis — The Rhiti or salt-streams, &c.—An Inscription—Incursions of the Lacedæmonians into Attica. 183

CHAP.

CONTENTS.

CHAP. XLII.
Extinction of the Eleusinian mysteries—Of Eleusis—Of the mystic temple, &c.—Other remains—Road to Megara. 188

CHAP. XLIII.
Proceed to Megara—Of the port and town Nisæa—Of Megara —The stone—An inscription—Dread of Corsairs—Of the Megaris—Our lodging, &c. 192

CHAP. XLIV.
Leave Megara—Vestiges of buildings—Of the Scironian rocks and way—The present road to Corinth—Pass the night in a cave—Coast by the Scironian way—Vestiges of Cromyon— —Of Sidús. 196

CHAP. XLV.
Land on the isthmus of Corinth---At Epidaurus and Methana--- On the islets in the gulf---At Ægina---On the island of Salamis 199

CHAP. XLVI.
Of Salamis---Islets---Fragments on Cynosura---Trophy for the battle of Salamis---The city---Village of Albanians---Old Salamis---The flower of Ajax. 201

CHAP. XLVII.
An antient oracle---The battle of Salamis---Flight of the Persian fleet. 204

CHAP. XLVIII.
Intended rout from Athens---Prepare for our departure---At the Piræus---Embark---Land on Munychia---Pass a haunted rock ---Land on an islet---On Ægina. 206

CHAP.

CONTENTS.

CHAP. XLIX.
Sail from Ægina---The island and town of Poro---The monastery---Way to Calaurea---Of the city---The remains---A goatherd. 209

CHAP. L.
Sail up the harbour of Trœzen --- Land on the peninsula of Methana---The bay or lake---Of Trœzen---The ruins — The Acropolis---The water---Of Damalá--- A proverbial saying. 213

CHAP. LI.
The gulf of Epidauria---Of Methana---An antient charm---A hot spring---The islets---Of Epidaurus---The harbour. 218

CHAP. LII.
Land in Epidauria---Set out on foot for the grove of Æsculapius ---At Ligurió---The evening---Remains by Ligurió. 221

CHAP. LIII.
The grove of Æsculapius---His statue and temple---Inscriptions ---The Stadium---The Theatre---Mount Cynortium---Water, &c.---Serpents 223

CHAP. LIV.
Leave Ligurió--- Nauplia --- Tiryns --- The river Inachus --- Old Argos --- The present town. 226

CHAP. LV.
Mycenæ near Argos---Agamemnon slain at Mycenæ---The city ruined---The temple of Juno---We miss the site. 229

CHAP.

CONTENTS.

CHAP. LVI.

We arrive at Nemea——Of the temple of Jupiter——The Nemean games——Ruin of the temple——Mount Apesas, &c. A village, and monastery. 231

CHAP. LVII.

To Cleonæ——Arrive at Corinth——The situation——The ports ——The city destroyed and repeopled——Described by Strabo ——By Pausanias——Taken by Alaric and the Turks—— Its present state——A ruin. 234

CHAP. LVIII.

Of the Isthmus——The place where vessels were drawn over—— Attempts to unite the two seas——A wall erected across—— The temple of Isthmian Neptune——The site. 240

CHAP. LIX.

The Archbishop of Athens restored——We leave Corinth—— Embark——Of Anticyra——The site. 244

CHAP. LX.

At Dystomo——An inscription——Ambryssus——The road to Anticyra. 246

CHAP. LXI.

Way from Ambryssus to Stiris——Of Stiris——Inscriptions. 247

CHAP. LXII.

Summary of the Life of St. Luke of Stiris. 249

CONTENTS.

CHAP. LXIII.

The monaſtery of St. Luke——The founder——The church—— The reliques of St. Luke——The tombs of the emperor Romanus and his queen——The hermitage. 252

CHAP. LXIV.

Of Bulis——Places on the coaſt between Bulis and the Iſthmus ——The bay of Livadoſtro——Aſcra——Mount Helicon ——The grove of the Muſes——Of the ſite, &c. 256

CHAP. LXV.

We leave Dyſtomo——The way called Schiſte——The road into Phocis from Bœotia——Of Orchomenus and Chæronea——We arrive at Delphi. 259

CHAP. LXVI.

Sanctity of Delphi——The Amphictyonic aſſembly——The oracle ——The temple——Its riches——Its decline. 260

CHAP. LXVII.

Site of Delphi——The court of the temple——Extinction of Apollo ——Veſtiges——An inſcription——Other inſcriptions—— Caſtalia. 264

CHAP. LXVIII.

Of mount Parnaſſus——The Corycian cave——Wheler's journey on mount Parnaſſus——Remarks——Some Albanians arrive at the monaſtery. 268

CHAP. LXIX.

Of Cirrha——Of Amphiſſa——The port of Delphi——We leave Delphi——Embark. 271

CHAP.

CONTENTS.

CHAP. LXX.

At Gallixithium———*At Thithavra*———*A plane-tree on the shore of the Morea*———*Site of Boſlitza*———*Ægium*———*The mouth of the gulf*———*Lepanto*———*The Caſtles*———*Arrive at Pátræ.* 273

CHAP. LXXI.

Of Patræ———*The city*———*Feaſt of Diana*———*The preſent town*———*The ſouth ſide of the gulf of Corinth*———*Neglect of travellers.* 276

CHAP. LXXII.

We leave Patræ———*On the coaſt of Ætolia*———*Flats*———*The river Achelous*———*The iſlands called Echinades*———*The Fiſhery*———*A monoxylo or ſkiff*———*Towns*———*Cauſe of the bad air in the gulf*———*Encroachments of the river.* 279

CHAP. LXXIII.

We ſail———*In the bay of Chiarenza*———*Cyllene*———*At Gaſtouni*———*At Elis*———*Its territory ſacred*———*The city*———*Veſtiges.* 282

CHAP. LXXIV.

Set out for Olympia———*Arrangement of the coaſt*———*At a monaſtery*———*The night*———*A tree-frog*———*At Pyrgo*———*Pitch our tent by a ruin*———*Gnats.* 286

CHAP. LXXV.

Of Piſa———*Of Olympia*———*Of the temple of Jupiter*———*The ſtatue*———*The great altar*———*Other altars*———*Riches of Olympia*———*Solemnity of the games*———*Herodes a benefactor*———*Ruin of Olympia.* 289

CONTENTS.

CHAP. LXXVI.

Vestiges of Olympia——Miráca——The river Alpheus. 294

CHAP. LXXVII.

Journey of Mr. Bocher——Ruin of a temple——Near Phigalia. 295

CHAP. LXXVIII.

Our situation——We return to Chiarenza——Arrive at Zante——Perform quarantine——Remove from the Lazaretto. 297

CHAP. LXXIX.

Of the island of Zante——The city——The Corinth-grape——Currants——Extract from Herodotus——The tar-springs——Remarks——Earthquakes——Not able to proceed——Occurrences at Zante——Embark for England. 299

ERRATA.

PAGE 3, l. 25, read " latin or"
7, l. 14, read " sea urchin" and " coast, full of prickles like a chesnut," Correct also, p. 177, l. 12. p. 208, l. 17.
8, l. antepenult. read " and a quarter"
28, l. 2, Note, " *by the*"
33, l. penult. " thirty five"
36, l. 27, " gulf, and".
    l. 28, " is pleasant, but too airy"
37, l. penult. " needs" l. ult." " in order to"
52, and p. 53, and p. 179, " Erechtheum" and " Erechtheus"
52, l. 13, l. 19, " Neptune-Erechtheus"
63, l. penult. " Thrasyllus"
75, l. 18, l. 19, " Jupiter, which is worth seeing, resembles the other
    " statues of him in size, except that those"
    l. 20, " are colossal, and is made"
    l. 28, " Colossus, which is".
78, l. 2. " adopted son"
93, l. 4, " had tents"
94, l. 23, " Ilithya"
101, l. 1, " city ı"
104, l. 4, " On a sudden"
    l. antepenult. " and, it"
106, l. 7, " conferring of" l. 9. " placing of"
107, l. 4, " except in name and"
120, l. penult. " πτον ;" l. ult. " *and what ?*"
127, l. 16, " beccafico"
130, l. 17, " less" and also, p. 193, l. 5. p. 228, l. 5.
132, l. 23, " sweetmeats"
139, l. 31, " and another"
176, l. 2, Note, " mitiget"
177, l. 16, " pinna marina"
180, l. 26, " of this"
183, l. 15, " silence ı" and at the bottom of the page " ı See what
    " is said of the Lesser Eleusinian Mysteries, p. 82."
185, l. 1, " it, is" l. 16, omit " or *the painted*"
197, l. 6, p. 198, l. 26, " Melicertes"
210, l. antepenult. " rowed"
238, l. 29, l. 30, " of too much consequence"
244, l. ult. " pop-guns. Our"
281, l. antepenult. " to and from the shore"
291, l. 21, " neither oil nor water"
293, l. 4, " connoisseur"
294, l. 7. " with the"
302, l. 22, " marish"

Lately Published.

(Inscribed by the Society of DILETTANTI to his Majesty)

IONIAN ANTIQUITIES;

OR,

Ruins of magnificent and famous Buildings in IONIA.

Sold by J. ROBSON, in Bond-Street, London.

ALSO,

(Inscribed to the Society of DILETTANTI)

INSCRIPTIONES ANTIQVAE,

PLERAEQVE NONDVM EDITAE:

IN ASIA MINORI ET GRAECIA, PRAESERTIM ATHENIS, COLLECTAE.

CVM APPENDICE.

Exscripsit ediditque R. CHANDLER, S. T. P.
COLL. MAGD. ET SOC. ANTIQ. SOCIVS.

OXONII M DCC LXXIV.

Prostant apud J. DODSLEY, JAC. ROBSON, et THO. CADELL, Londini;
et D. PRINCE, Oxonii.

ALSO,

TRAVELS IN ASIA MINOR.

TRAVELS
IN
GREECE.

CHAPTER I.

Our bark---We leave Smyrna---The sails and yards---We put into a creek---The vintage begun---Off Psyra---A storm------The night---We gain a port in Eubœa---Sail by Caryſtus---In a creek of Attica.

THE bark, engaged for our voyage from Smyrna to Athens, was one belonging to Hydre, a ſmall iſland or rather rock near Scyllæum, a promontory of the Peloponneſus oppoſite to Sunium in Attica. It had two maſts, with fourteen men. The hire was one hundred piaſters; and we agreed to pay a piaſter and a half a day, if we did not depart within ten days; and alſo, if we tarried beyond three days at Sunium or Ægina, at which places we purpoſed to touch in our way.

Our baggage and proviſions were put on board on Tueſday Auguſt 20, 1765. A gentle land-breeze, as uſual, ſprung up about midnight. We bade adieu to our friends the Engliſh conſul conful and Mr. Lee, who accompanied us to our boat; which rowed to the Frank Scale or Key for Europeans. We were hailed by a Turkish officer of the cuftoms, and immediately difmiffed. We reached our bark, and weighed anchor.

OUR veffel carried two triangular fails, each on a very long yard, thick at bottom, tapering upwards, like a bull-rufh, and faftened to the top of the maft, fo as to be moveable every way, like a lever on a pole, fuch as is ufed for drawing water out of wells. In tacking, the big end, which is always the lower, with the rigging, is fhifted over to the oppofite fide. The fharp end is very often high in the air apeak.

IN the morning the Inbat met us, and we put for fhelter into a fmall creek on the right hand, near the mouth of the gulf. The boys, climbing up the mafts with bare feet and holding by two ropes, beftrode the yards and gathered in the canvafs, furling it quite to the extremities. A Venetian fhip, which had failed from Smyrna fome days before, and was lying at anchor within the bay, afforded us an inftance of the flow progrefs, and confequently tedious voyages, for which that flag is noted and ridiculed in the Levant.

BETWEEN the mountains near us, by the fea fide, was a fmall green valley, in which were fcattered a few mean houfes. There the vintage was now begun; the black grapes being fpread on the ground in beds, expofed to the fun to dry for raifins; while in another part, the juice was expreffed for wine, a man, with feet and legs bare, treading the fruit in a kind of ciftern, with a hole or vent near the bottom, and a veffel beneath it to receive the liquor.

WHEN morning approached, the land-breeze re-commenced. The boys mounted the yards, and as they defcended, untied the knots of the fails very expeditioufly. Our captain knew every ifland, rock and cape; fteering from promontory to promontory.
One

One of the sailors, his brother, fell overboard; but swimming he was soon taken up. We came between Lesbos and Chios, passed by the north end of the latter, and, as Nestor did on his return from Troy, toward Psyra. This little island was reckoned forty stadia, or five miles in circuit[1]; and fifty stadia, or six miles and a quarter, from Melæna, a promontory of Chios. It lay opposite to the rugged tract called Arvisia, once famous for its nectar. The wind was northerly and strong, and it was apprehended would become contrary; being remarked to set commonly into the gulf of Thessalonica during the day, at this season; and to go back again, as it were, toward morning; in the same manner as the Inbat and land-breeze prevail alternately in the gulf of Smyrna. We endeavoured to get under the lee of Psyra, and succeeding, we sailed by a chapel of St. George standing on a head-land, when the captain and crew made their crosses very devoutly. The same ceremony was repeated soon after at one of the Panagia or Virgin Mary. We then opened the harbour of the town, and were desirous to put in, but the wind would not permit.

THE day had been cloudy, and distant flashes of pale lightning in the south, with screaming voices in the air, as was surmised, of some sea-bird flying to land, seemed to portend a blustering and disagreeable night. The captain, who was skilled in the previous signs of foul weather, prepared his bark by taking down the triangular main-sail, and hoisting a latin ro square one, as more manageable. The wind increasing and the sea running very high, our vessel laboured exceedingly. It was now total darkness, no moon or stars, but the sky expanding terribly on all sides with livid flames, disclosing the bright waves vehemently assailing, and every moment apparently swelling to overwhelm us. It thundered also, and rained heavily.

[1] Strabo p. 645. Cellarius has confounded the two islands, and made the city Chios, instead of Psyra, to be forty stadia in circuit. p. 12.

THE poop of our boat was covered, and would contain three perfons lying along or fitting. It was furnifhed with arms, and in a niche was a picture of the Panagia, of a faint, and of the crucifixion, on boards, with a lamp burning in a lanthorn. This feemed an eligible retreat from the noife and confufion on the open deck, where all hands were fully employed. The veffel fhook, and heeled to and fro exceffively; the violence of its motion fhifting me from fide to fide feveral times, though I ftrove to preferve my pofition unaltered. The captain at intervals looked in, and invoked his deities to affuage the wind and fmooth the waves; or, proftrate on his belly, infpected the compafs by the glimmering light of the lamp, and gave directions to the man at the helm. The tardy morning, as it were, mocked our impatience, while we continued beating the waves and tofling. At length it dawned, when we found we had been driven from our courfe; but the gale abated, leaving behind a very turbulent fwell.

THE following day was confumed in ftanding to and fro between the ifland Andros, and a cape now called D'Oro, but antiently Caphareus, the fouthern promontory of Euboea toward the Hellefpont; once noted for dangerous currents, and the deftruction of the Grecian fleet on its return from Troy. Before midnight we gained a fmall port beyond it; where we found at day-break a couple of goat-herds, with their flocks, traces of a wall, and of a chapel of the Panagia. On a rocky eminence was the ruin of a pharos erected, we were told, by a Corfair for the benefit of fignals, and to facilitate his entering in the dark.

GERÆSTUS, the fouthern promontory of Euboea toward Attica, was reckoned ten miles from Andros, and thirty-nine from the ifland Cea. Between it and Caphareus was a city named Caryftus, and near it a quarry, with a temple of *The marble Apollo*, from which they croffed to Alæ of Araphen in Attica. The columns cut there were much efteemed and celebrated for their beauty. It produced alfo a ftone, the
amianthus,

amianthus, which, when combed, was woven into towels. Plutarch relates, that some fibres only, or narrow threads, of this substance were discovered in his time; but that towels made of it, with nets and cawls used by women for their hair, were then extant, and, when soiled, were thrown into a fire, by which they were rendered white and clean, as by washing. We sailed by the town, which retains its antient name, in the morning. It stands at some distance from the shore; the houses rising on the bare slope of a rocky hill. The inhabitants have a very bad character. The lofty summits of Oche, the mountain above it, were covered with white clouds.

IN the evening we were again forced into a port or creek; but we had now gained the European continent, and were arrived in Attica. We moored to a rock, on which was a ruined chapel of the Panagia. This being Saturday, our mariners about sunset bore thither Labdanum to be used as incense, with coals of fire, and performed their customary devotions.

CHAP. II.

Set sail --- Of Hydre --- We pass the island Helene --- In the port of Sunium --- Of the town --- The temple of Minerva Sunias --- Hydriote vessels.

EARLY in the morning we steered with a favourable breeze toward Sunium, a promontory of Attica fronting the islands called Cyclades and the Ægean sea; distant three hundred stadia or thirty-seven miles and a half from the southermost promontory of Euboea named Leuce or *White*. The sun arose burnishing the silver deep, skirted by the Attic and Peloponnesian coasts. We had capes, mountains, and islands in view; and among the latter, the Hydriotes soon discovered their native rock, which they beheld, though bare and producing nothing, with the same partiality of affection, as if it were adorned with the golden fruits and perfumed by the aromatic gales of Scio; pointing it out, and expatiating on the liberty they possessed there.

HYDRE

6 TRAVELS IN GREECE.

HYDRE or Hydrea is on the coaſt of the Peloponneſus, and has been mentioned as lying in the way from Scyllæum to Hermione'. The inhabitants are maintained wholly by the ſea, to which the males are bred from their childhood. They now poſſeſſed, as we were told, above an hundred and twenty boats of various ſizes, ſome better armed for defence than ſeveral Engliſh veſſels frequenting the Archipelago. They are accounted the beſt ſailors in the Levant, boldly navigating in rough weather, and venturing to ſea at night, if in danger of being intercepted by an enemy or by pirates. They pay to the Grand Signior two purſes yearly, as caratch or tribute-money; which ſum, with expenſes, fees, and preſents, amounting nearly to two more, is aſſeſſed, at the rate of three piaſters a houſe. The captain-paſha ſends a galeote from Paros with officers, who receive it, and are entertained by a papas or Greek prieſt at the monaſtery by the ſea-ſide, below the town. No Turk reſides among them, and they enjoy the uſe of bells to their churches, without controul; a privilege on which they enlarge, as if alike pregnant with profit and delight.

WE now approached Cape Sunium, which is ſteep, abrupt, and rocky. On it is the ruin of the temple of Minerva Sunias, overlooking from its lofty ſituation the ſubject deep, and viſible from afar. We often loſt, and recovered again, the view of this beautiful object; ſailing on a wide canal, between Attica and Macroniſi² or *Long Iſland*. This was called antiently Helene, becauſe, it was ſaid, Helen had landed on it in her way to Lacedæmon, after Troy was taken. It ranges, like Eubœa, before the continent, and belonged to the Athenians; but was of little value, being rough and deſert. It was reckoned about

---

¹ Sailing from Scyllæum to Hermione was Point Bucephala, then the iſlands Haliuſa, Pityuſa, and Ariſteras; then the cape called Acra, then the iſland Tricrana, then a mountain projecting into the ſea, named Buporthmos, before which was the iſland Aperopia, and near it Hydrea. Pauſanias, p. 77.
² This iſland has been miſtaken for the Cranae of Homer. Vid. Strab. p. 398. Cellar. p. 830.

ſixty

TRAVELS IN GREECE.

fixty ftadia, or feven miles and an half long; five miles from Sunium, and as many from Cea, which lies beyond it.

THE waves, on our arrival near the promontory, broke gently, with a hollow murmur, at the foot of the rock beneath the temple. At the entrance of the fhining gulf was a little fleet of Hydriote veffels, eight in number, coming out with white triangular fails. We anchored within the cape in the port of Sunium, near three hours before mid-day; and landing, afcended to the ruin. Meanwhile our failors, except two or three who accompanied us, ftripped to their drawers to bathe, all of them fwimming and diving remarkably well; fome running about on the fharp rocks with naked feet, as if void of feeling; and fome examining the bottom of the clear water for the echinus or fea-chefnut, a fpecies of fhell-fifh common on this coaft, and now in perfection, the moon being nearly at the full.

SUNIUM was one of the demi or burrough-towns of Attica, belonging to the tribe named Attalis. It was fortified by the Athenians in the Peloponnefian war[1], as a fecure port for veffels with provifions. The fite, which has been long deferted, is overrun with bufhes of maftic, low cedars, and evergreens. The wall may be traced, running along the brow from near the temple, which it inclofed, down to the port. The mafonry was of the fpecies termed Pfeudifodomum. The fteep precipices and hanging rocks were a fufficient defence toward the mouth of the gulf. Some other fragments of folid wall remain, but nearly level with the ground. At the edge, near the port, the rock is fhelving, and refembles the cinder of a coal. There is a round well, and farther off at the mountain-foot was a pond, the water frefh, but hard and of a dark colour.

THE temple of Minerva Sunias was of white marble, and probably erected in the fame happy period with the great

[1] 4th Olymp. 91. Before Ch. 411.

temple

temple of Minerva called the Parthenon in the acropolis at Athens or in the time of Pericles, it having like proportions, though far inferior in magnitude. The order is Doric, and it appears to have been a fabric of exquisite beauty. It had six columns in front. Nine columns were standing on the southweſt side in the year 1676, and five on the oppoſite, with two antæ or pilaſters at the ſouth end, and part of the pronaos. The number is now twelve, beſides two in front and one of the antæ; the other lying in a heap, having been recently thrown down, as we were informed, by the famous Jaffier Bey, then captain of a Turkiſh galeote, to get at the metal uniting the ſtones. The ruin of the Pronaos is much diminiſhed. The columns next to the ſea are ſcaled and damaged, owing to their aſpect. We ſearched diligently for inſcriptions, but without ſucceſs, except finding on the wall of the temple many modern names, with the following memorial in Greek, cut in rude and barbarous characters, but with ſome labour : *Oneſimus remembered his Siſter Chreſte.* The old name Sunium is difuſed, and the cape diſtinguiſhed by its columns, *Capo Colonni.*

THE Hydriote fleet, which had ſailed out of the gulf when we arrived, returned on the following day, laden with corn from Cea, purchaſed for a Venetian armed ſhip, captain Alexander, who was then come to an anchor within the cape. This being a contraband cargo, was to be delivered clandeſtinely, and we were informed the boats had given to the commander of a Turkiſh cruiſer, which appeared in the offing, the ſum of fifteen piaſters each for his permiſſion to fulfil their contract without moleſtation. Sunium was reckoned three hundred and thirty ſtadia or forty-one miles and three quarters from the Piræus [1] or port of Athens.

[1] Strabo. In Pliny forty-two miles.

CHAP.

TRAVELS IN GREECE.

CHAP. III.

Of the island Ægina --- We sail by the island of Patroclus --- Our mariners --- We arrive at Ægina --- View from M. Panhellenius --- Story of Æacus --- Temple of Jupiter --- We set sail for the city of Ægina.

THE gulf included within the two promontories, Sunium and Scyllæum, contains several islands, of which Ægina is the principal. This island was surrounded by Attica, the Megaris or territory of Megara, and the Peloponnesus; each distant about one hundred stadia, or twelve miles and a half. In circumference it was reckoned one hundred and eighty stadia, or twenty-two miles and a half. It was washed on the east and south by the Myrtoan and Cretan seas. It is now called Eyina or Egina; the *g* soft and the *i* short. " What occasion is there, exclaims Strabo, to mention, that this is one of the islands which have been excessively renowned? since it was the country of Æacus; it has enjoyed naval dominion; and has disputed with Athens the prize of superior glory in the famous battle with the Persian fleet off Salamis."

THE distant hills continued hazy; but the wind being fair, we embarked on the second evening after our landing at Sunium, and setting sail, passed very near to a small island called Gaitharonesi (*Asses Island*), a naked rock, except a few bunches of thyme; not even a shrub growing on it; the clefts inhabited by wild pigeons. It once bore the name of Patroclus, by whom it was fortified with a wall and fosse. He was sent with some Egyptian triremes to assist the Athenians against Antigonus son of Demetrius. Sailing on, we had on our right hand the mountain Laurium, formerly noted for silver mines. The coast of Attica was bare and of a parched aspect.

C   WE

TRAVELS IN GREECE.

WE had now sea-room and a prosperous gale. The genius of the Greek nation prevailed, and was displayed in the festivity of our mariners. One of the crew played on the violin and on the lyre; the latter, an ordinary instrument with three strings, differing from the kitara, which has two and a much longer handle. The captain, though a bulky man, excelled, with two of his boys, in dancing. We had been frequently amused by these adepts. It mattered not whether the vessel was still in port, or rolling, as now, on the waves. They exerted an extraordinary degree of activity, and preserved their footing, for which a very small space on the deck sufficed, with wonderful dexterity. Their common dance, which was performed by one couple, consisted chiefly in advancing and retiring, expanding the arms, snapping the fingers, and changing places; with feats, some ludicrous, and to our apprehension indecent.

THE sun sat very beautifully, illuminating the mountain-tops, and was succeeded by a bright moon in a blue sky. We had a pleasant breeze, and the land in view, sailing as it were on a wide river. A smart gale following a short calm, and driving us along at a great rate, in the morning by sun-rise we had reached Ægina, and were entering a bay; the mountain Panhellenius, covered with trees, sloping before us, and a temple on its summit, near an hour distant from the shore, appearing as in a wood. The water being shallow, a sailor leaped overboard, carrying a rope to be fastened, as usual, to some stone or crag by the sea-side.

WE set out for the temple, which was dedicated to Jupiter Panhellenius, on foot, with a servant and some of the crew bearing our umbrellas and other necessaries. One of the sailors had on a pair of sandals made of goat-skin, the hairy side outward. The ascent was steep, rough, and stony, between bushes of mastic, young cedars, and fir-trees, which scented the air very agreeably. Some tracts were quite bare. On the eminence

nence our toil was rewarded by an extenfive view of the Attic and Peloponnefian coafts, the remoter mountains inland, and the fummits in the Ægean Sea; the bright furface, which intervened, being ftudded as it were with iflands; many lying round Ægina, toward the continent; and one, called antiently Belbina, ftretching out toward the mouth of the gulf. We faw diftinctly the acropolis of Athens, feated on a hill near the middle of a plain, and encompaffed with mountains, except toward the fea; a portion of its territory, covered with dufky olive-groves, looking black, as if under a dark cloud.

T H E name Panhellenius was probably given to this mountain from the temple, for which only it was noted. That fabric, as the Æginetans affirmed, was erected by Æacus, the renowned anceftor of the illuftrious family of the Æacidæ. He was reputed the fon of Ægina the daughter of Afopus by Jupiter, who tranfported her into this ifland, then uninhabited and called Oenone. To omit the fabulous account of its population; in his time Hellas was terribly oppreffed by drought; the god raining neither on the country without the ifthmus, nor on the Peloponnefus. The Delphic oracle was confulted. The Pythia replied, that Jupiter muft be rendered propitious by Æacus. The cities intreated him to be their mediator. He facrificed and prayed to Jupiter Panhellenius, and procured rain. Paufanias relates, that he faw the ftatues of the perfons deputed to attend him on that emergency, at the entrance of the Æacéum, a quadrangular wall of white ftone, by the city, inclofing fome antient olive-trees and a low altar; and alfo, that the other Greeks then concurred in affigning that reafon for the embaffy. On a fummit of Mount Sciron in Attica was a temple of Jupiter, furnamed Aphefius, from his remitting their calamity; and a ftatue of the Earth [1] in a fuppliant pofture, requefting Jupiter to fend her rain, which was in the acropolis at Athens, referred, it is moft likely, to the fame ftory.

[1] Paufanias, p. 57. See Bryant's Mythology, p. 414.

THE temple of Jupiter Panhellenius is of the Doric order, and had fix columns in front. It has twenty one of the exterior columns yet ftanding; with the two in the front of the pronaos and of the pofticum; and five of the number, which formed the ranges within the cell. The entablature, except the architrave, is fallen. The ftone is of a light brownifh colour, much eaten in many places, and by its decay witneffing a very great age. Some of the columns have been injured by boring to their centres for the metal. In feveral the junction of the parts is fo exact, that each feems to confift of one piece. Digging by a column of the portico of the naos, we difcovered a fragment of fine fculpture. It was the hind-part of a greyhound, of white marble, and belonged, it is probable, to the ornaments fixed on the freeze, which has a groove in it, as for their infertion. I fearched afterwards for this remnant, but found only a fmall bit, with fome fpars; fufficient to fhow that the trunk had been broken and removed. The temple was inclofed by a peribolus or wall, of which traces are extant. We confidered this ruin as a very curious article, fcarcely to be paralleled in its claim to remote antiquity. The fituation on a lonely mountain, at a diftance from the fea, has preferved it from total demolition amid all the changes and accidents of numerous centuries. Since the worfhip of Jupiter has been abolifhed, and Æacus forgotten, that has been its principal protection; and will, it is likely, in fome degree prolong its duration to ages yet remote.

WE continued our journies up the mountain, until our work was done, fetting out before fun-rife and returning to our bark in the evening. The heat of noon, during which we repofed under a tree or in the fhade of the temple, was exceffive. A fouth-eafterly wind fucceeded, blowing frefh, and murmuring amufively among the pines. On the third day toward evening, we defcended to the fhore, embarked haftily and unmoored; bringing away the carcafe of a pig on a wooden fpit, half roafted. We were apprehenfive left the wind, which at that feafon

commonly

TRAVELS IN GREECE. 13

commonly fets into the gulf in the day-time, and comes in a contrary direction foon after funfet, fhould fail, before we could reach the port of the antient city. The boys mounted to the fharp ends of the yards, high in air above the mafts, undid the knots of the fails, which were furled; and tied them anew with rufhes. We were towed out of the bay, and then pulling the ropes, the rufhes breaking fell down, and the canvafs fpread.

CHAP. IV.

Shoals and rocks --- A phænomenon --- We anchor in the mole of Ægina ---Of the city---Of the barrow of Phocus---Phreattys--- Of Oea --- The prefent town --- The ifland.

WE paffed round the eaftern end of the ifland, near a pointed rock called Turlo, and fometimes miftaken for a veffel under fail; the city Ægina fronting Libs or the fouth-weft. The coaft was moftly abrupt and inacceffible; the land within, mountainous and woody. Our crew was for fome time engaged in looking out for one of the lurking fhoals, with which it is environed. Thefe, and the fingle rocks extant above the furface, are fo many in number, and their pofition fo dangerous, that the navigation to Ægina was antiently reckoned more difficult than to any other of the iflands. The Æginetans, indeed, faid, they were purpofely contrived, and difpofed by Æacus to protect their property from piratical robbers, and for a terror to their enemies.

WE were now amufed by a very ftriking phænomenon. The fun was fetting; and the moon, then rifen in the eaftern or oppofite portion of the hemifphere, was feen adorned as it were with the beams of that glorious luminary, which appeared, probably from the reflexion or refraction of the atmofphere, not as ufual, but inverted, the fharp end pointing to the horizon, and the ray widening upwards.

THE

The evening was hazy, and the mountain-tops on the weſt and north-weſt enveloped in clouds; from which proceeded lightning, pale and forky, or reſembling the expanſion of a ball of fire. We were becalmed for a few minutes, but the breeze returned, and we moved pleaſantly along; the ſplendid moon diſcloſing the ſolemn hills, and the ſea as bright as placid. We now tacked, and ſtanding to the north-weſt, came to a barrow near the ſhore; and then doubling a low point of land, caſt anchor, about three hours after ſun-ſet, by a veſſel within the mole of the city Ægina.

The maritime genius of the old Æginetans was founded, like that of the preſent Hydriotes, upon neceſſity. This too produced among them the invention of ſilver coinage; their commerce requiring a medium, and their country furniſhing only ſuch unimportant articles for exportation, as rendered the venders proverbially contemptible. With this diſadvantage did the city Ægina become a rival of its neighbour Athens. Its ſite, which has been long forſaken, was now naked, except a few wild fig-trees, and ſome fences made by piling the looſe ſtones. It had produced corn, and was not cleared from the ſtubble. Inſtead of the temples mentioned by Pauſanias, we had in view thirteen lonely churches, all very mean, as uſual; and two Doric columns ſupporting their architrave. Theſe ſtand by the ſea-ſide toward the low cape; and, it has been ſuppoſed, are a remnant of a temple of Venus, which was ſituated by the port principally frequented. The theatre, which is recorded as worth ſeeing, reſembled that of the Epidaurians both in ſize and workmanſhip. It was not far from the private port; the ſtadium, which, like that at Priene, was conſtructed with only one ſide, being joined to it behind, and each ſtructure mutually ſuſtaining and propping the other. The walls belonging to the ports and arſenal were of excellent maſonry, and may be traced to a conſiderable extent, above, or nearly even with the water. At the entrance of the mole, on the left, is a ſmall

chapel

TRAVELS IN GREECE. 15

chapel of St. Nicholas; and oppofite, a fquare tower with fteps before it, detached, from which a bridge was laid acrofs, to be removed on any alarm. This ftructure, which is mean, was erected by the Venetians, while at war with the Turks, in 1693, as appears by an infcription cut in large characters on a piece of veined marble fixed in the wall. I copied it as exactly as its height and the powerful reflection of the fun would permit. Some letters remain of a more antient infcription in Greek.

   D x O O Δ ΗΜ Ο Σ
FRANCISCI MAVROCENI
DVCIS VENET &' CGMIVSSV
ALOYISIOM OCENICO
C. GVLPHI CVRANTE
   ERECTA
  A. MDCXCIII.

THE barrow, which we faw on the fhore, was probably that once by the Æacéum. It was defigned, it is related, for Phocus, and its hiftory as follows. Telamon and Peleus, fons of Æacus, challenged their half-brother Phocus to contend in the Pentathlum. In throwing the ftone, which ferved as a quoit, Peleus hit Phocus, who was killed; when both of them fled. Afterwards, Telamon fent a herald to affert his innocence. Æacus would not fuffer him to land, or to apologize, except from the veffel; or, if he chofe rather, from a heap caft up in the water. Telamon, entering the private port by night, raifed a barrow, as a token, it is likely, of a pious regard for the deceafed. He was afterwards condemned, as not free from guilt; and failed away again to Salamis. The barrow in the fecond century, when feen by Paufanias, was furrounded with a fence, and had on it a rough ftone. The terror of fome dreadful judgement to be inflicted from heaven had preferved it entire and unaltered to his time; and in a country depopulated and neglected, it may ftill endure for many ages.

                THE

THE form of trial inftituted on this occafion paffed early into Attica; where by the fea-fide, without the Piræus, at a place called Phreattys, was a tribunal, at which fugitives for involuntary murder were permitted to appear on any new accufation and to plead from their veffel; the judges fitting on the fhore. They were punifhed, if found guilty; but if acquitted, had liberty to depart and fulfil the term of their banifhment.

THE Æginetans preferved two famous ftatues, named Damia and Auxefia, or Ceres and Proferpine, at Oea, twenty ftadia or two miles and a half from the city. The Athenians demanded the yearly offerings, which the Epidaurians, from whom they were taken, had agreed to make to Minerva Polias and Erectheus; or the images, which they regarded as their property, being formed of their facred Olive, by command of the Delphic oracle. Their difpute is recorded by Herodotus; and Paufanias, in the fecond century, relates, that he faw the goddeffes and facrificed to them as at Eleufis.

THE prefent town, it may be conjectured, was Oea. It ftands on the acclivity of a fteep rock; which perhaps was preferred to the old fite, as lefs expofed to the ravages of corfairs and other plunderers. It is in the way to the mountain Panhellenius, from which it is feparated by a narrow valley, which winds and runs far into the ifland. It is diftant about three quarters of an hour from the fea, where neareft, the track narrow and rough. The houfes are mean, in number about four hundred, rifing on the flope, with flat roofs and terraces of gravel. It is remarkably free from gnats and other troublefome infects. The wells afford good water, but the air is accounted unhealthy. On a fummit above the town are fome windmills, and cifterns or refervoirs, with the rubbifh of a fortrefs erected by the Venetians in 1654. The houfes, which in 1676 amounted to about fourfcore, have been demolifhed, with the two churches; one of which was for the Latin or Catholic Greeks, and had in

it

it a monument of a Venetian governor, of marble. The Æginetans have a bishop, and so many churches, scattered over the island, that, as they affirm, the number equals the days in the year. We had this place in view at the temple of Jupiter, and afterwards I passed two days in it with a Greek of Athens, the governor; no Turk residing there. I then re-visited the ruin, and was near an hour and a half riding to it, though in a strait line it is not far off. I was mounted on a low mule, with a guide on foot, the track rough and bad.

THE soil of Ægina is, as described by Strabo, very stony, especially the bottoms, and naked, but in some places not unfertile in grain. Besides corn, it produces olives, grapes, and plenty of almonds. Perhaps no island abounds more in doves, pigeons, and partridges. Of the latter, which have red legs, we sprung several covies; and our caraboucheri or captain caught one with his hands. It has been related, that the Æginetans annually wage war with the feathered race, carefully collecting or breaking their eggs, to prevent their multiplying, and in consequence a yearly famine. They have no hares, foxes, or wolves. The rivers in summer are all dry, The vaiwode or governor farmed the revenue of the Grand Signior for twelve purses'. About half this sum was repaid yearly by the caratch-money, or poll-tax.

' A purse is 500 piasters.

CHAP. V.

We arrive in the Piræus --- Of the ports of Athens --- Phalerum and Munychia --- Remark on Phalerum --- Piræus --- The town --- The long walls --- Other fortifications --- Their state under the Romans --- Present state of Phalerum and Munychia --- Of the Piræus --- Inscriptions.

THE vicinity of Ægina made Pericles style it the eye-sore of the Piræus. It was distant only twenty miles. We sailed in the afternoon with a fair wind, and in the evening anchored in this renowned haven. We were hailed from the custom-house, and the captain went on shore. On his return, we had the satisfaction to hear that the plague had not reached Athens. We intrusted our recommendatory letters to a person departing for the city. Some Greeks, to whom the captain had notified his arrival, came on board early in the morning. The wine circulated briskly, and their meeting was celebrated, as usual among this lively people, with singing, fiddling, and dancing. We left them, and were landed by the custom-house, exceedingly struck with the solemn silence and solitude of this once crouded emporium.

ATHENS had three ports near each other, the Piræus, Munychia, and Phalerum. Of these the Piræus is formed by a recess of the shore, which winds, and by a small rocky Peninsula spreading toward the sea. A craggy brow, called Munychia, separates it from the Phalerian and Munychian ports, which indent the narrow isthmus, on the opposite or eastern side. It was an antient tradition that this whole peninsula had been an island lying before the coast. The city was not more than twenty stadia or two miles and a half from the sea by Phalerum; but the distance is perhaps increased. From the port it was thirty five stadia, or four miles a quarter and a half; and more from Munychia,

Munychia, which is beyond. From the Piræus it was forty ſtadia or five miles, and, it is related, the city-port was once as far.

PHALERUM was ſaid to have been named from Phalerus, a companion of Jaſon in the Argonautic expedition. Theſeus ſailed from it for Crete; and Meneſtheus, his ſucceſſor, for Troy; and it continued to be the haven of Athens to the time of Themiſtocles. It is a ſmall port, of a circular form, the entrance narrow, the bottom a clean fine ſand, viſible through the tranſparent water. The farm of Ariſtides and his monument, which was erected at the public expenſe, were by this port. Munychia is of a different form or oval, and more conſiderable; the mouth alſo narrow.

THE traveller accuſtomed to deep ports and bulky ſhipping may view Phalerum with ſome ſurprize; but Argo is ſaid to have been carried on the ſhoulders of the crew; the veſſels at the ſiege of Troy were drawn up on the ſhore, as a bullwark, before the camp; and the mighty fleet of Xerxes conſiſted chiefly of light barks and gallies. Phalerum, though a baſin, ſhallow and not large, may perhaps even now be capable of receiving an armament like that of Meneſtheus, though it conſiſted of fifty ſhips.

THE capital port was that called Piræus. The entrance of this is narrow, and formed by two rocky points; one belonging to the promontory of Eetion; the other, to that of Alcimus. Within were three ſtations for ſhipping; Kantharus, ſo named from a hero; Aphrodiſium, from a temple of Venus; and Zea, the reſort of veſſels laden with grain. By it was a demos or borough-town of the ſame name before the time of Themiſtocles, who recommended the exchanging its triple harbour for the ſingle one of Phalerum, both as more capacious, and as better ſituated for navigators. The wall was begun by him, when Archon, in the ſecond year of the ſeventy-fifth Olympiad, four hundred and ſeventy ſeven years before Chriſt; and afterwards he urged the

Athenians to complete it, as the importance of the place deferved. This whole fortification was of hewn ftone, without cement or other material; except lead and iron, which were ufed to hold together the exterior ranges or facings. It was fo wide that the loaded carts could pafs on it in different directions; and it was forty cubits high, which was about half what he had defigned. The bones of this great man, when tranfported from Magnefia by the Mæander, were, with propriety, depofited in the Piræus, near the biggeft port, probably Kantharus, by which were the arfenals. "When you are got within the elbow, which projects from the promontory of Alcimus, where the water is fmooth, you are near the fite of his tomb." It was in fhape like an altar or round, and on a large bafement.

THE Piræus, as Athens flourifhed, became the common emporium of all Greece. Hippodamus an architect, celebrated, befides other monuments of his genius, as the inventor of many improvements in houfe-building, was employed to lay out the ground. Five porticoes, which uniting formed the *long portico*, were erected by the ports. Here was an agora or market-place; and farther from the fea, another called Hippodamia. By the veffels were dwellings for the mariners. A theatre was opened, temples were raifed, and the Piræus, which furpaffed the city in utility, began to equal it in dignity. The cavities and windings of Munychia, natural and artificial, were filled with houfes; and the whole fettlement, comprehending Phalerum and the ports of the Piræus, with the arfenals, the ftore-houfes, the famous armoury, of which Philo was the architect, and the fheds for three hundred, and afterwards four hundred, triremes, refembled the city of Rhodes, which had been planned by the fame Hippodamus. The ports, on the commencement of the Peloponnefian war, were fecured with chains. Centinels were ftationed, and the Piræus was carefully guarded.

IT was the defign of Themiftocles to annex the Piræus to the city by *long walls*. The fide defcending to Phalerum was

begun

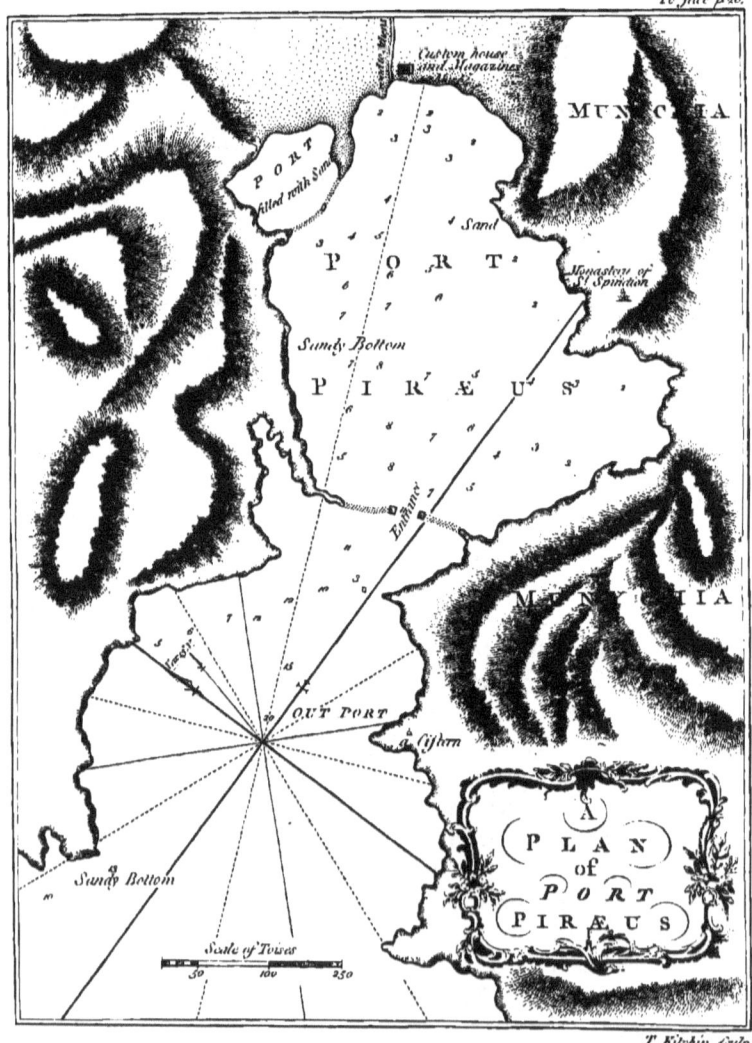

begun. Cimon then furnished money, and made a foundation with chalk and massive stones, where the ground was wet and marshy. Pericles completed it, and erected the opposite wall. The Peloponnesian war impending, he was attentive to the fortifications in general. Callicrates was his architect.

THE four hundred tyrants, who in the first year of the ninety-second Olympiad [1] usurped the government of Athens, knowing that their power depended on the possession of the Piræus, walled about the promontory Eëtion. Soon after the Lacedæmonians insisted on the demolition of *the long walls*, except only ten stadia, or a mile and a quarter, on each side; and obtained it under the thirty tyrants [2]. Thrasybulus, the brave patriot by whom these were expelled, fortified Munychia. Conon resolved to restore the walls of the Piræus and *the long walls*; and Demosthenes, to render the Piræus yet more secure, added a double fosse.

THE Piræus was reduced with great difficulty by Sylla, who demolished the walls, and set fire to the armoury and arsenals. In the civil war it was in a defenceless condition. Calenus, lieutenant to Cæsar, seized it, invested Athens, and ravaged the territory. Strabo, who lived under the emperors Augustus and Tiberius, observes, that the many wars had destroyed *the long walls*, with the fortress of Munychia, and had contracted the Piræus into a small settlement by the ports and the temple of Jupiter Saviour. This fabric was then adorned with wonderful pictures, the works of illustrious artists; and on the outside, with statues. In the second century, besides houses for triremes, the temple of Jupiter and Minerva remained, with their images in brass; and a temple of Venus, a portico, and the tomb of Themistocles. By Munychia was then a temple of Diana. By Phalerum was a temple of Ceres, of Minerva, and,

[1] Before Christ, 410.
[2] The city had expended not less than 1000 talents on the arsenal. They sold it to be removed for three talents. It was restored by Lycurgus.

at

at a diſtance, of Jupiter; with altars of the *unknown gods* and of the heroes.

WE found by Phalerum and Munychia a few fragments, with rubbiſh. Some pieces of columns and a ruined church probably mark the ſite of one of the temples. In many places the rock, which is naked, has been cut away. On the brow toward Munychia a narrow ridge is left ſtanding, with ſmall niches and grooves cut in it, as by the lake of Myûs, perhaps to receive the offerings made to the marine deities on landing; or before embarking, to render them propitious; and for the inſertion of votive tablets, as memorials of diſtreſs and of their aſſiſtance. One ſtone is hollowed ſo as to reſemble a centry-box. The walling of the Piræus muſt have been greatly expedited by theſe quarries, which are mentioned by Xenophon. At Phalerum the ſoil appeared ſhallow, but produces corn. No trees or buſhes grow there.

THE port of the Piræus has been named Porto Lione, from the marble lion ſeen in the chart, and alſo Porto Draco. The lion has been deſcribed as a piece of admirable ſculpture, ten feet high; and as repoſing on its hinder parts. It was pierced, and, as ſome have conjectured, had belonged to a fountain. Near Athens, in the way to Eleuſis, was another, the poſture couchant, probably its companion. Both theſe were removed to Venice by the famous general Moroſini², and are to be ſeen there, before the arſenal. At the mouth of the port are two ruined piers. A few veſſels, moſtly ſmall-craft, frequent it. Some low land at the head ſeems an incroachment on the water. The buildings are a mean cuſtom-houſe, with a few ſheds; and by the ſhore on the eaſt ſide, a warehouſe belonging to the French; and a Greek monaſtery dedicated to St. Spiridion. On the oppoſite ſide is a rocky ridge, on which are remnants of the antient wall, and of a gateway toward Athens. By the

² See Muſeum Venetianum, t. 2.

water

water edge are vestiges of building; and going from the custom-house to the city on the right hand, traces of a small theatre in the side of the hill of Munychia [1].

ONE of the marbles, which we brought from Athens, relates to the sale of this theatre; containing a decree for crowning with olive a person, who had procured an advance in the price; and also for crowning the buyers, four in number. On another marble, the honour of a front seat in the theatre, with an olive-crown and several immunities and privileges, is conferred on one Callidamus; and it is enacted, that the crown be proclaimed by the herald in the full assembly, to demonstrate that the Piræensians had a proper regard for men of merit. This inscription is not more remarkable for its antiquity, which is very great, than for its fine preservation, being as fair as when first reposited in the temple of Vesta. A third contained the conditions, on which the Piræensians leased out the sea-shore, and salt-marshes, the Theséum and other sacred portions. It is dated in the archonship of Archippus, about three hundred and eighteen years before Christ.

CHAP. VI.

We set out for Athens --- Two roads described by Pausanias --- The barrow of Euripides --- The public cisterns --- M. Lycabettus --- We arrive at the French convent --- Reception at Athens.

AFTER viewing the monastery of St. Spiridion and the ports, we returned to the custom-house, and waited to hear from Athens, not without some impatience. We saw the Acropolis or citadel, with the great temple of Minerva, from the window. An archon, named Ianáchi Isofime, to whom we had sent, arrived before noon, attended by a servant, to welcome

[1] It is mentioned by Thucydides, Xenophon, and the orator Lysias. *Meursii Piræus*, p. 1940.

us;

us; and was followed by a capuchin-friar, then refiding in the French convent at Athens. We were detained until the fun was on the decline, when we fet forward, mounted on affes or on horfes laden with our baggage.

PAUSANIAS defcribes two ways from the ports to Athens. By the road from Phalerum was a temple and ftatue of Juno, the building half-burned, and without a door or roof; remaining, with a temple of Ceres by the port, unrepaired, as a memorial of the enmity of the barbarians under Mardonius. By the entrance of the city was a tomb of the Amazon Antiope. On the other road, which led from the Piræus, were ruins of the walls erected by Conon; with fepulchral monuments, among which, thofe of Menander and Euripides were the moft noted. That of the latter poet was a cenotaph or mound of earth without his afhes. By the city-gate was the fepulchre of a foldier, who was reprefented ftanding near his horfe, the fculpture by Praxiteles. The inclofures, which now intervene, may have occafioned fome fmall alteration in the courfe of the two roads. They were nearly in the fame direction, and not far afunder.

AFTER paffing the fite of the theatre and the termination of the rocky peninfula, we had on the right hand a level fpot covered with ftones, where, it is probable, was the remoter agora of the Piræus. Farther on by the road-fide is a clear area within a low mound, formed perhaps by concealed rubbifh of the walls of the temple of Juno. We then entered among vineyards and cotton-grounds, with groves of olive-trees. On one fide rifes a large barrow, it is likely, the cenotaph of Euripides. In a tree was a kind of couch, fheltered with boughs, belonging to a man employed to watch there during the vintage. The foul weather we experienced at fea had extended to Attica, where heavy fhowers had fallen, with terrible thunder and lightning, flooding the land, and doing much damage. An Albanian peafant was expecting the return of the archon, who was one of the annual magiftrates

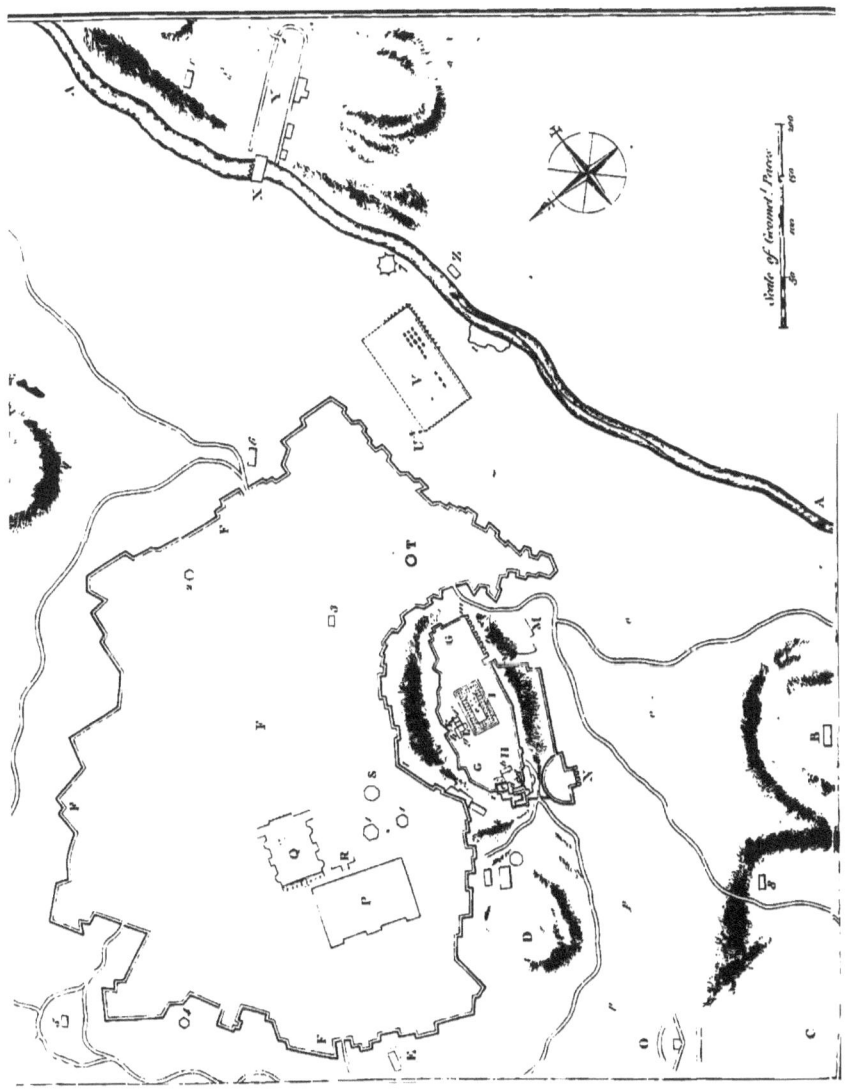

magiſtrates called Epitropi or Procurators, with a preſent of very fine grapes, on which we regaled; and another, who was retiring with his leather bucket, hanging flaccid at his back, enabled us to get water from a well about mid-way.

BEYOND the vineyards are the public ciſterns, from which water is difpenſed to the gardens and trees below, by direction of the owners, each paying by the hour, the price riſing and falling in proportion to the ſcarcity or abundance. In the front is a weeping willow, by which is inſerted a marble with an antient ſepulchral inſcription in fair characters. Beyond the ciſterns is the mountain once called Lycabettus, lying before the Acropolis. It is bare or covered with wild ſage and plants, except where the ſcanty ſoil will admit the plough. It was formerly in repute for olives. We ſaw behind the ciſterns a marble ſtatue, ſedent; as we ſuppoſed, of a philoſopher. It was ſunk in the ground and the face much injured, but, we were told, had been diſcovered, not many years before, entire.

THE road, dividing at the ciſterns, branches through the plain, which is open and of a barren aſpect. The way to the left of Lycabettus, which antiently led to the Piræan gate, now paſſes on between the ſolitary temple of Theſeus, and the naked hill of the Areopagus, where the town begins. On that ſide is alſo a track leading over Lycabettus. We proceeded by the way to the right, on which, at ſome diſtance from the ciſterns, is an opening in the mountain, and a rocky road worn with wheels, ſeparating the hill of the Muſéum from Lycabettus; and once leading to the Melitenſian gate, which was before the Acropolis.

WE kept on in the plain, and croſſed the dry bed of the Iliſſus. On our left were the door-ways of antient ſepulchres hewn out in the rock; the Muſéum, and on it the marble monument of Philopappus; and then the lofty Acropolis, beneath which we paſſed. Before us was a temple ſtanding on

E   the

the farther bank of the Iliſſus; and ſome tall columns, of vaſt ſize, the remains of the temple of Jupiter Olympius. We arrived at the French convent, which is at this extremity of the town, infinitely delighted and awed by the majeſty of ſituation, the ſolemnity and grandeur of ruin, which had met us.

EARLY in the morning we were viſited by the French conful, Monſieur de Gaſpari; and by the archons or principal Greeks in a body. With the latter came an Italian named Lombardi, who had reſided ſeveral years at Athens, and who was known to one of my companions. This man was well received by the Turks, who regarded him as a Mahometan, and as he affected humility and poverty, had beſtowed on him the appellation of *Derviſh*. He offered to ſerve us, and we found it our intereſt to employ him. He attended us on our viſit of ceremony to Achmet Aga, the chief Turk of Athens; to the vaiwode or governor of the city; to the diſdar or officer who commands in the Acropolis; to the mufti; the archbiſhop, and archons; interpreted for us, and adjuſted the preſents neceſſary to be made for the purchaſe of permiſſion to examine the antiquities and of protection during our ſtay; with the ſmaller gratuities to inferior perſons. We were pleaſed with the civil behaviour of the people in general, and enjoyed a tranquillity to which we had long been ſtrangers.

CHAP.

CHAP. VII.

The city of Cecrops --- Athens burned by the Perfians, &c. --- Under the Macedonians --- Receives a Roman garrifon --- Defaced by Sylla --- State under the Roman emperors --- Governed by a pro-conful --- Kindnefs of Hadrian --- The city-wall reftored --- Befieged and taken --- Favoured by Conftantine the Great --- In danger from the Goths --- Sacked by Alaric --- A chafm in its hiftory --- Under various mafters after the twelfth century --- Unknown in the fixteenth --- Antient extent of the walls.

IT was the boaft of the early Athenians, that their origin was from the land which they inhabited, and their antiquity co-equal with the fun. The reputed founder of their city was Cecrops, who, uniting a body of the natives[1] then living difperfed and in caves, fettled on the rock of the Acropolis. He was there fecure from inundation, a calamity much dreaded after the deluge which had happened under Ogyges, one hundred and ninety years before. The hill was nearly in the centre of his little territory; rifing majeftically in the middle of the plain, as if defigned by nature for the feat of government. The town and its domain were called Cecropia, but the name of the former was afterwards changed in honour of Minerva. Her difpute with Neptune was faid to have happened in this reign, and on the fecond day of the month called Boedromion. Neptune difplayed his power by ftriking the rock with his trident, when falt-water arofe; and Minerva, by producing the olive-tree, which, it is related, was long peculiar to Attica. This town was watered by a copious fountain, which failed after an earthquake. Beneath it, lived artificers and hufbandmen, chiefly on the fouth fide, until the time of Thefeus; the houfes not fpreading then in every direction round about, as in fubfequent ages. A wandering people, called Pelafgi, were firft employed

---

[1] Before Troy was taken, 355 years.

employed to level the fummit of the rock, and to encompafs it with a wall, which they completed, except on the fouth, where the deficiency was fupplied by trunks of olive-trees and palifades. The entrance was by nine gates. Afterwards Cimon, fon of Miltiades, erected the wall on the fouth fide with the spoils he had taken in the Perfian war.

THE tyranny of Pififtratus was eftablifhed by his getting poffeffion of the Acropolis or citadel, from which he could command and overawe the town below. His fon Hippias was expelled, and then followed the invafion by Darius, and the battle of Marathon. Thirty three years after this, Athens was taken, and fet on fire by Xerxes; and in the next year, by his general Mardonius; but, on the victories of Platæa and Salamis, it emerged from ruin to fuperior luftre and extended dominion. The Peloponnefian war then enfued; the *long walls* were demolifhed; and it was even propofed to raze the city and lay wafte the plain.

THE victory obtained over the Thebans at Mantinea left Athens at leifure to indulge in elegant diffipation. A poet was preferred to a general, and vaft fums were expended on plays and public fpectacles. At this period Philip of Macedonia was afpiring to the empire of Greece and Afia. Alexander, his fon, facrificed an hecatomb to Minerva at Athens, and fortified the Piræus to keep the city in fubjection. On his death the Athenians revolted, but were defeated by Antipater, who garrifoned Munychia. They rebelled again, but the garrifon and oligarchy were re-inftated. Demetrius[1] the Phalerean, who was made governor, beautified the city, and they erected to him three hundred and fixty ftatues, which, on his expulfion, they demolifhed; except one in the Acropolis. Demetrius Poliorcetes withdrew the garrifon and reftored the democracy, when

---

[1] This Demetrius was author of the antient and famous Chronicon infcribed on marble at Paros, and now preferved, but not entire, at Oxford. See *Daniel a LXX.* p. 480. *Rome,* 1772.

they

TRAVELS IN GREECE.

they deified him, and lodged him in the Opisthodomos or the back part of the Parthenon, as a guest to be entertained by their Minerva. Afterwards they decreed, that the Piræus, with Munychia, should be at his disposal; and he took the Muséum. They expelled his garrison, and he was persuaded by Craterus a philosopher, to leave them free. Antigonus Gonatas, the next king, maintained a garrison in Athens; but on the death of his son Demetrius, the people, with the assistance of Aratus, regained their liberty; and the Piræus, Munychia, Salamis, and Sunium, on paying a sum of money.

PHILIP, son of Demetrius, encamping near the city, destroying and burning the sepulchres and temples in the villages, and laying their territory waste, the Athenians were reduced to sollicit protection from the Romans, and to receive a garrison, which remained until the war with Mithridates, king of Pontus, when the tyrant Aristion made them revolt.

ARCHELAUS, the Athenian general, unable to withstand the Roman fury, relinquished the *long walls*, and retreated into the Piræus and Munychia. Sylla laid siege to the Piræus, and to the city, in which Aristion commanded. He was informed, that some persons had been overheard talking in the Ceramicus and blaming Aristion for his neglect of the avenues about the Heptachalcos, where the wall was accessible. Sylla resolved to storm there, and about midnight entered the town at the gate called Dipylon or the Piræan; having levelled all obstacles in the way between it and the gate of the Piræus. Aristion fled to the Acropolis, but was compelled to surrender by the want of water, when he was dragged from the temple of Minerva and put to death. Sylla burned the Piræus and Munychia, and defaced the city and suburbs, not sparing even the sepulchres.

IN the civil war, the Athenians took the side of Pompey. Cæsar generously refused to punish the city, which afterwards

caressed

careffed his murderers. They next joined Antony, who gave them Ægina and Cea, with other iflands. Auguftus was unkind to them, and they revolted, four years before he died. Under Tiberius, the city was declining, but free, and regarded as an ally of the Romans. The high privilege of having a lictor to precede the magiftrates was conferred on it by Germanicus; but he was cenfured as treating with too much condefcenfion a mixture of nations, inftead of genuine Athenians, which race was then confidered as extinct.

THE emperor Vefpafian reduced Achaia to a province paying tribute and governed by a pro-conful. Nerva was more propitious to the Athenians; and Pliny, under Trajan his fucceffor, exhorts Maximus to be mindful whither he was fent, to rule genuine Greece, a ftate compofed of free cities. " You will " revere the gods and heroes their founders. You will refpect " their priftine glory and even their age. You will honour them " for the famous deeds, which are truly, nay for thofe which " are fabuloufly, recorded of them. Remember, it is Athens you " approach." This city was now entirely dependent on Rome, and was reduced to fell Delos and the iflands in its poffeffion.

HADRIAN, who was at once emperor and an archon of Athens, gave the city laws compiled from Draco, Solon, and the codes of other legiflators; and difplayed his affection for it by unbounded liberality. Athens reflourifhed, and its beauty was renewed. Antoninus Pius, who fucceeded, and Antoninus the philofopher, were alfo benefactors.

THE Barbarians, in the reign of Valerian, befieging Theffalonica, all Greece was terrified, and the Athenians reftored their city-wall, which had been difmantled by Sylla, and afterwards neglected.

UNDER the next emperor, who was the archon Gallienus, Athens was befieged, the archontic office ceafed, and the Strategus or general who had before acted as overfeer of the
agora

agora or market, then became the fupreme magiftrate. Under Claudius, his fucceffor, the city was taken but foon recovered.

It is related, that Conftantine, when emperor, gloried in the title of general of Athens, and rejoiced exceedingly on obtaining from the people the honour of a ftatue with an infcription, which he acknowleged by a yearly gratuity of many bufhels of grain. He conferred on the governor of Attica and Athens the title of *grand duke*, μεγας δουξ. That office was at firft annual, but afterwards hereditary. His fon Conftans beftowed feveral iflands on the city, to fupply it with corn.

In the time of Theodofius the firft, three hundred and eighty years after Chrift, the Goths laid wafte Theffaly and Epirus, but Theodore, general of the Achæans, by his prudent conduct preferved the cities of Greece from pillage and the inhabitants from being led into captivity. A ftatue of marble was erected to him at Athens by order of the city; and afterwards one of brafs, by command of the emperor, as appears from an infcription in a church dedicated to a faint of the fame name, not far from the French convent. It is on a round pedeftal, which fupports a flat ftone ferving for the holy table. Eudocia the wife of Theodofius the fecond was an Athenian.

The fatal period now approached, and Athens was about to experience a conqueror more favage even than Sylla. This was Alaric, king of the Goths; who, under the emperors Arcadius and Honorius, overran Greece and Italy, facking, pillaging, and deftroying. Then the Peloponnefian towns were overturned, Arcadia and Lacedæmon were laid wafte, the two feas by the Ifthmus were burnifhed with the flames of Corinth, and the Athenian matrons were dragged in chains by Barbarians. The invaluable treafures of antiquity, it is related, were removed; the ftately and magnificent ftructures converted into piles of ruin; and Athens was ftripped of every thing fplendid or remarkable.

Synefius,

Synefius, a writer of that age, compares the city to a victim, of which the body had been confumed, and the hide only remained.

AFTER this event, Athens became an unimportant place, and as obfcure as it once had been famous. We read that the cities of Hellas were put into a ftate of defence by Juftinian, who repaired the walls, which at Corinth had been fubverted by an earthquake, and at Athens and in Bœotia were impaired by age; and here we take a long farewel of this city. A chafm of near feven hundred years enfues in its hiftory, except that, about the year 1130, it furnifhed Roger the firft, king of Sicily, with a number of artificers, whom he fettled at Palermo, where they introduced the culture of filk, which then paffed into Italy. The worms had been brought from India to Conftantinople in the reign of Juftinian.

ATHENS, as it were, re-emerges from oblivion in the thirteenth century, under Baldwin, but befieged by a general of Theodorus Lafcaris, the Greek emperor. It was taken in 1427 by Sultan Morat. Boniface, marquis of Montferrat, poffeffed it, with a garrifon; after whom it was governed by Delves, of the houfe of Arragon. On his death, it was feized with Macedonia, Theffaly, Bœotia, Phocis, and the Peloponnefus, by Bajazet; and then, with the ifland Zante, by the Spaniards of Catalonia in the reign of the Greek emperor Andronicus Palæologus the elder. Thefe were difpoffeffed by Reinerius Acciaioli, a Florentine; who, leaving no legitimate male iffue, bequeathed it to the ftate of Venice. His natural fon, Antony, to whom he had given Thebes with Bœotia, expelled the Venetians. He was fucceeded in the dukedom by his kinfman Nerius, who was difplaced by his own brother named Antony, but recovered the government, when he died. Nerius, leaving only an infant fon, was fucceeded by his wife. She was ejected by Mahomet on a complaint from Francus fon of the fecond Antony, who confined her at Megara, and made away with her;

but

but, her fon accufing him to Mahomet the fecond, the Turkifh army under Omar advanced, and he furrendered the citadel in 1455; the Latins refufing to fuccour him, unlefs the Athenians would embrace their religious tenets. Mahomet, it is related, when he had finifhed the war with the defpot of the Morea, four years after, furveyed the city and Acropolis with admiration. The Janizaries informed him of a confpiracy, and Francus Acciaioli, who remained lord of Bœotia, was put to death. In 1464 the Venetians landed at the Piræus, furprized the city, and carried off their plunder and captives to Eubœa.

It is remarkable that after thefe events Athens was again in a manner forgotten. So lately as about the middle of the fixteenth century, the city was commonly believed to have been utterly deftroyed, and not to exift, except a few huts of poor fifhermen. Crufius, a learned and inquifitive German, procured more authentic information from his Greek correfpondents refiding in Turkey, which he publifhed in 1584; to awaken curiofity and to promote farther difcoveries. One of thefe letters is from a native of Nauplia, a town near Argos in the Morea. The writer fays, that he had been often at Athens, and that it ftill contained things worthy to be feen, fome of which he enumerates, and then fubjoins, " but why do I dwell " on this place? It is as the fkin of an animal, which has been " long dead."

The walls of Athens, when the city was in its profperity, with the Piræus, were one hundred and ninety-five ftadia, or twenty-four miles, a quarter, and a half, in circumference; the calculation being made as follows.

The wall encompaffing the Piræus with Munychia, fixty ftadia, or feven miles and a half.

The *long walls* joining the Piræus to the city, north-fide, forty ftadia, or five miles; fouth-fide, thirty ftadia, or four miles, a quarter, and a half.

THE exterior city wall joining the *long walls*, forty-three ſtadia, or five miles, a quarter, and a half.

THE middle or interior wall, between the *long walls*, ſeventeen ſtadia, or two miles and half a quarter.

BY this computation, the circuit of the city-wall alone was ſixty ſtadia, or ſeven miles and a half. The part toward Hymettus and Pentele, the mountains on the eaſt and north-eaſt, was of brick. The plain alſo was then covered with demi or towns, and with villas richly furniſhed.

CHAP. VIII.

Of modern Athens --- The antiquities --- The citadel --- Its antient and preſent ſtate --- Remark.

ATHENS is placed by geographers in fifty three degrees of longitude. Its latitude was found by Mr. Vernon, an Engliſh traveller, to be thirty eight degrees and five minutes. It is now called (Ἀθήνη) *Athini*, and is not inconſiderable, either in extent or the number of inhabitants. It enjoys a fine temperature, and a ſerene ſky. The air is clear and wholeſome, though not ſo delicately ſoft as in Ionia. The town ſtands beneath the Acropolis or citadel, not encompaſſing the rock, as formerly, but ſpreading into the plain, chiefly on the weſt and north-weſt. Corſairs infeſting it, the avenues were ſecured, and in 1676 the gates were regularly ſhut after ſunſet. It is now open again, but ſeveral of the gateways remain, and a guard of Turks patroles at midnight. Some maſſes of brick-work, ſtanding ſeparate, without the town, belonged perhaps to the antient wall, of which other traces alſo appear. The houſes are moſtly mean, and ſtraggling; many with large areas or courts before them. In the lanes, the high walls on each ſide, which are commonly white-waſhed, reflect ſtrongly the heat of the ſun.

The

The streets are very irregular; and antiently were neither uniform nor handsome. They have water conveyed in channels from mount Hymettus, and in the Bazar or market-place is a large fountain. The Turks have several mosques and public baths. The Greeks have convents for men and women; with many churches, in which service is regularly performed; and besides these, they have numerous oratories or chapels, some in ruins or consisting of bare walls, frequented only on the anniversaries of the saints to whom they are dedicated. A portrait of the owner on board is placed in them on that occasion, and removed when the solemnity of the day is over.

BESIDES the more stable antiquities, of which an account will be given in the sequel, many detached pieces are found in the town, by the fountains, in the streets, the walls, the houses, and churches. Among these are fragments of sculpture; a marble chair or two, which probably belonged to the Gymnasia or theatres; a sun-dial at the catholicon or cathedral, inscribed with the name of the maker; and, at the archiepiscopal house close by, a very curious vessel of marble, used as a cistern to receive water, but once serving, it is likely, as a public standard or measure. Many columns occur; with some maimed statues; and pedestals, several with inscriptions, and almost buried in earth. A custom has prevailed, as at Chios, of fixing in the wall, over the gateways and doors of the houses, carved stones, most of which exhibit the funereal supper. In the courts of the houses lie many round stelæ, or pillars, once placed on the graves of the Athenians; and a great number are still to be seen applied to the same use in the Turkish burying grounds before the acropolis. These generally have concise inscriptions containing the name of the person, and of the town and tribe, to which the deceased belonged. Demetrius the Phalerean, who endeavoured to restrain sepulchral luxury, enacted, that no person should have more than one; and that the height should not exceed three cubits. Another species, which resembles our modern head-stones, is sometimes adorned with sculpture, and has an epitaph in verſe. We ſaw a few mutilated Hermæ. Theſe were buſts on long quadrangular baſes, the heads frequently of braſs, invented by the Athenians. At firſt they were made to repreſent only Hermes or Mercury, and deſigned as guardians of the ſepulchres, in which they were lodged; but afterwards the houſes, ſtreets, and porticoes of Athens, were adorned with them, and rendered venerable by a multitude of portraits of illuſtrious men and women, of heroes and of gods: and, it is related, Hipparchus, ſon of Piſiſtratus, erected them in the demi or borough-towns, and by the road ſide, inſcribed with moral apophthegms in elegiac verſe; thus making them vehicles of inſtruction.

The acropolis, aſty, or citadel, was the city of Cecrops. It is now a fortreſs, with a thick irregular wall, ſtanding on the brink of precipices, and incloſing a large area, about twice as long as broad. Some portions of the antient wall may be diſcovered on the outſide, particularly at the two extreme angles; and in many places it is patched with pieces of columns, and with marbles taken from the ruins. A conſiderable ſum had been recently expended on the ſide next Hymettus, which was finiſhed before we arrived. The ſcaffolding had been removed to the end toward Pentele, but money was wanting, and the workmen were withdrawn. The garriſon conſiſts of a few Turks, who reſide there with their families, and are called by the Greeks *Caſtriani* or the ſoldiers of the caſtle. Theſe hollow nightly from their ſtation above the town, to approve their vigilance. Their houſes overlook the city, plain, and gulf, but the ſituation is as airy as pleaſant, and attended with ſo many inconveniences, that thoſe who are able and have the option prefer living below, when not on duty. The rock is lofty, abrupt, and inacceſſible, except the front, which is toward the Piræus; and on that quarter is a mountainous ridge, within cannon-ſhot. It is deſtitute of water fit for drinking, and ſupplies are daily carried up in earthen jars, on horſes and aſſes, from one of the conduits in the town.

The

TRAVELS IN GREECE.

The acropolis furnifhed a very ample field to the antient virtuofi. It was filled with monuments of Athenian glory, and exhibited an amazing difplay of beauty, of opulence, and of art; each contending, as it were, for the fuperiority. It appeared as one entire offering to the deity, furpaffing in excellence, and aftonifhing in richnefs. Heliodorus, named Periegetes, *the guide*, had employed on it fifteen books. The curiofities of various kinds, with the pictures, ftatues, and pieces of fculpture, were fo many and fo remarkable, as to fupply Polemo Periegetes with matter for four volumes; and Strabo affirms, that as many would be required in treating of other portions of Athens and of Attica. In particular, the number of ftatues was prodigious. Tiberius Nero, who was fond of images, plundered the acropolis, as well as Delphi and Olympia; yet Athens, and each of thefe places, had not fewer than three thoufand remaining in the time of Pliny. Even Paufanias feems here to be diftreffed by the multiplicity of his fubject. But this banquet, as it were, of the fenfes has long been withdrawn; and is now become like the tale of a vifion. The fpectator views with concern the marble ruins intermixed with mean flat-roofed cottages, and extant amid rubbifh; the fad memorials of a nobler people; which, however, as vifible from the fea, fhould have introduced modern Athens to more early notice. They who reported it was only a fmall village, muft, it has been furmifed, have beheld the acropolis through the wrong end of their telefcopes.

When we confider the long feries of years, which has elapfed, and the variety of fortune, which Athens has undergone, we may wonder that any portion of the old city has efcaped, and that the fite ftill furnifhes an ample fund of curious entertainment. Atticus is reprefented by Cicero as receiving more pleafure from the recollection of the eminent men it had produced, than from the ftately edifices and exquifite works of antient art, with which it then abounded. The traveller need not be fo refined to derive fatisfaction even now from feeing Athens.

CHAP.

CHAP. IX.

Of Pericles---Of his buildings---Entrance of the acropolis---The propylea---Story of the architect---The temple of victory, or right wing of the propylea---The left wing---Present state of the propylea---Of the temple---Ignorance of the Turks and Greeks---Of the left wing---The propylea when ruined---Inscription on a pedestal.

IT was the fortune of Athens, while flourishing in glory, dominion, and revenue, to produce Pericles, a man as distinguished by the vastness of his ideas, as by the correctness of his taste, and as eloquent as splendid. His enemies declaiming against his temples and images, and comparing the city with its gilding and painting to a vain woman hung with jewels, he took occasion to show, it was wisdom to convert the prosperity of a state, sufficiently prepared for war, into its perpetual ornament by public works, which excited every liberal art, moved every hand, and dispensed plenty to the labourer and artificer, to the mariner and merchant ; the whole city being at once employed, maintained, and beautified by itself. " Think " ye, said he, it is much I have expended ?" Some answered, " very much. Be mine then, he replied, the whole burthen, " and mine the honour of inscribing the edifices raised for you." But the multitude refused, and calling out, bade him take from the treasury and spare not.

THE architects employed by Pericles were possessed of consummate skill in their profession, and Phidias was his overseer. The artificers in the various branches were emulous to excel the materials by their workmanship. To grandeur of proportion were added inimitable form and grace. The vigour of one administration accomplished what appeared to require the united efforts of many ; yet each fabric was as mature in perfection, as

if

if it had been long in finishing. Plutarch affirms, that, in his time, the structures of Pericles alone demonstrated the relations of the antient power and wealth of Hellas not to be romantic. In their character was an excellence peculiar and unparallelled. Even then they retained all their original beauty. A certain freshness bloomed upon them, and preserved their faces uninjured; as if they possessed a never-fading spirit, and had a soul insensible to age. The remains of some of these edifices, still extant in the acropolis, cannot be beheld without admiration.

THE acropolis has now, as formerly, only one entrance, which fronts the Piræus. The ascent is by traverses and rude fortifications furnished with cannon, but without carriages and neglected. By the second gate is the station of the guard, who sits crofs-legged under cover, much at his ease, smoking his pipe, or drinking coffee; with his companions about him in like attitudes. Over this gateway is an inscription in large characters on a stone turned upside down, and black from the fires made below. It records a present of a pair of gates.

GOING farther up, you come to the ruins of the propylea, an edifice, which graced the entrance into the citadel. This was one of the structures of Pericles, who began it when Euthymenes was archon, four hundred thirty-five years before Christ. It was completed in five years, at the expence of two thousand and twelve talents. It was of marble, of the doric order, and had five doors, to afford an easy passage to the multitudes, which resorted on business or devotion to the acropolis.

WHILE this fabric was building, the architect, Mnesicles, whose activity equalled his skill, was hurt by a fall, and the physicians despaired of his life; but Minerva, who was propitious to the undertaking, appeared, it was said, to Pericles, and prescribed a remedy, by which he was speedily and easily cured.

It

It was a plant or herb growing round about the acropolis, and called afterwards parthenium.

The right wing [1] of the propyléa was a temple of victory. They related that Ægeus had stood there, viewing the sea, and anxious for the return of his son Theseus, who was gone to Crete with the tributary children to be delivered to the Minotaur. The vessel, which carried them, had black sails suiting the occasion of its voyage; and it was agreed, that, if Theseus overcame the enemy, their colour should be changed to white. The neglect of this signal was fatal to Ægeus, who, on seeing the sails unaltered, threw himself down headlong from the rock, and perished. The idol was named *Victory without wings*; it was said, because the news of the success of Theseus did not arrive, but with the conqueror. It had a pomegranate in the right hand, and an helmet in the left. As the statue was without pinions, it was hoped the goddess would remain for ever on the spot.

On the left wing of the propyléa, and fronting the temple of Victory, was a building decorated with paintings by Polygnotus, of which an account is given by Pausanias. This edifice, as well as the temple, was of the doric order, the columns fluted, and without bases. Both contributed alike to the uniformity and grandeur of the design; and the whole fabric, when finished, was deemed equally magnificent and ornamental. The interval between Pericles and Pausanias consists of several centuries. The propyléa remained entire in the time of this topographer, and, as will be shown, continued nearly so to a much later period. It had then a roof of white marble, which was unsurpassed either in the size of the stones, or in the beauty of their arrangement; and before each wing was an equestrian statue.

---

[1] Pausanias, p. 20. Των δε Προπυλαιων εν δεξια — εν αριστερα οικηματι εχει γραφας.— Wheler, p. 358, and Spon, p. 137, not attending enough to this passage, have mistaken one wing for the other; substituting the right and left of the human body, for the right and left of the propyléa.

THE propyléa have ceafed to be the entrance of the acropolis. The paffage, which was between the columns in the centre, is walled up almoft to their capitals, and above is a battery of cannon. The way now winds before the front of the antient ftructure, and, turning to the left hand among rubbifh and mean walls, you come to the back part, and to the five door-ways. The foil without is rifen higher than the top of the two fmaller. There, under the vault and cannon lies an heap of large ftones, the ruin of the roof.

THE temple of Victory, ftanding on an abrupt rock, has its back and one fide unincumbered with the modern ramparts. The columns in the front being walled up, you enter it by a breach in the fide, within the propyléa. It was ufed by the Turks as a magazine for powder, until about the year 1656; when a fudden explofion, occafioned by lightning, carried away the roof, with a houfe erected on it, belonging to the officer who commanded in the acropolis, whofe whole family, except a girl, perifhed. The women of the Aga continued to inhabit in this quarter, but it is now abandoned and in ruins.

THE cell of the temple of Victory, which is of white marble, very thick, and ftrongly cemented, fufficiently witneffes the great violence it has undergone; the ftones in many places being disjointed, as it were, and forced from their original pofition. Two of thefe making an acute angle, the exterior edges touching, without a crevice; and the light abroad being much ftronger than in the room, which has a modern roof and is dark; the portion in contact becoming pellucid, had illumined the vacant fpace with a dim colour, refembling that of amber. We were defired to examine this extraordinary appearance, which the Greeks regarded as a ftanding miracle, and which the Turks, who could not confute them, beheld with equal aftonifhment. We found in the gap fome coals, which had been brought on a bit of earthen ware for the purpofe of burning

G incenfe

incenfe, as we fuppofed, and alfo a piece of wax-taper, which probably had been lighted in honour of the faint and author of the wonder; but our Swifs unfortunately carrying his own candle too far in, the fmoke blackened the marble, and deftroyed the phænomenon.

THE building oppofite to the temple has ferved as a foundation for a fquare lofty tower of ordinary mafonry. The columns of the front are walled up, and the entrance is by a low iron gate in the fide. It is now ufed as a place of confinement for delinquents; but in 1676 was a powder magazine. In the wall of a rampart near it are fome fragments of exquifite fculpture, reprefenting the Athenians fighting with the Amazons. Thefe belong to the freeze, which was then ftanding. In the fecond century, when Paufanias lived, much of the painting was impaired by age, but fome remained, and the fubjects were chiefly taken from the Trojan ftory. The traces are fince vanifhed.

THE pediment of the temple of Victory, with that of the oppofite wing, is defcribed as remaining in 1676; but on each building a fquare tower had been erected. One of the fteps in the front of the propyléa was entire, with the four columns, their entablature and the pediment. The portico, to which the five door-ways belonged, confifted of a large fquare room, roofed with flabs of marble, which were laid on two great marble beams and fuftained by four beautiful columns. Thefe were Ionic, the proportions of this order beft fuiting that purpofe, as taller than the Doric; the reafon it was likewife preferred in the pronaos of the temple of Victory. The roof of the propyléa, after ftanding above two thoufand years, was probably deftroyed, with all the pediments, by the Venetians in 1687, when they battered the caftle in front, firing red-hot bullets, and took it, but were compelled to refign it again to the Turks in the following year. The exterior walls, and, in particular, a fide of the temple of Victory, retain many marks of their hoftilities.

PAUSANIAS

PAUSANIAS was really, or pretended to be, ignorant, to whom the equeftrian ftatues before the wings of the propyléa belonged. One of the pedeftals, which remains, will fupply this deficiency. The whole is immured, except the front; which has been much battered by cannon-fhot; and on this, my companions, while bufied in meafuring and drawing, difcovered fome Greek letters, high above the ground. After repeated trials, in which I was affifted by a pocket-telefcope, I procured the infcription, which may be thus tranflated; "The " people have erected Marcus Agrippa, fon of Lucius, thrice " conful, the friend of Caius." The third confulate of Marcus Agrippa falls on the year of Rome, feven hundred and twenty fix[1], when his colleague was the Caius here recorded, Caius Cæfar Octavianus the feventh time conful, who was dignified by the Roman fenate in this memorable year with the title of Auguftus; by which he was diftinguifhed after the fixteenth of February. The confulate commenced on the Calends or firft of January. It follows, that the pedeftal was infcribed between this day, and the fixteenth of the fucceeding month; or, at fartheft, before the notification of this fignal and recent honour had arrived in Greece; for afterwards to have omitted the name Auguftus, would have been an affront both to Caius and to the fenate. The two friends, it is likely, were joined in the Athenian decree, and as Agrippa graced the approach to the propyléa on the left hand, Caius was on the right. The theatre in the Ceramicus was called for fome time *the Agrippéum*, probably as a compliment to this Agrippa. No dog or goat was fuffered to enter the propyléa.

[1] Before Chrift, 27.

CHAP. X.

Of the parthenon --- Of the statue of Minerva --- Of Phidias --- The statue remaining after Julian --- When removed --- The temple when ruined --- Described in 1676 --- Present state --- The pediments --- Other sculptures --- Copied by Mr. Pars.

THE chief ornament of the acropolis was the parthenon or great temple of Minerva, a most superb and magnificent fabric. The Persians had burned the edifice, which before occupied the site, and was called hecatompedon, from its being an hundred feet square. The zeal of Pericles and of all the Athenians was exerted in providing a far more ample and glorious residence for their favourite goddess. The architects were Callicrates and Ictinus; and a treatise on the building was written by the latter and Carpion. It was of white marble, of the doric order, the columns fluted and without bases, the number in front eight; and adorned with admirable sculpture. The story of the birth of Minerva was carved in the front pediment; and in the back, her contest with Neptune for the country. The beasts of burthen, which had conveyed up the materials, were regarded as sacred, and recompensed with pastures; and one, which had voluntarily headed the train, was maintained during life, without labour, at the public expense.

THE statue of Minerva, made for this temple by Phidias, was of ivory, twenty six cubits or thirty nine feet high. It was decked with pure gold to the amount of forty four talents,[1] so disposed by the advice of Pericles as to be taken off and weighed, if required. The goddess was represented standing, with her vestment reaching to her feet. Her helmet had a Sphinx for the crest, and on the sides were Griffins. The head of Medusa was on her breast-plate. In one hand she held her spear, and in the other supported an image of Victory about four

[1] Forty talents valued, according to Herodotus, at thirteen times the weight in silver will amount to above 120,000*l.* sterling.

cubits

cubits high. The battle of the Centaurs and Lapithæ was carved on her fandals; and on her fhield, which lay at her feet, the war of the gods and giants, and the battle of the Athenians and Amazons. By her fpear was a ferpent, in allufion to the ftory of Erichthonius; and on the pedeftal, the birth of Pandora. The Sphinx, the Victory, and Serpent, were accounted eminently wonderful. This image was placed in the temple in the firft year of the eighty feventh Olympiad [1], in which the Peloponnefian war began. The gold was ftripped off by the tyrant Lachares, when Demetrius Poliorcetes compelled him to fly. The fame plunderer plucked down the golden fhields in the acropolis, and carried away the golden Victories, with the pretious veffels and ornaments provided for the Panathenæan feftival.

IT was obferved of Phidias, that as a ftatuary he excelled more in forming gods than men; a fhort encomium containing the fubftance of a panegyric. The Minerva of Athens, with a ftatue, which he made afterwards, of Jupiter at Olympia, raifed him far above competition in ivory. Such an artift deferved to be generoufly treated, but Phidias had enemies as well as his patron. He had inferted in the fhield of Minerva a beautiful figure of Pericles, without his knowlege, fighting with an Amazon, the face partly concealed; a hand with a fpear, extended before it, feeming defigned to prevent the likenefs from being perceived. Much envy and obloquy followed, when that, with his own image, was detected. Phidias was reprefented as an old man and bald, but with a ponderous ftone uplifted in his hands; and this figure, cementing, as it were, the whole work, could not be removed without its falling in pieces. He was accufed of having embezzled fome ivory, by charging more for the fcales of the ferpent than had been confumed. He fled to Elis, and was killed by the people, to fecure their Jupiter from a rival.

[1] Before Chrift, 430. Pericles furvived only two years and a half.

MINERVA had been too long in poffeffion, and was too firmly eftablifhed, to be eafily expelled from Athens. The partiality of Conftantine the Great, it is probable, averted from this city the tide of reformation, and preferved to the tutelary goddefs, and its deities, in general, their facred portions and revenues, their temples and cuftomary rites. The emperor Julian, in a letter to the Athenians, reminds them, that when he was fummoned by Conftantius the deftroyer of his family to a court filled with his enemies, he had left them reluctantly, weeping plentifully, as many of them could witnefs, ftretching forth his hands toward the acropolis, and fupplicating Minerva to fave and protect him: and, he affirms, fhe did not abandon or give up her fervant, as had been manifeft; but was always his guide, accompanying him with guardian angels, which fhe had taken from the fun and moon. His beard had been fhaven, and the philofophic cloke relinquifhed at the command of Conftantius. Julian was transformed into a courtier and foldier, but he retained his affection for Athens and for Minerva, to whom he facrificed every morning in his clofet. The orator Libanius coincided with his own belief, when he affirmed to him, that none of his exploits had been atchieved without the Athenian goddefs, and that fhe had been continually his counfel and co-adjutor. Minerva preferved her ftation in the acropolis under his fucceffors Valentinian and Valens.

THE extirpation of Gentilifm at Athens feems to have been accomplifhed by Alaric and his Goths. Indeed, one hiftorian [1] relates, that this Barbarian, on his irruption into Greece through the ftraits of Thermopylæ, haftened to Athens, expecting an eafy conqueft, as he could cut off the communication with the Piræus, and the city was too large to be defended by the inhabitants; but that, on his approach, he beheld Minerva armed on the battlements and preparing to fally forth; with Achilles,

---

[1] Zozimus, p. 512.

ftanding

standing before the wall, and terrible, such as he is described by Homer when he appeared to the Trojans after the death of Patroclus; that Alaric, dismayed by these spectres, was induced to treat; and being admitted with a small party into the city, was conducted to the Bath, entertained by the principal persons, and gratified with valuable presents; and that he then led his army toward the Isthmus, leaving Athens and Attica unspoiled. But this is the narrative of a Pagan, zealous for the credit of the proscribed deities; and it has been proved, that Athens suffered with the other cities of Greece. The potent and revered idol of Minerva then, it is likely, submitted to their common plunderer, who levelled all their images without distinction, alike regardless whether they were heaven-descended or the works of Phidias.

THE parthenon remained entire for many ages after it was deprived of the goddess. The Christians converted it into a church, and the Mahometans into a mosque. It is mentioned in the letters of Crusius, and miscalled *the pantheon*, and the temple of *the unknown god*[1]. The Venetians under Koningsmark, when they besieged the acropolis in 1687, threw a bomb, which demolished the roof, and, setting fire to some powder, did much damage to the fabric. The floor, which is indented, still witnesses the place of its fall. This was the sad forerunner of farther destruction; the Turks breaking the stones, and applying them to the building of a new mosque, which stands within the ruin, or to the repairing of their houses and the walls of the fortress. The vast pile of ponderous materials, which lay ready, is greatly diminished; and the whole structure will gradually be consumed and disappear.

THE temple of Minerva in 1676 was, as Wheler and Spon assert, the finest mosque in the world, without comparison. The Greeks had adapted the fabric to their ceremonial by con-

[1] See also, Modern Universal History, v. 5. p. 417.

structing

structing at one end a semicircular recess for the holy tables, with a window; for before it was enlightened only by the door, obscurity being preferred under the heathen ritual, except on festivals, when it yielded to splendid illuminations; the reason, it has been surmised, why temples are commonly found simple and unadorned on the insides. In the wall beneath the window were inserted two pieces of the stone called Phengites, a species of marble discovered in Cappadocia in the time of Nero; and so transparent, that he erected with it a temple to Fortune, which was luminous within, when the door was shut. These pieces were perforated, and the light which entered, was tinged with a reddish or yellowish hue. The picture of the Panagia or Virgin Mary, in Mosaic, on the ceiling of the recess, remained; with two jasper columns belonging to the skreen, which had separated that part from the nave; and within, a canopy supported by four pillars of porphyry, with corinthian capitals of white marble, under which the table had been placed; and behind it, beneath the window, a marble chair for the archbishop; and also a pulpit, standing on four small pillars in the middle aile. The Turks had white-washed the walls, to obliterate the portraits of saints and the other paintings, with which the Greeks decorate their places of worship; and had erected a pulpit on the right hand for their Iman or reader. The roof was disposed in square compartments; the stones massive; and some had fallen in. It had been sustained in the pronaos by six columns, but the place of one was then supplied by a large pile of rude masonry; the Turks not having been able to fill up the gap more worthily. The roof of the naos was supported by colonnades ranging with the door, and on each side; consisting of twenty two pillars below, and of twenty three above. The odd one was over the entrance, which by that disposition was left wide and unembarrassed. In the portico were suspended a few lamps, to be used in the mosque at the seasons, when the Musselmen assemble before day-break, or to be lighted up round the minaret, as is the custom during their Ramazan or Lent.

It

TRAVELS IN GREECE. 49

IT is not eafy to conceive a more ftriking object than the parthenon, though now a mere ruin. The columns within the naos have all been removed, but on the floor may be feen the circles, which directed the workmen in placing them; and, at the farther end is a groove acrofs it, as for one of the partitions of the cell. The recefs erected by the Chriftians is demolifhed, and from the rubbifh of the ceiling the Turkifh boys collect bits of the Mofaic, of different colours, which compofed the picture. We were told at Smyrna, that this fubftance had taken a polifh, and been fet in buckles. The cell is about half demolifhed, and in the columns, which furrounded it, is a large gap near the middle. On the walls are fome traces of the paintings. Before the portico is a refervoir, funk in the rock, to fupply the Turks with water for the purifications cuftomary on entering their mofques. In it on the left-hand is the rubbifh of the pile erected to fupply the place of a column; and on the right, a ftaircafe, which leads out on the architrave, and has a marble or two with infcriptions, but worn fo as not to be legible. It belonged to the minaret, which has been deftroyed.

THE travellers, to whom we are indebted for an account of the mofque, have likewife given a defcription of the fculpture then remaining in the front. In the middle of the pediment was feen a bearded Jupiter, with a majeftic countenance, ftanding, and naked; the right arm broken. The thunder-bolt, it has been fuppofed, was placed in that hand, and the eagle between his feet. On his right was a figure, it is conjectured, of Victory, clothed to the mid-leg; the head and arms gone. This was leading on the horfes[1] of a car, in which Minerva fat, young and unarmed; her head-drefs, inftead of a helmet, refembling that of a Venus. The generous ardour and lively fpirit vifible in this pair of celeftial fteeds, was fuch as befpoke the hand of a mafter, bold and delicate, of a Phidias or Praxi-

---

[1] Thefe horfes are mentioned in a letter to Crufius.

H   teles.

teles. Behind Minerva was a female figure, without a head, fitting, with an infant in her lap; and in this angle of the pediment was the emperor Hadrian with his arm round Sabina, both reclining, and feeming to regard Minerva with pleafure. On the left fide of Jupiter were five or fix other trunks to complete the affembly of deities, into which he received her. Thefe figures were all wonderfully carved, and appeared as big as life. Hadrian and his confort, it is likely, were complimented by the Athenians with places among the marble gods in the pediment, as benefactors. Both of them may be confidered as intruders on the original company, and poffibly their heads were placed on trunks, which before had other owners. They still poffefs their corner, and are eafy to be recognized, though not unimpaired. The reft of the ftatues are defaced, removed, or fallen. Morofini was ambitious to enrich Venice with the fpoils of Athens, and by an attempt to take down the principal group haftened their ruin. In the other pediment is a head or two of fea-horfes finely executed, with fome mutilated figures; and on the architrave beneath them are marks of the fixtures of votive offerings, perhaps of the golden fhields, or of feftoons fufpended on folemn occafions, when the temple was dreffed out to receive the votaries of the goddefs.

IT is to be regretted that fo much admirable fculpture as is ftill extant about this fabric fhould be all likely to perifh, as it were immaturely, from ignorant contempt and brutal violence. Numerous carved ftones have difappeared; and many, lying in the ruinous heaps, moved our indignation at the barbarifm daily exercifed in defacing them. Befides the two pediments, all the metopes were decorated with large figures in alto relievo, of which feveral are almoft entire on the fide next Hymettus. Thefe are exceedingly ftriking, efpecially when viewed with a due proportion of light and fhade, the fun rifing behind the mountain. Their fubject is the fame as was chofen for the fandals of Minerva, or the battle of the Centaurs and Lapithæ. On the freeze of the cell was carved in baffo relievo, the folemnity of a facrifice to Minerva; and

and of this one hundred and seventy feet are standing, the greater part in good preservation; containing a procession on horseback. On two stones, which have fallen, are oxen led as victims. On another, fourteen feet long, are the virgins called Canephori, which assisted at the rites, bearing the sacred canisters on their heads, and in their hands each a taper; with other figures, one a venerable person with a beard reading in a large volume, which is partly supported by a boy. This piece, now inserted in the wall of the fortress, is supposed to have ranged in the centre of the back front of the cell. The sacrifice designed to be represented was probably that performed at stated times by the Athenian cavalry; and perhaps the figure last mentioned is the herald praying for the prosperity of the Athenians and Plataeensians, as was usual, in commemoration of their united bravery at Marathon. We purchased two fine fragments of the freeze, which we found inserted over door-ways in the town; and were presented with a beautiful trunk, which had fallen from the metopes, and lay neglected in the garden of a Turk.

The marquis de Nointell, ambassador from France to the Porte in the year 1672, employed a painter to delineate the freeze; but his sketches, the labour of a couple of months, must have been very imperfect, being made from beneath, without scaffolding, his eyes straining upwards. Mr. Pars devoted a much longer time to this work, which he executed with diligence, fidelity, and courage. His post was generally on the architrave of the colonnade, many feet from the ground, where he was exposed to gusts of wind, and to accidents in passing to and fro. Several of the Turks murmured, and some threatened, because he overlooked their houses; obliging them to confine or remove the women, to prevent their being seen from that exalted station. Besides views and other sculptures, he designed one hundred ninety six feet of bass-relief in the acropolis.

CHAP. XI.

Of the Erectheum---Temple of Neptune --- Temple of Minerva Polias --- Story of Pandrosos --- Present state of the temples of Neptune and Minerva --- Of the Pandroseum---Business of the virgins called Canephori --- Images of Minerva --- The treasury --- Inscriptions.

WE proceed now to the cluster of ruins on the north side of the parthenon, containing the Erectheum and the temple of Pandrosos, daughter of Cecrops.

NEPTUNE and Minerva, once rival deities, were joint and amicable tenants of the Erectheum, in which was an altar *of Oblivion*. The building was double, a partition-wall dividing it into two temples, which fronted different ways. One was the temple of Neptune Erectheus, the other of Minerva Polias. The latter was entered by a square portico connected with a marble skreen, which fronts toward the propylea. The door of the cell was on the left hand, and at the farther end of the passage was a door leading down into the Pandroseum, which was contiguous.

BEFORE the temple of Neptune Erectheus was an altar of Jupiter *the supreme*, on which no living thing was sacrificed, but they offered cakes without wine. Within it was the altar of Neptune and Erectheus; and two, belonging to Vulcan and a hero named Butes, who had transmitted the priesthood to his posterity, which were called Butadæ. On the walls were paintings of this illustrious family, from which the priestess of Minerva Polias was also taken. It was asserted that Neptune had ordained the well of salt water and the figure of a trident in the rock, to be memorials of his contending for the country.

The

The former, Paufanias remarks, was no great wonder, for other wells, of a fimilar nature were found inland; but this, when the fouth wind blew, afforded the found of waves.

THE temple of Minerva Polias was dedicated by all Attica, and poffeffed the moft antient ftatue of the goddefs. The demi or towns had other deities, but their zeal for her fuffered no diminution. The image, which they placed in the acropolis, then the city, was in after ages not only reputed confummately holy, but believed to have fallen down from heaven in the reign of Erichthonius. It was guarded by a large ferpent, which was regularly ferved with offerings of honied cakes for his food. This divine reptile was of great fagacity, and attained to an extraordinary age. He wifely withdrew from the temple, when in danger from the Medes; and, it is faid, was living in the fecond century. Before the ftatue was an owl; and a golden lamp. This continued burning day and night. It was contrived by a curious artift, named Callimachus, and did not require to be replenifhed with oil oftener than once a year. A brazen palm-tree, reaching to the roof, received its fmoke. Ariftion had let the holy flame expire, while Sylla befieged him, and was abhorred for his impiety. The original olive-tree, faid to have been produced by Minerva, was kept in this temple. When the Medes fet fire to the acropolis, it was confumed; but, they afferted, on the following day, was found to have fhot up again as much as a cubit. It grew low and crooked, but was efteemed very holy. The prieftefs of Minerva was not allowed to eat of the new cheefe of Attica; and, among her perquifites, was a meafure of wheat, and one of barley, for every birth and burial. This temple was again burned when Callias was Archon[1], twenty four years after the death of Pericles. Near it was the tomb of Cecrops, and within it Erectheus was buried.

IT was related in the mythology of Athens, that Minerva intrufted to Aglauros, Herfe, and Pandrofos, a cheft; which

[1] Before Chrift, 404. Pericles died of the plague in the 4th Olymp. 87.

fhe

she strictly enjoined them not to open. It contained Erectheus or Erichthonius, an infant, the offspring of Vulcan and of the Earth; guarded by a serpent. Curiosity prevailing, the two elder sisters disobeyed. The goddess was gone to Pallene for a mountain; intending to blockade the entrance of the acropolis. A busy crow met her, on her return, and informed her what had passed, when she dropped the mountain, which was afterwards called Lycabettus; and, displeased with the officious talebearer, commanded that no crow should ever again visit the acropolis. The guilty sisters were seized with a frenzy, and threw themselves down one of the precipices. Pandrosos was honoured with rites and mysteries. She was joined with Minerva, and when a heifer was sacrificed to the goddess, it was accompanied with a sheep for Pandrosos. This story is alluded to by Homer, who mentions the temple of Minerva, with the offerings of bulls and young sheep made annually by the Athenians. Crows, as I have often observed, fly about the sides of the rock, without ascending to the height of the top; and Lucretius asserts that not even the smoking of the altars, when they might expect food, could entice them thither; which he sensibly attributes, not to the dread of Minerva, as the Greek poets sung, but to the nature of the place.

The ruin of the Erecthéum is of white marble, the architectural ornaments of very exquisite workmanship, and uncommonly curious. The columns of the front of the temple of Neptune are standing with the architrave; and also the skreen and portico of Minerva Polias, with a portion of the cell retaining traces of the partition-wall. The order is Ionic. An edifice revered by antient Attica, as holy in the highest degree, was in 1676 the dwelling of a Turkish family; and is now deserted and neglected; but many ponderous stones and much rubbish must be removed, before the well and trident would appear. The former, at least, might probably be discovered. The portico is used as a powder-magazine; but we obtained permission to dig and to examine the outside. The door-way of the

the veſtibule is walled up, and the ſoil riſen nearly to the top of the door-way of the Pandroſéum. By the portico is a battery commanding the town, from which aſcends an amuſing hum. The Turks fire from it, to give notice of the commencement of Ramazan or of their Lent, and of Bairam or the Holy-days, and on other public occaſions.

The Pandroſéum is a ſmall, but very particular building, of which no ſatisfactory idea can be communicated by deſcription. The entablature is ſupported by women called Caryatides. Their ſtory is thus related. The Greeks, victorious in the Perſian war, jointly deſtroyed Carya, a city of the Peloponneſus, which had favoured the common enemy. They cut off the males, and carried into captivity the women, whom they compelled to retain their former dreſs and ornaments, though in a ſtate of ſervitude, The architects of thoſe times, to perpetuate the memory of their puniſhment, repreſented them, as in this inſtance, each with a burthen on her head, one hand uplifted to it, and the other hanging down by her ſide. The images were in number ſix, all looking toward the parthenon. The four in front, with that next to the propyléa, remain, but mutilated, and their faces beſmeared with paint. The ſoil is riſen almoſt to the top of the baſement on which they are placed. This temple was open or latticed between the ſtatues; and in it alſo was a ſtunted olive-tree, with an altar of Jupiter Hercéus ſtanding under it. The propyléa are nearly in a line with the ſpace dividing it from the parthenon; which diſpoſition, beſides its other effects, occaſioned the front and flank of the latter edifice to be ſeen at once by thoſe who approached it from the entrance of the acropolis.

The deities of the acropolis had a variety of miniſters and inferior ſervants, whoſe dwellings were near their temples. In particular, at a ſmall diſtance from the temple of Minerva Polias lived two virgins, called Canephori, which continued ſome time with the goddeſs, and, when the ſeaſon of her feſtival approached,

were

were employed as follows in the night-time. They placed on their heads fomething, they knew not what, which they received from the prieſteſs, who was reputed equally ignorant; and defcended with it into a fubterraneous paffage in the city, not far from the temple of *Venus in the gardens*; where they exchanged one myſterious load for another, and returned to the acropolis. They were then difmiffed and two new virgins admitted in their room. Paufanias wondered much at this cuſtom. One of thefe virgins, after her difcharge, was honoured by the council and people with a ſtatue, as appears from an infcription extant in the town. The houfes, it may be prefumed, were judiciouſly arranged in ſtreets, forming avenues to the temples; where now are mean cottages, narrow lanes, walls, and rubbifh. The rock in many places is rugged, and bare, or cut into fteps, perhaps to receive marble pavement, or the foundation of a building.

BESIDES the ſtatue of Minerva Polias, which was of olive, and that in the parthenon, the acropolis poffeffed a third, which was of braſs, and fo tall that the point of the fpear and the creſt of the helmet were vifible from Sunium. It was an offering made with a tenth of the fpoils taken at Marathon, and dedicated to the goddefs. The artiſt was Phidias. It remained to the time of Arcadius and Honorius; and Minerva, it was faid, appeared to Alaric, as reprefented in this image. There were likewife fome images of her, which efcaped the flames, when Xerxes fet fire to the acropolis. Thefe, in the fecond century, were entire, but unufually black, and mouldering with age. Many invaluable curiofities were then preferved in the temples.

AT the commencement of the Peloponnefian war, Pericles, to animate the Athenians, harangued on the flouriſhing ſtate of the republic, and on the riches of the acropolis, in money, in gold and filver, in private and public offerings, facred utenfils, the fpoils of the Medes, and the like; befides the forty talents, which,

which, if wanted, might be borrowed from Minerva. The treafury was in the Opifthodomos or back part of the parthenon [1]; where the Athenians afterwards lodged Demetrius Poliorcetes. The pretious effects of Minerva and of the other deities were amaffed, and regiftered on marble. The tutelary gods were Jupiter Saviour, and Plutus, who had wings and eyes. The keys of this place, and of the gates of the acropolis, were intrufted with the Prytanes; one of whom, chofen by lot, had them in his cuftody, but for a night only and a day, when he was called the Epiftates or prefident; and then refigned them to a fucceffor. The precaution of jealoufy regulated and limited the command in this manner, left a tyranny fhould be eftablifhed on the poffeflion of the public treafure and of the acropolis.

THE marbles, which recorded thefe riches of the Athenians, have not all perifhed. We difcovered fome, which I carefully copied, among the rubbifh at the farther end of the parthenon; and purchafed one of a Turkifh woman living in the acropolis. Another had been conveyed down to the French convent, and, after we left it, was placed as a ftep in the ftaircafe of a kitchen erected by the friar. All thefe infcriptions, which are very antient, commemorate jewels, Victories, and crowns of gold, rings, and a variety of curiofities confecrated by eminent perfons; giving fome, though an inadequate, idea of the nature and quality of the treafure. Another marble, which has been engraved at the expenfe of the fociety of DILETTANTI, was difcovered at a houfe not far from the temple of Minerva Polias, placed, with the infcribed face expofed, in the ftairs. The owner, who was branded for fome unfair dealing with the appellative *Jefüt* or *the Jew*, prefixed to his name, feeing me beftow fo much labour in taking a copy, became fearful of parting with the original under its value. When the bargain

---

[1] The Opifthodomos is defcribed by the fcholiaft on Ariftophanes as a double wall, with a door, behind the temple of Minerva Polias; but this feems to be a miftake, unlefs he intended to mark the fituation of the pofticum of the parthenon, as behind the portico of Minerva Polias.

was at length concluded, we obtained the connivance of the Difdar, his brother, under an injunction of privacy, as otherwife the removal of the ftone might endanger his head, it being the property of the Grand Signior. Muftapha delivered a ring, which he commonly wore, to be fhown to a female black flave, who was left in the houfe alone, as a token; and our Swifs, with affiftants and two horfes, one reputed the ftrongeft in Athens, arrived at the hour appointed, and brought down the two marbles, for which he was fent, unobferved; the Turks being at their devotions in the mofque, except the guard at the gate, who was in the fecret. The large flab was afterwards rendered more portable by a mafon. We faw many other infcribed marbles, befides thefe; fome fixed in the walls, or in the pavement of the portico of the mofque; fome in the floors and ftairs of the houfes; or lying in the courts, and among rubbifh; all which we were permitted to copy; the Turks even prying into corners, and difcovering feveral, which they had often paffed before without notice.

CHAP. XII.

Front of the hill of the acropolis --- The cave of Apollo and Pan --- A fountain and ftatue --- The pelafgicon and long rocks --- An infcription --- The theatre of Bacchus --- The Athenians fond of gladiators --- A grotto and choragic monument --- The Odéum of Pericles and Atticus Herodes.

THE rock of the acropolis fpreads in front, floping down from before the propyléa and out-works; and is covered with Turkifh fepulchres and grave-ftones; among which ftands a fmall mofque. At the foot is a deep narrow vale, with a road leading through, between the hill and Lycabettus or the mountain, which lies before it. On one fide, the burying-grounds are bounded by a bare craggy rock, with a track paffing over it

toward

toward the temple of Theseus. We shall leave this, which was the hill of the areopagus, on the left hand, and descend by the way most frequented; intending to survey the out-side of the acropolis, keeping it on the right, until we have completed the circuit.

AND first, below the right wing of the propyléa or the temple of Victory, is a cave, once sacred to Apollo and Pan. It appears to have been adorned with votive tablets; and before it are some masses of brick-wall, remnants of a church, founded, it is probable, on the removal of their altars, to insult them, and to prevent their votaries from cherishing a superstitious veneration of the spot. Apollo, one of its owners, deserved, instead of worship, to have been tried and condemned for a rape, which, it was believed he committed in this cave on Creusa, daughter of Erectheus, who exposed in it afterwards the child, Ion, from whom the Ionians of Europe and Asia were named. As to Pan, it is related, that on the landing of the Medes at Marathon, Phidippides, being sent to summon the Lacedæmonians, was met by him in Arcadia, when he declared an affection for the Athenians, and promised to be their ally. A temple, on mount Parthenius near Tegea, remaining in the second century, was erected, they affirmed, on the very place of the interview. He was believed to have attended at Marathon, and to have contributed largely to the victory, by striking the enemy with the species of terror from him called Panic. Miltiades rewarded him with a statue, and on the pedestal was an inscription, which is preserved among the epigrams ascribed to Simonides. Moreover, he was inserted in the catalogue of Athenian divinities. The goat-footed god quitted his habitation on the mountain, and, according to Lucian, settled at Athens, living in the cave under the acropolis, a little beneath the pelasgic wall; where the people still continued to assemble two or three times a year, to sacrifice a he-goat to him, to feast and be merry.

By the road-side before you come to the town, is a fountain, in the wall on the left hand, supplied probably by the same spring as the well once in the temple of Neptune; for the water descends from the acropolis, and is not fit for drinking. Farther on is a statue of Isis inserted in the wall on the right hand; a ruined church; and the gateway of the out-work next the town. We shall turn up on the right, and keep in the out-skirt, on the side of the hill.

The Athenians permitted the Pelasgi, who fortified the acropolis, to dwell beneath, and bestowed on them a portion of land to cultivate, as a reward for their labour. Afterwards, they accused them of a conspiracy, and of way-laying their sons and daughters, who went for water to the fountain called Enneacrunus; drove them out of Attica, and execrated the spot on which they had lived, making it unlawful to dig, or sow, or build there; the transgressors to be apprehended, carried before the archon, and fined. It was the advice of the Delphic oracle, that the pelasgicon should be kept rough and naked; but, on the invasion by the Peloponnesians, the people flocking into the city, that spot[1], with the temples, except a few which could not be forced open, and the towers of the *long walls*, received inhabitants. The pelasgicon probably comprehended the acclivity, or vacant space, on this side above the houses, which now produces grain; and perhaps it was forbidden to be occupied for the security of the fortress, which on that quarter was most liable to be surprized by treachery or carried by assault. Some large single rocks, which lie there, and have rolled down from above, disparted by their own weight, or the violence of earthquakes, are, it is likely, those called antiently the *long rocks* and mentioned as near the cave of Apollo and Pan.

The hill of the acropolis is more abrupt and perpendicular, as well as narrower, at the extremity or end opposite to the

[1] The pelasgicon is mistaken for a temple by the interpreter of Thucydides, l. 2.

propyléa

propyléa. There, beneath the wall, is a cavern, the roosting-place of crows and daws. A long scaffold was standing against the outside of the fortress above, and many large stones had fallen down. One was inscribed and contained a decree of the tribe named Pandionis. In this record, Nicias is praised and honoured with a crown, because he had obtained a victory with a chorus of boys at the Dionysia or festival of Bacchus, and with one of men at the Thargelia or festival of Apollo; and it is ordered, that if any other person had conquered, since the archonship of Euclid, either with boys or men, at the festivals specified, his name should likewise be engraved; and that the subsequent curators should add the names of such as proved victorious, while they were in office. Religion furnished Athens with a great variety of spectacles and amusements. The festivals were celebrated with gymnic exercises, music, and plays. The public sometimes defrayed the expense of the choruses, but that burthen was commonly laid upon rich citizens, who had attained to the age of forty years. Rewards were proposed for superior excellence, and the victory was eagerly desired. The glory of individuals reflected lustre on the community, to which they belonged; and the tribes were emulous to surpass each other. It was a splendid contention, the parties vying in the display of spirit and generosity. The conquerors were distinguished and applauded, and their names registered on marble. The archonship of Euclid coincides with the second year of the ninety fourth Olympiad [1], and was an æra in the chronology of Athens.

WE proceed now to the side of the acropolis, which is toward mount Hymettus; leaving the town, which before extended beneath on our left into the plain. The hill, near this end, is indented with the site of the theatre of Bacchus, by which is a solitary church or two. This was a very capacious edifice, near the most antient temple of Bacchus, and adorned

[1] Before Christ, 401.

with

with images of the tragic and comic poets. Some stone-work remains at the two extremities, but the area is ploughed, and produces grain. The Athenians invented both the drama and the theatre, the latter originally a temporary structure of wood; but, while a play of Æschylus was acting, the scaffolds fell; and it was then resolved to provide a solid and durable fabric. The slope of the hill, on which perhaps the spectators had been accustomed to assemble, was chosen for the building; and the seats disposed in rows rising one above another, each resting on the rock as its foundation.

WHILE Athens continued independent, the stage was ennobled by the glorious produce of Attic genius; by the solemn chorus; by a Sophocles, and a Menander. When Rome had prevailed, it was degraded and prostituted to the savage combats of gladiators; and in the time of Trajan, the Athenians exceeded even the Corinthians in their relish of that cruel pastime. These assembled without their city, in a torrent-bed, capable of containing the multitude, and of no account; where, it is said, no one would even bury a free person; but the Athenians hired and armed miscreants of all denominations, whom they encouraged to fight in the theatre sacred to Bacchus; so that some, it often happened, were slain in the very chairs belonging to the hierophant and priests. Apollonius Tyanæus, when at Athens, was invited to the theatre; but he refused to enter a place so polluted with human gore; and affirmed in a letter, that the Athenians, unless they speedily desisted from this barbarous practice, would soon sacrifice hecatombs of men, instead of heifers, to their goddess. He wondered that Minerva had not forsaken her temple; and that Bacchus had not removed, as preferring the purer mountain of Cithæron.

IN the rock above the theatre is a large cavern, perhaps an antient quarry, the front ornamented with marble pilasters of the Corinthian order, supporting an entablature, on which are three inscriptions. Over that in the middle, is a female figure,
which

which had loft its head in the year 1676, mounted on two or three fteps, fedent. On one fide is a marble fun-dial, moved awry from its proper pofition. It is of a kind antiently very common[1], as is evident from the great number ftill in ufe about Athens, particularly in the tract called *the gardens*, where many are fet on the mud-walls, often with very rude gnomons. Above the cavern, are two columns, ftanding on the fteep flope, between the foot of the caftle-wall and the fedent figure. They are of unequal heights, and have triangular capitals. On each of thefe a tripod has been fixed, as is evident from the marks of the feet, which may be feen from the battlements of the fortrefs. The Greeks have converted the cave into a chapel, which is called Panagia Spiliótiſſa, *The Virgin of the Grotto*. The fides of the rock within are covered with holy portraits. The door is rarely open, but I was once prefent at the celebration of mafs, when it was lighted up with wax-candle, and filled with fmoke of incenfe, with bearded priefts, and a devout croud; the fpectacle fuiting the place, which is at once folemn and romantic. The tripods, which decorated this monument, were obtained by chorufes exhibited in the theatre below, probably at the Dionyfia; and confecrated to Bacchus. The firft infcription informs us of the author and age, as well as of the occafion of the building. " Thrafyllus, fon of Thrafyllus of
" Deceleia, dedicated *the tripod*; having, when he provided a
" chorus, conquered with men for the tribe Hippothoontis.
" Evius of Chalcis was mufician. Neæchmus was Archon.
" Carcidamus fon of Sotis was teacher." This archonfhip falls on the firft year of the cxvth Olympiad, three hundred and twenty years before Chrift. The other infcriptions are records of a fimilar nature. " The people provided a chorus. Pytha-
" ratus was archon; the prefident of the games was Thraficles,.
" fon of Thafyllus, of Deceleia. The tribe Pandionis con-
" quered in the conteft of men. Nicocles of Ambracia was

---

[1] Lord Befborough has a fmall one in his choice and curious collection of antiquities at Roehampton. See the form in Paciaudius.

" mufician

"musician. Lysippus an Arcadian was teacher." The third has a like preamble, and refers to the same year, but to another class of competitors. "The tribe Hippothoontis conquered in the contest of boys. Theon of Thebes was musician. Pronomus a Theban was teacher." Pytharatus was archon in the second year of the cxxviith Olympiad[1], so that Thrasycles presided and procured other tripods, to be placed on the family monument, forty nine years after it was erected by Thrasyllus his father. Deceleia was a borough-town of the tribe Hippothoontis. On one of the tripods was represented the story of Apollo and Diana killing the children of Niobe. It is mentioned by Pausanias; who then proceeds to relate, that he had seen this Niobe on mount Sipylus. The figure[2] over the grotto was probably intended to represent that celebrated phantom, which he has described; the idea of placing the statue there corresponding with her story, and being suggested both by the tripod, and by the tragedies, which were acted in the theatre, containing her unhappy catastrophe.

GOING on from the theatre of Bacchus, you have an extensive cornfield, once part of the Ceramicus within the city, on the left hand, now bounded by the bed of the Ilissus, beyond which are rocks; and before you, on an eminence, is the monument of Philopappus. At some distance from the theatre begins an out-work of the fortress, standing on antient arches, supposed to be the remains of a stoa or portico, which was connected with the theatre called the Odéum[3]. This fabric was designed

[1] Before Christ, 271.
[2] If it be conjectured that this figure represented a Tribe, the answer is, that no instance of such personification has been produced.
Pausanias may be cited as mentioning statues or pictures of *the people*, but this is a mistranslation. Demus was an Athenian of singular beauty, the son of Pyrilampes a friend of Pericles. v. *Meursius Pop. Ath.* p. 774. p. 779. *Att. Lect.* p. 1867.
[3] Pausanias, p. 23. describing the acropolis, mentions that Attalus had offered the war of the giants, the battle of the Athenians and Amazons, &c. which were (προς τῷ τοιχι τῷ Νοτιῳ) against the south wall, and each as much as two cubits.

Among

designed by Pericles for the musical contests, which he regulated and introduced at the Panathenæan solemnity. The building was finished by Lycurgus son of Lycophron. It contained many rows of seats and marble columns. The roof was constructed with the masts and yards of Persian ships, and formed to imitate the pavilion of Xerxes. Here was the tribunal of the archon or supreme magistrate; and here the Athenians listened to the Rhapsodists rehearsing the poems of Homer, and to the songs in praise of the patriots Harmodius and Aristogiton and Thrasybulus. Aristion and Sylla set it on fire; the former, when he fled to the acropolis, because the timber would have enabled the enemy to raise machines for an attack without loss of time. King Ariobarzanes the second, named Philopator, who reigned in Cappadocia not long after[1], restored it; and in a stable is an inscription, which has belonged to a statue of him erected by the persons, whom he appointed the overseers. He was honoured also with a statue by the people, as appears from another inscription. Before the entrance were statues of the kings of Egypt; and within, a Bacchus worth seeing. This was the edifice in being when Pausanias published his Attica. Afterwards, as he informs us, it was rebuilt by Atticus Herodes in memory of his wife Regilla. This lady was a Roman of high extraction, and died of ill usage, which Herodes was supposed to have abetted; but he put his house into mourning, refused a second consulate on account of his affliction, and dedicated her female ornaments in the temple at Eleusis. This fabric was roofed with cedar, and Greece had not a rival to it in dimensions and magnificence. The wall of the inner front of the proscenium is still standing, very lofty, with open arches; serving as part of an out-work of the castle; and beyond it, turning up toward the castle-gate, a portion of the exterior wall

---

Among the prodigies which were supposed to have pre-signified the event of the war between Antony, who was stiled *a new Bacchus*, and Cæsar, was this; the Bacchus in the combat with the Giants was loosened by a hurricane and borne into the theatre beneath. Plutarch.

[1] From the year of Rome 692 to 712. v. *Corsin. Inscriptiones Atticæ.*

of the right wing is vifible. On the right hand, within the gate, is the way into the area, which was fown with wheat; as was alfo the circular fweep of the hill on which the feats once ranged. In the wall of the profcenium on this fide is a fmall niche or cavity, with a low entrance. The Dervifhes have a *teckeh* or place of worfhip above, with a room, in which the bow-ftring, when a Turk is fentenced to be ftrangled, is commonly adminiftered. A way leads from that part, within the out-work, to a door at the end next the theatre of Bacchus, and in that line Paufanias appears to have afcended to the front of the acropolis. Going on from the Odéum, without turning, you defcend among Turkifh fepulchres, and by the burying-grounds, into the vale at the foot of the hill.

CHAP. XIII.

Of the areopagus --- The tribunal when extinct --- The pnyx --- Account of pnyx.

IN the preceding chapter we have mentioned the hill of the areopagus. This place is defcribed by Paufanias as oppofite to the cave of Apollo and Pan. In Lucian, Mercury, arriving at Athens with Juftice, who is fent by Jupiter to hold a court on areopagus, bids her fit down on the hill, looking toward pnyx, while he mounts up to the acropolis and makes proclamation for all perfons concerned to appear before her. Juftice defires to be informed, before he goes, who it was fhe beheld approaching them, with horns on his head, hairy legs, and a paftoral pipe in his hand. Mercury relates the ftory of Pan, and fhowing her the cave, his dwelling, tells her, that feeing them from it, not far off, he was coming, it was likely, to receive them. The hill before noted is proved to have been that of the areopagus by its fituation both with refpect to the cave and to pnyx, of which place we fhall treat next. It is afcended by fteps cut in

the

the rock, and by it, on the fide next to the temple of Thefeus, is a fmall church of St. Dionyfius, near one ruined and a well now choked up, in which, they tell you, St. Paul on fome occafion was hid. The *upper council* of Athens affembled in the areopagus, and a writer of the Auguftan age has recorded the clay-roof of the fenate-houfe there as very antient and ftill exifting. Paufanias informs us, that he faw on the fide next the acropolis, within the inclofure or wall, a monument and altar of Œdipus, and, after much enquiry, found that his bones had been removed thither from Thebes.

THE areopagus was long the feat of a moft ferious, filent, folemn, and impartial tribunal. The end of this court of judicature is as obfcure as its origin, which was derived from very remote antiquity. It exifted, with the other magiftracies, in the time of Paufanias. The term of its fubfequent duration is not afcertained; but a writer, who lived under the emperors Theodofius the elder and younger, mentions it as extinct. The actions for murther were introduced by the archon called *the king*, who laying afide his crown, which was of myrtle, voted as a common member; and thefe caufes were ufually tried in the open air, that the criminal and his accufer might not be under the fame roof. It was the bufinefs of a herald to deliver a wand to each of the judges.

WE have taken notice more than once of a valley between the hill of the acropolis and Lycabettus. That region of the antient city was called Cœle or *The hollow*. By the fide of the mountain, beyond the way formerly called *Through* Cœle, nearly oppofite to the rock of the areopagus, is a large, naked, femicircular area or terrace fupported by ftones of a vaft fize, the faces cut into fquares. A track leads to it between the areopagus and the temple of Thefeus. As you afcend to the brow, fome fmall channels occur, cut perhaps to receive libations. The defcent into the area is by hewn fteps, and the rock within is fmoothed down perpendicularly in front, extending to the fides,

fides, not in a ftrait line, but with an obtufe angle at the fteps. This place has been miftaken for the areopagus, and for the odéum, but was the Pnyx.

Pnyx was a place of public affembly, not boafting the curious labour of a theatre, but formed with the fimplicity of primitive times. There the citizens met to tranfact their affairs; and by law no perfon could be crowned elfewhere, on a decree of the people. The bufinefs was done afterwards in the theatre of Bacchus; but they continued to chufe the magiftrates and to vote the ftrategus or prætor in pnyx, which was hallowed by command of an oracle. The furniture on record is a ftone or altar, on which certain oaths were taken; a pulpit for the orators; and a fun-dial, made on the wall when Apfeudes was archon [1]. The pulpit, which before looked toward the fea, was turned a contrary way by the thirty tyrants, who confidered naval dominion as the parent of democracy. A portion of the rock near the entrance, within, was probably left for the altar to be placed on it; and a broad ftep or bank, on each fide by the perpendicular wall, was intended perhaps to raife the magiftrates who prefided, and perfons of fuperior rank, above the croud. The grooves, it may be conjectured, were for tablets containing decrees and orders. The circular wall, which now reaches only to the top of the terrace, it is likely, was higher and ferved as an inclofure. Excepting this, and the accceffion of foil, with the removal of the altar, the pulpit, and the fun-dial, pnyx may be deemed to have undergone no very material alteration. It had formerly many houfes about it, and that region of the city was called by its name. Cimon, with Elpinice his fifter, lived in Pnyx; and Plato relates of the earlier Athens, that it had extended on one fide of the acropolis toward the rivers Eridanus and Iliffus, and on the other had comprized Pnyx, having beyond it mount Lycabettus.

[1] Before Chrift, 434.

C H A P.

CHAP. XIV.

Story of Thefeus --- A temple erected to him --- The decorations --- Prefent ftate of the temple --- The fculptures --- Gymnafium of Ptolemy.

WE proceed now to the temple of Thefeus. This moft renowned hero, it is related, was born at Trœzen a city of the Peloponnefus, and was the fon of Neptune and Ægeus king of Athens by Æthra daughter of Pittheus. His mother conducted him, when fixteen years old, to a rock, beneath which Ægeus had depofited his fword and flippers. She directed him to bear thefe pledges to Athens; and he refolved to go by land, though the way was full of perils. In Epidauria he was ftopped by Periphetes, whom he flew, and afterwards carried about his weapon, which was a club, in imitation of Hercules. Sinis or Pityocamptes, whofe haunt was by the Ifthmus of Corinth, had been accuftomed to faften to bended pines the unfortunate perfons, whom he could feize, to be torn in pieces by their elaftic violence. On him Thefeus retaliated. He killed Phœa the terrible fow of Crommyon, and mother of the famous Caledonian boar. He then entered the Megaris and encountered Sciron, whom he threw into the fea. It was the practice of this monfter to force paffengers to wafh his feet by a precipice called Chelone, and to kick them unexpectedly down. By Eleufis, Cercyon made him wreftle for his life, and was overcome. By the Eleufinian Cephiffus, he flew Polypemon furnamed Procruftes, compelling him to undergo the fame torture which he was ufed to inflict on travellers; fitting their bodies to his beds, either by tenfion or amputation. Paffing the Cephiffus, he was hofpitably entertained by the Phytalidæ. He arrived at Athens on the eighth of Hecatombæon or July. He wore his hair platted, and a garment, which reached to his heels.

heels. Ægeus, on feeing the fword, acknowleged him for his fon. After this, Thefeus fubdued Pallas, who had rebelled; and drove the Marathonian bull alive into the city, where it was facrificed to Apollo Delphinius. He failed to Crete, deftroyed the Minotaur, and efcaped out of the Labyrinth, affifted by a clew given him by Ariadne, daughter of Minos. He made Athens the capital of all Attica, and inftituted the Panathenæan feftival. He defeated the Amazons. He aflifted Adraftus in recovering the bodies of the dead Argives from the Thebans, and flew Creon their king. He was prefent at the marriage-feaft of Pirithous; and aiding, with the Lapithæ, to expell the Centaurs, who were intoxicated, and offered violence to the women. He was fifty years old, when he feized Helen, a girl not marriageable, as fhe was dancing in a temple at Sparta. His abettor was Pirithous, who, in return, required his company on a like expedition, which proved unfortunate. It was to procure for him the daughter of Pluto, king of the Molofli; or, as mythologifts relate, they meditated a rape of Proferpine, and defcended into hell, but were detained there, condemned to fit on a rock without power to rife. Hercules obtained liberty for Thefeus. In the mean time the Tyndaridæ had invaded Attica, and taken Aphidna, where Helen was, concealed, with Æthra his mother, whom they carried away into captivity. The Athenians received them into the city as friends at the perfuafion of Meneftheus, whom they made king. Thefeus returned to Athens, but was foon compelled to fly. He took refuge in the ifland of Scyros, where he was killed by Lycomedes, the king, who pufhed him down a precipice.

IT was the popular opinion at Athens, after the battle of Marathon, that the fpectre of Thefeus had been feen fighting againft the Medes. The Pythia directed the Athenians to remove his relics to their city, and to honour him as a hero. His bones, with a brazen helmet and a fword lying near them, were difcovered by Cimon fon of Miltiades; who tranfported them

from

TRAVELS IN GREECE. 71

from Scyros, about eight hundred years after he died. The Athenians received them with splendid proceffions and facrifices; and rejoiced, as if he were come again in perfon. They inftituted facred rites for him, as for a God, and erected an heroum or monument on the Colonus Hippius, and a temple in the city, on which they conferred the privilege of an afylum. This building, which was called the Theféum, was in fubfequent ages reputed fo exceedingly holy, that with the Parthenon and another temple, it was generally adored.

THE temple of Thefeus was decorated with (γραφαι) reprefentations of the Athenians fighting with the Amazons, and of the battle of the Centaurs with the Lapithæ. Thefeus was diftinguifhed, as having killed a Centaur, while the others were engaged in equal combat. The third wall required explanation, as Paufanias obferves, partly from time, partly becaufe Micon had not expreffed the whole ftory. Minos, it was faid, had required Thefeus to prove he was the fon of Neptune, by recovering a fignet, which he threw into the fea; and they related, that he arofe with it and with a golden crown prefented to him by Amphitrite. It was Micon who painted Thefeus and the Athenians fighting with the Amazons in the Stoa or Portico called Pœcile. He was alfo a ftatuary.

THE temple of Thefeus is of the Doric order, and in the ftyle of its architecture greatly refembles the Parthenon. Though a very antient fabric, it is entire, except the roof, which is modern, and vaulted, with an aperture or two for the admiffion of light. The pavement has been removed, and the walls are bare. It is a Greek church, dedicated to St. George, as good a hero as Thefeus. A recefs for the holy table has been erected, as in the Parthenon, but in the pronaos; and decorated with portraits of faints. The entrance is in the fide of the cell, at a low door, which is kept locked, except on the feftival, when mafs is celebrated. It is plated with iron, and much battered; the Turks firing at it with bullets to try the force of their

powder,

powder, the goodnefs of their pieces, or their own dexterity at a mark. In the corner, within, ftands a circular marble, which has ferved as a font. From the infcriptions, which range in four columns, it appears to have belonged to the Prytanéum. Among the names of travellers on the wall is that of Mr. Vernon [1]. The cell has been painted on the outfide with figures of faints, unlefs thefe traces, which are faint, may be referred rather to the pencil of Micon. An attentive fpectator will difcover likewife fome architectural ornaments and mouldings, with ftars in the foffits of the lacunaria of the portico [2]. The pofticum has been injured by lightening. The fubftruction is vifible, except on the fide next the areopagus, where the foil reaches nearly to the top of the ftep.

THE fculptures ftill extant about this temple, though much impaired, witnefs the hand of a mafter, and furnifh abundant proof, that Thefeus was its owner. The exploits of this hero and of Hercules were carved on the metopes, in fixteen compartments, in alto relievo, and the following fubjects are intelligible, viz. Thefeus killing the fow of Crommyon; throwing Sciron from a rock into the fea; wreftling with Cercyon; deftroying the Minotaur; driving the bull of Marathon to Athens: Hercules ftrangling the Neméan lion; with Iolaus deftroying the hydra; receiving the golden apples from a nymph, one of the Hefperides. Mr. Pars copied thefe with the bafs reliefs of the pronaos and pofticum, except a few ftones defigned by Mr. Stuart. In the fculpture of the pofticum, it is remarkable, that Thefeus is diftinguifhed in the fame manner as by Micon. He is killing a Centaur, whom he has thrown on the ground, backwards. In another piece two Centaurs are burying one of the Lapithæ in a pit alive, laying over him a

---

[1] See his letter relating to Greece, and particularly to Athens. *Philofoph. Tranf.* n. 124. For an account of the author, fee *Wood's Athen. Oxon.* 2d Ed. v. 2. col. 599, 600.

[2] Mr. Pars found out the method ufed in drawing the echinus or *eggs and anchors*, from the marks of the compaffes on the wall.

large

TRAVELS IN GREECE. 73

large ftone. On another is the battle with the Thebans, and Creon dead. Two figures with fhields may be Hercules and his companion Iolaus defcending into hell, where they find Thefeus and Pirithous fitting on rocks, and between them a female, perhaps Metanoia or Repentance.

THE temple of Thefeus was near the Gymnafium of Ptolemy, which was not far from the agora or market-place. In the gymnafium, befides other ftatues, was one of the founder in brafs. A remnant of maffive wall in the town, not far from the temple, is fuppofed to have been part of that building.

CHAP. XV.

A marble arch or gate-way---The temple of Jupiter Olympius---Not finifhed before Hadrian---Number of ftatues, &c.---The ruin ---Of the water of Athens---An aquæduct---Of the Eridanus and Iliffus---Remark---An antient bridge.

AFTER the temple of Thefeus no ruin occurs without the town, keeping the acropolis, as before, on the right hand, until we come oppofite to the end of the rock, where the fcaffold was ftanding. There, at fome diftance in the plain, is a marble gate, which feparated the old city from Hadrianopolis or New Athens. It is related, that Thefeus erected a ftela or column on the ifthmus of Corinth, which remained above an hundred years, to the time of Codrus, when it was demolifhed by the Peloponnefians. It had infcriptions in Greek. On one fide, " Here is Peloponnefus, not Ionia;" and on the other " Here " is not Peloponnefus, but Ionia." The gate, ferving as a boundary, is infcribed in capitals in like manner. Over the arch on one fide, " What you fee is Athens, the old city of " Thefeus;" and on the other front, " What you fee is the " city of Hadrian, and not of Thefeus." We dug down to

L the

the basement, and with much difficulty procured ladders sufficiently long and strong to ascend and measure the upper part. From the traces of painting on the walls above, it appears that a church has been erected against it. This fabric, which is of the Corinthian order, with the tower of the Winds and other structures at Athens, is seen to disadvantage from the accession of soil round about it. Beyond it, within the region of new Athens, is the majestic ruin of the temple of Jupiter Olympius.

Deucalion was said to have erected the first temple of Jupiter on this spot; and the place of his burial was shown near it to prove that he had lived at Athens. Pisistratus the second founder dying, his sons carried on the work; but after they were slain, so many difficulties occurred, that it remained for ages unfinished; a specimen of the only temple in the world designed with a grandeur worthy of the ruler of heaven; and exciting astonishment in every beholder. About four hundred years after Pisistratus, Antiochus Epiphanes promised to complete it; and Cossutius, a Roman, the architect, is extolled for his noble ideas of magnitude in the cell, and for disposing the columns and the entablature with an exact symmetry, which testified his exquisite knowlege and skill. It is likely he was employed in fitting up the inside of the fabric, in which, as well as in the Parthenon, were colonnades. The temple was a dipteros and hypæthros, or with double rows of columns and open to the sky; though not, as was most common, with ten, but with eight, columns in front. Rome afforded no example of this species. It was one of the four marble edifices, which had raised to the pinnacle of renown the architects[1], who planned them; men, it is said, admired in the assembly of the gods for their wisdom and excellence.

Sylla, when he punished Athens, dared to plunder even Jupiter Olympius, and removed columns and brazen thresholds

---

[1] Antistates, Callæschros, Antimachides, and Porinus were the earlier architects employed on this fabric.

to adorn the capitol at Rome. The structure still continuing imperfect, the kings in alliance with Augustus agreed to finish it by contribution, and jointly dedicate it to the Genius of the emperor. Afterwards, by command of Caligula, the image of Jupiter was transported to the capitol, where the god submitted to lose his own head, which was broken off, and to accept in its room that of a monster less civil to him even than Sylla. It was reserved for Hadrian to put the last hand to a work, on which Athens had expended seven thousand eighty-eight talents, and which Antiochus, with united kings, had been ambitious of completing. This achievement of the emperor was celebrated in a hymn sung at the sacrifice, when he dedicated the fabric to Jupiter, more than seven hundred years after its foundation by Pisistratus; and he acquired from it the title of Olympius. He placed in the temple an uncommon serpent brought from India.

We shall insert here an extract from Pausanias relating to this temple. " The image of Jupiter is worth seeing, not
" for its similitude to other statues in size, for those of the
" Romans and Rhodians are not colossal, but as made of ivory
" and gold, and with art, as will be perceived by those who
" consider its magnitude. The statues of Hadrian there are
" two of Thasian marble, and two of Egyptian. The Athe-
" nian Colonies stand in brass before the columns. The whole
" inclosure is about four stadia, half a mile, in circumference,
" and full of statues; for one of Hadrian was dedicated by
" each of the cities, and Athens has exceeded them all by
" offering the Colossus, (which was behind the temple and
" worthy of notice.) The antiquities within the inclosure are
" a brazen Jupiter, and a temple of Saturn and Rhea, and the
" portion of this goddess who is called Olympia. There the
" pavement is rent asunder as much as a cubit; and they relate,
" that after the Deucalionéan flood the chasm afforded a passage
" to the water; and they cast yearly into it wheat flower mixed
" with honey. And, besides a statue of Isocrates, there is a

" brazen

"brazen tripod supported by Persians, of Phrygian marble, worth seeing." Of the pedestals, which belonged to these statues, several are found scattered about in the town, fixed in the walls, or half buried in earth; and some of the inscriptions are preserved. Among them is that of one of the Thasian images, which I saw immured at a church, and copied. Within the peribolus or inclosure is part of another, a massive piece of white marble, lying, probably near its original site, the face, which is inscribed with very large characters, downwards. From these it appears that the priest of the temple at the time of their erection was named Tiberius Claudius Atticus, and, it is supposed, was the famous Herodes. The inclosure has been demolished, but a terrace of considerable extent is still sustained by part of the wall, which on the side next to the Ilissus is strengthened with buttresses.

THE ruin of the temple of Jupiter Olympius consists of prodigious columns, tall and beautiful, of the Corinthian order, fluted; some single, some supporting their architraves; with a few massive marbles beneath; the remnant of a vast heap, which only many ages could have consumed and reduced into so scanty a compass. The columns are of very extraordinary dimensions, being about six feet in diameter, and near sixty in height[1]. The number without the cell was one hundred and sixteen or twenty. Seventeen were standing in 1676; but, a few years before we arrived, one was overturned, with much difficulty, and applied to the building a new mosque in the Bazar or market-place. This violence was avenged by the Bashaw of Negropont, who made it a pretext for extorting from the vaiwode or governor fifteen purses; the pillar being, he alledged, the property of their master, the Grand Signior. It was an angular column and of consequence in determining the dimensions of the fabric. We regretted, that the fall of this mighty mass had not been postponed until we came, as it would have afforded an opportunity of inspecting and measuring some members, which we

[1] Ruins of Athens, p. 39.

found

found far too lofty to be attempted. On a piece of the architrave suppôrted by a couple of columns, are two parallel walls, of modern mafonry, arched about the middle, and again near the top. You are told it has been the habitation of a hermit, doubtlefs of a Stylites ; but of whatever building it has been part, and for whatever purpofe defigned, it muft have been erected thus high in air, while the immenfe ruin of this huge ftructure was yet fcarcely diminifhed, and the heap inclined fo as to render it acceffible. It was remarked that two ftones of a ftep in the front had coalefced at the extremity, fo that no juncture could be perceived; and the like was difcovered alfo in a ftep of the Parthenon. In both inftances it may be attributed to a concretory fluid, which pervades the marble in the quarry. Some portion remaining in the pieces, when taken green as it were, and placed in mutual contact, it exfuded and united them by a procefs fimilar to that in a bone of an animal when broken and properly fet.

THE water antiently conveyed in channels to the city and to the Piræus, coming from fources in the mountains, which abound with ore, was hard, and had a fcum fwimming on the furface, fuch as may be ftill feen at the public cifterns, was unfit to drink, and applicable folely to other ufes. The wells afforded a more wholfome fluid, but were the occafion of many quarrels. Solon enacted that all, who lived within four ftadia, or half a mile, of a public well, fhould have the privilege of drawing from it ; that thofe who were more remote fhould provide their own water, but fhould be allowed a certain quantity daily from the next well, if they found none on digging ten fathom deep. The tranfgreffors were fined by the Epiftates or præfect of the waters. The city now abounds in wells, fome houfes having three or four, in confequence of thefe early and wife regulations.

NEW Athens was fupplied with water by the munificence of Hadrian from remote fources, at a vaft expenfe. He founded a very extenfive aquædud, of which many piers are yet ftanding

in

in the tract beneath Cephifia, or Cevrifha, as that village is now called. It was finifhed by his fon and fucceffor Antoninus Pius in his third confulate. The water was partly conveyed by a duct running along the fide of the adjacent hill, and diftributed to the town from a refervoir or ciftern cut in the rock, and fronted with an arcade of marble, of the Ionic order. One half of this remains, confifting of two columns and the fpring of the arch. The foil is rifen fome feet round about the fhafts. Over the columns is half the infcription[1], which was copied entire by Spon from a manufcript then two hundred years old, and was as follows :

The part remaining.
IMP. CAESAR T. AELIVS
AVG. PIVS COS. III TRIB. POT. II. P. P. AQVAEDVCTVM IN NOVIS
CONSVMMAVIT

The part fupplied.
HADRIANVS ANTONINVS
ATHENIS COEPTVM AD IVO HADRIANO PATRES VO
DEDICAVITQ.

The ftate of this ruin was the fame in 1676 as now. It ftands beneath the mountain of St. George, antiently, it is fuppofed, Anchefmus; and is about a mile from the gate of Hadrian. The fpace between, where once was new Athens, is now ploughed and fowed.

On the left hand, returning from the aquædua, is the bed of the Iliffus; and higher up, the junction of it and of the Eridanus. The water of this river was fo bad that the cattle

---

[1] In the Modern Univerfal Hiftory it is made to refer to New Athens in Delos. See volume of Chronology, p. 1031.

would

would scarcely drink of it. The Iliſſus is now, as it ever was, an occaſional torrent. In ſummer it is quite dry. During our reſidence at Athens, I ſeveral times viſited the bed, after ſnow had fallen on the mountains, or heavy rain, hoping to ſee it filled to the margin, and ruſhing along with majeſtic violence; but never found even the ſurface covered; the water lodging in the rocky cavities, and trickling from one to another.

AND here it may be remarked, that the poets who celebrate the Iliſſus as a ſtream laving the fields, cool, lucid, and the like, have both conceived and conveyed a falſe idea of this renowned water-courſe. They may beſtow a willow fringe on its naked banks, amber waves on the muddy Mæander, and hanging woods on the bare ſteep of Delphi, if they pleaſe; but the foundation in nature will be wanting; nor indeed is it eaſy for a deſcriptive writer, when he exceeds the ſphere of his own obſervation, to avoid falling into local abſurdities and untruths.

GOING on by the bed of the Iliſſus, as before, toward the town, you come to a ruinous bridge of three arches, the ſtones maſſive, and without cement. A piece of ordinary wall, ſtanding on it, is part of a monaſtery, which was abandoned after the Turks took Athens. The ingenious Frenchman [1], who, in a view of this ſpot, has exhibited the bridge ſtanding in a full ſtream, may juſtly plead, that the ſame liberties have been indulged to the painter as to the poet.

[1] See Le Roy

CHAP. XVI.

The stadium --- Rebuilt by Atticus Herodes --- Present state --- A temple by the Ilissus --- Once the Eleusinium --- The lesser mysteries --- Temple of Diana the huntress --- The fountain Callirhoe or Enneacrunus --- Scene of a dialogue of Plato --- Changed.

THE bridge over the bed of the Ilissus, mentioned in the preceding chapter, is opposite to the stadium called the Panathenæan from a solemn festival of all the Athenians, at which the games were held there. By uniting the two banks it made the crossing easy, and prevented any inconvenience if a flood happened. The rewards of victory in the gymnic exercises performed in the stadium were a crown of olive, and a jar of most pretious oil, the produce of holy trees called Moriæ. These were twelve in number, immediate descendants from the original olive of Minerva Polias, planted in the Academy, and on account of their sanctity untouched by the Lacedæmonians, when they invaded Attica. In it private merit was emblazoned by public gratitude, the herald proclaiming the honorary decrees of the people, with the names of the persons presented with statues and golden crowns; and it was regarded as a glorious recompense, to be distinguished and applauded in this assembly. The emperor Hadrian presided, when at Athens, and furnished a thousand wild beasts to be hunted for their diversion. The stadium was one of the works of Lycurgus, and the ground-plat a torrent-bed, which he smoothed.

THE stadium of Lycurgus was much decayed, when Atticus Herodes, pleased with a crown, which had been conferred on him, and with his reception at the Panathenæa, rose up and addressing the company, promised the Athenians to provide for them, and for the Greeks who should repair to the next solemnity,

lemnity, and for thofe who fhould contend at it, a new ftadium of white marble. This was completed in four years, chiefly from the quarries on mount Pentele, and is extolled as without a rival, and as unequalled by any theatre. " What indeed, " fays Paufanias, is not alike pleafing to thofe, who have heard " of it, but is a wonder to thofe who have feen it, is the " ftadium of Herodes the Athenian. One may guefs at the " magnitude from hence. It is a mountain beginning at a " diftance, beyond the Iliffus, of a lunar form, reaching to the " river-bank, ftrait and double." The author, it feems, would infinuate, that the magnificence of Herodes was a topic not very agreeable. By the will of his father the people were entitled to a large bequeft; but among his papers were found vouchers for fums borrowed to a great amount. Herodes had balanced the old debt with the legacy. This had raifed a clamour; many murmuring, as defrauded of their due; and thefe affirmed, it was indeed a Panathenæan ftadium, for that all the Athenians paid for it. On one fide was a temple of Fortune, with a ftatue of ivory.

WHEN the Panathenæa, with the other fpectacles, ceafed, the ftadium became as ufelefs as the odéum or theatre, and was treated in like manner. The mountain, on which quarries were exhaufted, has been totally ftripped of its marble covering. The feats were continued in rows very high up, on the fide next the fea; the flopes favouring fuch a difpofition. At the two extremities by the Iliffus is fome ftone-work. The area, which produces grain, has been exactly meafured, and found to be fix hundred and thirty Englifh feet long. On the left hand, going up it, near the top, is a fubterraneous paffage through the mountain, once under the feats. This was a private way, by which the prefident of the games, the magiftrates, and priefts entered to take their places, after the fpectators were met; and by which, it has been furmifed, thofe who contended and were unfuccefsful made their retreat. Such avenues were not uncommon in the ftadiums of Greece.

GOING on from the ſtadium without croſſing the Iliſſus, you have a ſolitary church on the left hand at a diſtance, and before you a temple of white marble ſeated on the rock by the ſide of the river. This has been transformed, as well as the Parthenon and the temple of Theſeus, into a church, named *St. Mary on the rock*. It was abandoned by the Greeks, as defecrated, after the Romiſh maſs had been celebrated in it, in 1672, by order of the marquis de Nointell. On the wall next Hymettus are lines of one or two ſmall ſundials, and in the vaulted roof is the trunk of a little female ſtatue. Some traces remain of figures and of architectural ornaments painted in the inſide. An exact view of this temple is given in *The Ruins of Athens*, to which valuable work the reader is here referred. The fabric has ſuſtained ſome damage ſince, the exterior column next to the Iliſſus, in the front, being ruined, and the capital lying on the rock, much maimed. The ſubſtruction of the oppoſite end is ſo impaired, that it is likely a farther downfall will ſoon enſue; when the materials will be removed, as wanted, and the ſite in a few years become hardly diſtinguiſhable.

THE antients preferred particular ſituations for the temples of certain deities. A place, without the city, which men had no occaſion to approach, but at ſet times, and to ſacrifice, was commonly choſen for Ceres; ſhe requiring, that it ſhould be kept pure by chaſte religion and ſanctity of manners. The temple before deſcribed has ſtood on ſuch a ſpot, and, it is believed, was the famous Eleuſinium belonging to Ceres and Proſerpine, before which was a ſtatue of Triptolemus, mentioned by Pauſanias, who then enters on a detail of his ſtory, but, as he aſſerts, was prevented from proceeding in it and in his account of the temple by a dream; and therefore paſſes on to topics, of which he was at liberty to treat without reſerve. This place was regarded by the people with the ſame reverence as the Parthenon and Theſeum.

THE *Leſſer Myſteries*, which belonged to Proſerpine were ſolemnized yearly in the month Antheſterion or February, in the region

region called Agræ, which was beyond the Iliſſus. They who aſpired to initiation were forewarned to come with clean hands and hearts, and a knowlege of the Greek tongue; beſides an awful ſenſe of the great holineſs of thoſe antient things to which they were about to be introduced. The herald commanded all murderers, magicians, and wicked or impious perſons to depart. The aſſembly was purified by a ſolemn luſtration on the myſtic banks of the Iliſſus. The ceremony was accompanied with prayer and ſacrifice, the victim a young pig. When the rites had been fulfilled, they were admitted into the Eleuſinium, probably in companies; for it is deſcribed as a ſmall building. Afterwards, they were ſtiled Myſtæ, and were expected to obſerve certain injunctions, of which one was to abſtain from eating red mullet, a delicacy ſacred to Ceres. One year at leaſt intervened, before they could attain to the *Greater Myſteries*, to which theſe were preparatory. Secrecy impenetrable, with night, veiled the whole tranſaction. This initiation was in the popular opinion of no trivial conſequence. The neglect of it is among the crimes imputed to Socrates. Greeks, Romans, and perſons from remoter countries, of both ſexes, were deſirous to partake of it, and Athens at the ſeaſon was crouded with devotees; receiving yearly into the Eleuſinium more people, than repaired to ſome other cities.

BEYOND the Eleuſinium, in Agræ, was a temple of Diana Agræa. She was repreſented bearing a bow, and named Agrotera, *the huntreſs*. It was ſaid, ſhe had hunted there on her firſt arrival from Delos. When the Medes landed at Marathon, the Athenians made a vow to her, to offer a goat for each of the enemy whom they ſhould kill; but ſhe proved ſo very propitious, that a ſufficient number of victims could not be procured, and they decreed to ſacrifice yearly five hundred, as was the cuſtom in the time of Xenophon. From this event ſhe was named Euclea, or *Glorious*. Her temple was erected from the ſpoils, which they dedicated, and in 1676 was a church called

M 2 *(Stávroſis*

(Stávrofis Petru, or *Stavroménu Petru) St. Peter's Crucifixion.* It was of white marble, and the floor Mofaic. The fite is now occupied by the church mentioned as on our left coming from the ftadium, a recent and mean ftructure, with fragments of columns and marbles lying in and about it. The Mofaic pavement was ordinary, much broken, and covered with dirt, fwarming, as we experienced, with large fleas. A fkull or two and fome human bones were fcattered on it. We found there an Ionic capital with marks of the compaffes ufed in forming the volute.

BENEATH the Eleufinium, in a rocky dell, is a fmall church with fome buildings, and trees, and veftiges of the fountain Callirhoe, or, as it was called after Pififtratus had furnifhed it with *nine pipes,* Enneacrunus. This was without the gate of Diochares, and near the Lycéum; the water copious, clear, and fit to drink. The current is now conveyed into the town, and only the holes, at which it iffued into the ciftern, remain. Thefe are in the rocky bank next to the temple of Jupiter Olympius, which is in the way to the gate dividing the cities of Thefeus and Hadrian, and not remote. At a little diftance is a modern ruinous fountain.

IN one of the dialogues of Plato, Socrates is reprefented as meeting Phædrus, who was going from a houfe by the temple of Jupiter Olympius toward the Lycéum, which was without the city. Perceiving, as they walked, that he had a book in his left hand, under his garment, Socrates propofed turning out of the road, and fitting down by the Iliffus. Phædrus confents, pointing to a lofty plane-tree as a proper place; and obferving, that as both had their feet naked, it would not be difagreeable to wet them, efpecially at that time of the year and day. The converfation changes to a local ftory, that Boreas had carried off Orithyia, daughter of Erectheus, as fhe was fporting by the Iliffus, not by the fountain, but two or three ftadia lower down, where was the croffing over to go to the temple of Diana Agræa,

and

TRAVELS IN GREECE. 85

and where was the altar of Boreas. On their arrival at the chosen spot, Socrates admires it, like a stranger or one rarely stirring out of the city into the hilly country round about. He praises the large and tall tree; the thicket of Agnus Castus, high and shady, then in full flower and fragrant; the cool delicious fountain running near, with the girls by it, and the images, which made it seem a temple of the Nymphs and Achelous; the grateful and sweet air; the shrill summer-chorus of locusts; and the elegance of verdure, prepared as it were to meet the reclining head.

THE vicinity of Enneacrunus has ceased to deserve encomiums like those bestowed on it by Socrates, since it has been deprived of the waste water of the fountain, which chiefly nourished the herbage and the plane-tree. The marble-facing and the images are removed; and the place is now dry, except a pool at the foot of the rock, down which the Ilissus commonly trickles. The water, which overflows after rain, is used by a currier, and is often offensive. The church in this dell occupies, it is probable, the site of the altar of the Muses, to whom, among other deities, the Ilissus was sacred. One lower down stands perhaps where Boreas had an altar. This God was believed to have assisted the Athenians in the Persian war, and was on that account honoured with a temple. By the Ilissus Codrus was slain.

CHAP. XVII.

The Muséum --- Monument of Philopappus --- Sepulchres --- The Cimonian sepulchres --- The eminence fronting the acropolis.

FOLLOWING the course of the Ilissus from Enneacrunus you have the theatre of Bacchus and the Odéum at a distance on the right hand. The intermediate plain, which made part of the *Ceramicus within the city*, has in several places the

scattered

scattered stones and rubbish of its former edifices. By the bed of the river are some masses of brick-work and traces of building; with a solitary church founded on a small rock. Farther on is the mountainous range lying before the Acropolis, of which the portion next to the Ilissus was called the Muséum, and, was said to have received its name from Musæus, a disciple of Orpheus, who, it was related, sung, and, dying of old age, was buried there. The summit was fortified by Antigonus and his son Demetrius Poliorcetes; but a small body of the Athenians succeeded in an attempt to scale, and expelled the garrison of Macedonians. The path of the wall, which ascended the hill, may be seen, when the ground is free from corn and herbage.

PAUSANIAS informs us, that a monument had been erected on the Muséum for a Syrian[1], but conceals his name. A part of it is still extant, with inscriptions. The ruin is of white marble, a portion of a semicircle, the convex side toward the Piræus. It consists of two niches, and on the left was a third, which, it is supposed, completed the symmetry of the structure. In the first niche on the right is a statue sedent; and underneath, an inscription in Greek, " King Antiochus, " Son of King Antiochus." In the middle niche is another statue and inscription, " Philopappus, son of Antiochus Epi- " phanes, of Bisa." This place was one of the demi or towns of the tribe Antiochis, which had its name from king Antiochus, who had been a great benefactor to the Athenians. These were the ancestors of the person, who, it is probable, filled the third niche. He is recorded on a pilaster between the two statues in a Latin inscription, which, it has been conjectured, was continued on the pilaster now missing. His name was Caius Julius Antiochus Philopappus, and he lived under Trajan. The posterity of king Antiochus were removed by Pompey to Rome,

---

[1] Pausanias, p. 24. See a comment on this passage in *Daniel by the LXX*. p. 629. Rome 1772. The author of the Dissertation makes Musæus to have been Moses, and Moses the Syrian here mentioned.

and

and reduced to the rank of citizens. The Syrian of Paufanias, it is fuppofed, was this Philopappus, one of his defcendants. From the infcription it appears that he attained to the dignity of conful, but, as he is not regiftered in the confular tables, it is moft likely that he was only *defigned*, and did not furvive to take the chair. The emperor is ftiled in the infcription OPTVMVS, which title was not beftowed on him before the year of Chrift one hundred and fifteen[1]. On the bafement beneath the pilafter is a bold relievo reprefenting a perfon in a chariot drawn by four horfes, preceded by attendants and followed by Victory; the figures as large as life. The foil beneath is wafhed away, and the bare rock with the fubftruction is vifible; the fpectator ftanding fome feet below the intended level. Near it is rubbifh of a church. We employed an old Albanian to watch nightly on our fcaffold, to prevent the ropes from being pilfered.

IN the fide of the rock of the Muféum next to the Iliffus, are the fepulchres, which we noted in our way from the Piræus. Some time after Solon, it was enacted at Athens, that no fepulchre fhould have more labour beftowed on it than could be performed by ten men in three days; that the roof fhould be plain; and that no Hermæ or Mercurial ftatues fhould be allowed. Thefe perhaps are of a remoter antiquity, and were defigned for no vulgar tenants; but, though manfions of the illuftrious dead, they have long fince been ftripped of their marble-facings and ornaments, and are now open, and defiled; ferving chiefly to fhelter cattle from the fun.

WE now enter the valley at the foot of the hill of the acropolis, in which is a track leading between Pnyx and the Areopagus, toward the temple of Thefeus. This region was called Cœle, or *the Hollow*. On the left hand is a gap in the

---

[1] v. *Fabrett. ad Col. Traj.* In the following year the title Parthicus was confirmed to Trajan. *Dio.* This does not occur among the titles on the pilafter, and the omiffion will afcertain the date, if it be fuppofed that the infcription was not continued.

mountain,

mountain, where, it is believed, was the Melitenſian gate; and within, is a ſepulchre or two in the rock. Going on, other ſepulchres hewn in the ſide of the mountain, like thoſe firſt mentioned, occur; and here again we may regret that no friendly inſcription informs us of their reſpective owners; but theſe were named *The Cimonian ſepulchres*. Herodotus relates, that the ſepulchre of Cimon, father of Miltiades, was fronting the acropolis, beyond the way called *Through Cæle*; and that near him were interred his mares, which had obtained for him three victories at Olympia. Cimon, ſon of Miltiades, died in Cyprus, and Thucydides the hiſtorian was ſlain in Thrace; but the relics of each were tranſported to the burying-place of their family. The ſepulchre of Thucydides was by that of Elpinice, the ſiſter of Cimon, in Cœle, not far from the Melitenſian gate, and in it was a ſtela or column inſcribed " Thucydides ſon of Olorus, of Alimus." There alſo was ſhown a tomb of Herodotus.

THE aſcent to the brow is farther on the left hand, beyond Pnyx; and by the track are ſmall channels, already mentioned, cut in the rock, perhaps to receive libations. From that eminence, on which the Perſians, and before them the Amazons, encamped near the Areopagus, the Venetians battered the acropolis with four mortars and ſix pieces of cannon, in 1687, when the roof of the Parthenon was deſtroyed. This event was remembered by a little old man living at Athens, who conducted me to a ruined windmill above Pnyx as ſtanding on or near the ſpot from which the bomb was thrown.

CHAP.

CHAP. XVIII.

Of the gate called Dipylon --- Abſtract of Pauſanias --- The Pompeium, &c. --- Statues of Jupiter and Hadrian --- Of Harmodius and Ariſtogiton --- Paintings in Pœcile --- The region called Melite --- The Agora --- The altar of Pity.

WE ſhould proceed next to the antiquities within the preſent town, but theſe have been publiſhed with accuracy and fidelity by two of our countrymen, one of whom was my companion in this expedition. To their work I refer the curious reader; and, to complete our view of this illuſtrious city, ſhall now diveſt Pauſanias of the digreſſions, which obſcure his method, and follow him, as it were unembarraſſed, in his ſurvey; ſubjoining ſome farther account of a few of the places, and ſuch remarks on their ſituation as may contribute to enlarge our knowlege of the general topography of antient Athens. But firſt we ſhall treat of the gate Dipylon.

DIPYLON was the gate at which Sylla entered from the Piræus, and was ſometimes called the *Piræan Gate*. It led toward Thria and Eleuſis, and was likewiſe called the *Thriaſian* and the *Sacred Gate*. A region *within* and a ſuburb *without* it being named the Ceramicus, it was alſo called *the Gate of the Ceramicus*. Being placed as it were in the mouth of the city, it was larger and wider than the other gates, and had broad avenues to it. One was from the Agora or *market-place*, a portion of the inner Ceramicus; which was on the ſide of the Acropolis next mount Hymettus. At this the citizens could march out in battle-array, paſſing, it ſhould ſeem, through Cœle: The principal ſlaughter made by Sylla was about the Agora, in the Ceramicus; and when the citadel was reduced, he incloſed there and decimated the Athenians.

N PAUSANIAS

90   TRAVELS IN GREECE.

PAUSANIAS, on his arrival in the city from the Piræus, notes firſt an edifice called the Pompeium, and a temple of Ceres near it; and then the ſtoas or porticoes, adorned with braſs ſtatues, extending from the gate, which was Dipylon, into the Ceramicus. He begins with the ſtoa named *the Mercuries*, which had temples of the gods; the gymnaſium of Mercury; the houſe of Polytion, then ſacred to Bacchus; and after it, a building with ſtatues. This brings him into the Ceramicus. He then returns to the ſtoa on the right, which had ſtatues and was called *the Royal*; becauſe there was the tribunal of the archon ſtiled *the King*. The aſcent of the Areopagus being long and wearifome to old men, the venerable ſenate ſometimes met in this portico. There ſtood Jupiter Eleutherius, or *the Deliverer*; and the emperor Hadrian. The ſtoa of Jupiter was behind. This he deſcribes next; with the temple of Apollo Patrous, which was near; the Metróum or temple of Cybele; the Senate-houſe of the Five-hundred; the Tholus; and higher up, a range of ſtatues, among which were the ten heroes ſtiled the Eponymi; and Attalus, Ptolemy, and Hadrian, from whom likewiſe tribes were named; and after theſe, beſides others, Lycurgus, and Demoſthenes. Near this ſtatue was a temple of Mars, probably at the Areopagus; and then, not far off, the ſtatues of Harmodius and Ariſtogiton; then the ſtatues before the entrance of the Odeum; then the Odéum; the fountain Enneacrunus; the Eleuſinium beyond it; and more remote, the temple of Diana Euclea in Agræ. The author returns into the city, and begins again, above the Ceramicus and *royal Portico*, with the Hephæſtéum or temple of Vulcan and Minerva, by which was a temple of Venus Urania; then, going toward the portico called Pœcile, was the Hermes Agoræus or Mercury of the Agora; and near it, a gate[1], on which was a trophy

[1] By the gate near the Mercury of the Agora, wine was ſold *Att. Lect.* p. 1884. That perhaps is the gate mentioned by Plutarch. Ἴως δὲ εἰκότως ἐυψαι τε οςτε ἅμα γινίυτι πρὸ τῶν Ἱππαδὼν πυλῶν. in *Hyperide*. βελεύθηςιον τιχνῶν ἀκοδιμηται παςᾳ ταῖς τε Κεραμεικε πύλας ἢ ϖοῤῥω τῶν Ἱππιων. *Philoſtrat.* p. 577.

for

for a victory obtained by the Athenian cavalry from a general of Caſſander. In the Agora was an altar of Pity. This abſtract comprizes a portion of the old city by Dipylon, the region in the front of the Acropolis and the plain on the ſide next Hymettus, or, the Ceramicus *within the city*, of which the Agora was part; and extends into the ſuburb, beyond the Iliſſus.

THE Pompeium was a building in which all the neceſſaries for the ſolemn feſtivals were prepared, and the veſſels of gold and ſilver were kept, to be delivered to the bearers appointed at the Panathenæan and other grand proceſſions. The mention of this place, of Polytion, and of the Mercuries, will remind the claſſical reader of the enormities of Alcibiades. He made uſe of the conſecrated plate at his table, and refuſed to reſtore it; he imitated the myſteries of Eleuſis in the houſe of Polytion, wearing a ſtole and perſonating the hierophant or chief prieſt; and in the night he defaced all the Mercuries, except one. In the Tholus, which was a round building, ſometimes called Scias, were ſmall images of ſilver, and there the magiſtrates ſtiled Prytanes ſacrificed and feaſted.

THE portico of Jupiter Eleutherius and *the Royal* were near to each other. The ſtatue of Jupiter Eleutherius was erected on the defeat of the Medes. The inſcription gave him likewiſe the title of *Saviour*. Hadrian, who was ranked with him, had been, as Pauſanias adds, a great benefactor to other cities of the empire, but above all to Athens. A pedeſtal now remains, as we ſuppoſed, in its place, at ſome diſtance from the temple of Theſeus, in the way to the Piræus, almoſt buried in earth. After digging about it, we diſcovered the inſcription, " To the Saviour and founder the emperor Hadrian Olym-" pius."

THE ſtatues of Harmodius and Ariſtogiton were of braſs, and very antient. They had been carried away into Perſia by

Xerxes, and were restored to the Athenians by Alexander after Darius was conquered. They were near five hundred years old, when it was decreed that Brutus and Caffius, the murderers of Cæsar, should be placed next them. Arrian, who lived under the emperor Antoninus, has recorded them as remaining by the way, which was then used, up to the Acropolis, as nearly opposite to the Metróum, and not far from an altar of Eudanemus standing on the pavement and known to persons who had been initiated at Eleusis.

The Royal portico seems to have ranged with Pœcile [1]. The paintings in the latter exhibited the Athenians and Lacedæmonians drawn up in battle-array, about to engage, at Œnoe near Argos. In the middle of the wall were the Athenians and Theseus fighting with the Amazons. Next these was the taking of Troy, with the kings assembled in council; Ajax, and, among the female captives, Cassandra, whom he had violated. Lastly, there was the battle of Marathon.

By the Hephæstéum, and Euryfacéum or Heroum of Euryfaces, near the Agora, was the Colonus Agoræus or *hill of the Agora*; called also Misthius, from its being a place where servants were hired. It was behind the *long Portico*, (probably *Pœcile* and *the Royal* united) and had given its name to that part, which was otherwise termed Melite. Euryfaces was the son of Ajax, and had lived in Melite; as also Themistocles, who erected there a temple to Diana Aristobula after vanquishing the Persian fleet at Salamis; and there was likewise the house of Phocion, and the Melanippéum or Heroum of Melanippus son of Theseus. The extent of Melite is not defined; but it was contiguous with Cœle, for the Cimonian monuments in that region were near the Melitenfian gate. It probably approached or comprized the theatre, as in Melite was a large house where the tragedians studied their parts; and it comprehended the Eleusinium, for in Melite Hercules was initiated into the Lesser Mysteries, and had a temple. Melite bordered on Colyttus.

[1] απο της Ποικιλης κ, της τα Βασιλεως Στοας εισιν οι Ερμαι καλεμενοι. *Athen. Att.* p. 827.

The

THE Agora was a large open fpot, fubdivided into ftations for fellers of provifions and a variety of other articles, fome of which were fheltered by fheds or ftandings from the fun. The city-guard, confifting of a thoufand men, once had their tents in the middle, but afterwards was removed to the Areopagus. It was furrounded with temples, porticoes, and ftatues, but the extent of it is not defined. The altars of Apollo and Cybele are placed in it; as alfo the ftatues of Conon and his fon Timotheus. Thefe two were near the Perifchœnifma, a portion of it, by the altar of the twelve gods, confifting of an area of fifty feet, encompaffed with a rope, the tribunal of the archon ftiled *the king*, who fate there with the other archons; a party of the guard preventing the approach of improper perfons. Moreover, the ftatues of Harmodius and Ariftogiton were in the Agora; and that of Solon, which ftood before Pœcile. Lycurgus and Demofthenes and the two patriots are alfo on record as in the Ceramicus. Xenophon recommends, that at the public feftivals, the Athenian cavalry fhould be marched round the Agora, beginning from *the Mercuries*; and pay refpect to the temples and ftatues of the gods, as they paffed; and when the circuit was finifhed, fhould gallop off in fquadrons from *the Mercuries* as far as the Eleufinium. The proceffion, he imagines, if fo regulated, would prove highly pleafing to the deities as well as to the fpectators.

THE altar of Pity or Philanthropy, in the Agora, was exceedingly antient. It was faid, that the Heraclidæ had fled to it from Euryftheus, and that a herald, as he was dragging them from it, was flain by the Ephebi or youth of Athens, who continued to wear mourning for the outrage to the time of Atticus Herodes, when the colour of their chlamys or cloke was changed from black to white. Of all the Greeks, the Athenians alone, Paufanias tells us, regarded this deity, as ufeful in the cafualties of life and the manifold changes of human affairs. He remarks that the Athenians, who had eftablifhed the duties of philanthropy,

thropy, had alſo poſſeſſed more religion than any other people; and he adds, that ſuch as had excelled in piety were attended in proportion by good fortune. The altar, which remained under Julian, has been deſcribed as ſhaded with trees, among which was an olive known to ſuppliants and laurels decked with fillets; as frequented by the wretched and ever wet with their tears; as hung with treſſes of hair, and with the votive garments of perſons who had been relieved.

CHAP. XIX.

Abſtract of Pauſanias --- Of the temple of the Dioſcuri and of Agraulos --- Columns of different kinds of marble --- Of the Delphinium --- Of the temple of Venus in the gardens.

IN the preceding chapter we have accompanied Pauſanias from the gate Dipylon into the region called Agræ, whither he will now conduct us by a different way, on the oppoſite ſide of the Acropolis, and, as it were, through the preſent town. He begins with the Gymnaſium of Ptolemy, and then notes the temple of Theſeus, with the temple of the Dioſcuri; and above it, that of Agraulos. The Prytanéum was near; and, going from it into the lower parts of the city, there was a temple of Serapis; and, not far from this, the place where Theſeus and Pirithous made their fatal compact¹; near which was a temple of Ilythia. This brings him to the temple of Jupiter Olympius dedicated with the ſtatue by the emperor Hadrian, who had alſo erected temples of Juno and of Jupiter Panhellenius, and a Pantheon, in which his acts were inſcribed; and *there* were edifices richly adorned, and books, and the Gymnaſium of Hadrian. Theſe buildings, it may be obſerved, were in New Athens. The peribolus or incloſure of the Olympiéum contained alſo a temple of Saturn and Rhea, and a ſacred portion of the

¹ Vide Sophocl. Oedip. Col. v. 1588.

goddeſs

TRAVELS IN GREECE.

goddefs ftiled Olympia. Near the Olympiéum was Apollo Pythius, and the Delphinium or temple of Apollo Delphinius; from which the author paffes to the temple of Venus *in the gardens*, Cynofarges, the Lycéum, the Iliffus and Eridanus, the region called Agræ, the temple of Diana, and the Stadium.

THE temple of the Diofcuri, which was called alfo the Anacéum, with that of Aglauros, ftood on the hill of the Acropolis near the front. The Perfians under Xerxes endeavoured to fet fire to the palifades, which then fecured the entrance of the fortrefs; difcharging arrows with burning flax from Areopagus; but got poffeffion by climbing a precipice, before deemed inacceffible, beyond the gates, oppofite to the temple of Aglauros. Pififtratus fummoned the people to attend at the Anacéum, came forward from the Acropolis, and addreffed them in a low voice; while his guards removed their arms, unperceived, and fecured them in the temple of Aglauros. It was in this temple the military oath was adminiftered to the young Athenians, when they attained to the age of twenty years and were enrolled among the citizens.

AMONG the ill-matched columns in the churches are feveral of the marble imported by Hadrian, for his Pantheon and Gymnafium. In the former were one hundred and twenty from Phrygia, and in the latter one hundred from Libya. The produce of the Attic quarries is white; that of the Phrygian[1] white variegated with different colours.

ÆGEUS lived by the Delphinium; and in it was a fpot fenced about, where, it was faid, the cup fell with the poifon, which, at the inftigation of Medea, he tendered to Thefeus, before he knew him to be his fon. A Mercury to the eaft of the temple was called *The Mercury at the gate of Ægeus*.

[1] See Ruins of Athens, p. 39.

THE temple of Venus *in the gardens* was without the walls, though not remote from the town, as may be inferred from the ſtory of the Canephori. A church in the ſkirt of Athens, with an extenſive court before it, perhaps now occupies the ſite. It is called Panagía Spiliótiſſa, *St Mary of the cavern*, poſſibly from the ſubterraneous paſſage, which may ſtill exiſt. On the outſide in the wall, is fixed an inſcription relating to the temple of Venus, and recording the donations of a pious female, who gloried in the titles of candle-lighter and interpreter of dreams to the goddeſs. It is imperfect at the beginning, but commemorates her offering the pediment over the chancel, and a Venus, perhaps a puppet, which ſhe had made and dreſſed.

CHAP. XX.

Abſtract of Pauſanias --- The Prytanéum --- Of the ſtreet called The Tripods and a monument remaining --- Inſcriptions --- The Dionyſium --- Other temples --- Of Pandion and of the goddeſs Rome, &c. in the Acropolis --- The fountain Empedo --- Ceſſation of the magiſtracies at Athens ---- Of the Panathenæan proceſſion.

PAUSANIAS returns again into the city, and begins from the Prytanéum, keeping the Acropolis on his right hand nearer than before; a ſtreet, called *The Tripods*, leading from the Prytanéum toward the theatre of Bacchus, by which was the moſt antient temple of that god. The incloſure contained two temples, with two images. He then obſerves, that near the temple of Bacchus and the theatre, was the ſtructure formed in imitation of the tent of Xerxes, or the odéum; and after mention of the Mithridatic war, and of the cruelty of Sylla in the Ceramicus, treats of the ſtatues in the theatre, and notes on the ſouth wall of the Acropolis, which was toward it, a golden Ægis and head of Meduſa offered by king Antiochus; and a

cavern

cavern above the theatre, in the rock. He then goes on from the theatre to the front of the Acropolis, marking on the way the tomb of Talos, a nephew and scholar of Dædalus, who, regarding him as a rival, pushed him down a precipice; the temple and fountain of Æsculapius; and after it, the temple of Themis, before which was a barrow of Hippolytus, and a temple of Venus Pandemus. There was also the temple of Tellus Curotrophus and Ceres Chloe [1]. Pausanias then enters the Acropolis, and, after treating of the Propylea, mentions that he saw other articles there, and a temple of Diana Brauronia; describes the Parthenon, beyond which was a brazen Apollo; and, seeing a statue of Olympiodorus, digresses concerning the Muséum, which hill was within the old city-wall; and returns to the Erectheum and Pandroséum. Going down from the Acropolis, not into the city beneath, but below the Propyléa, he takes notice of a fountain near the cave of Apollo and Pan, and of the Areopagus, by which was a temple of the Furies; enumerates the tribunals, which were several besides Delphinium, Heliæa, and the Palladium; observes of the vessel used in the Panathenæan procession, which was shown by the Areopagus, that it was no longer a curiosity, but was much inferior to one at Delos; describes the Academy, a suburb near Dipylon; and proceeds to the Demi or towns more remote from the city.

The Prytanéum was a large edifice, in which the magistrates called Prytanes met to deliberate, and a daily allowance was provided for those persons who were entitled to their diet from the public. There was a statue of the goddess Peace, and of Vesta, with the perpetual fire. The building was thrown down by an earthquake in the sixth year of the Peloponnesian war. At a church called *Great St Mary*, in the town, is an antient arch, some remains of excellent masonry, and three columns supporting an architrave; which ruin, from its situation, may with great reason, be supposed to have been the Pry-

[1] Vide *Sophocl. Oedip.* Επι Κολων, v. 1641.

tanéum.

tanéum. A large area, in which it ſtands, was incloſed with a wall, having the fourth ſide or front decorated with columns. Of this a conſiderable portion is entire, but much encumbered, and concealed by houſes, magazines, and ſhops. It is publiſhed in *The Ruins of Athens*. The effect, in its preſent condition, is ſo ſtriking, that it was long miſtaken for the temple of Jupiter Olympius; but its magnificence, as has been juſtly remarked, is of a ſober ſtyle, ſhowing the œconomy of a republic rather than the profuſion of an Aſiatic king or Roman emperor.

THE conſecrated ſtructures, which embelliſhed the ſtreet called *The Tripods*, were probably noted for the offerings placed on them even more than for their own beauty. A fabric deſigned only to diſplay a tripod did not admit of great dimenſions. The choragic monument of Lyſicrates, which is yet extant, near the eaſtern end of the hill of the Acropolis, is but a ſmall edifice, though exquiſitely elegant. It may be ſeen, as in its original ſtate, in *The Ruins of Athens*. The number of theſe fabrics was conſiderable, but that is the only one undemoliſhed. During our reſidence at the French convent, it ſerved as a cloſet for a Greek, the ſervant of the Capuchin, to ſleep in. The Tripods were of braſs and very valuable for their workmanſhip. There was the Satyr, which Praxiteles eſteemed his maſter-piece; and on a cell or dome near it was a Satyr, a boy, giving a cup to Bacchus. It may appear no improbable conjecture that the monument of Lyſicrates was intended to ſupport the ſecond Tripod, for an analogy may be diſcovered between its ſubject and the ſculpture on the freeze[1]; as at the monument of Thraſyllus, above the theatre of Bacchus, between the ſtory on the Tripod and a ſtatue of Niobe.

THE deſtruction of the ſtreet called *the Tripods* may juſtly be regretted, as the monuments it contained were erected by eminent perſons, and at an æra when arts and the republic flou-

[1] See Ruins of Athens, Pl. X, XI, XXVI. Philoſtratus has deſcribed a picture, in which the transformation of the Pirates was repreſented, p. 761.

riſhed.

rished. If still extant, even their antiquity would deserve respect. The monument of Lysicrates, which remains, was constructed three hundred and thirty years before Christ. Thrasyllus was victorious only ten years after. I copied the inscription of one erected before the introduction of the Ionic alphabet, which consisted of twenty four letters, from a marble in the house of an Albanian woman near the Convent. In this the common formulary is not completed, for the name of the archon, under whom the Tripod was obtained, is omitted, though the stone is in good preservation and room was not wanting. This circumstance enables us to ascertain the date to the first year of the xcivth Olympiad[1], which the Athenians styled the year of anarchy, because the archon, not being duly elected, was disowned by them. Euclid succeeded in the following year, and the Attic alphabet, which had only sixteen letters, prevailed until after his archonship. The inscription of another was found on a stone at the mouth of an oven. It is imperfect, but very old, the letters in rows and ranging at equal distances. On a Doric architrave over the gate of the Bazar or market, near the ruin of the Prytanéum, is the inscription of one erected a year or two before that of Thrasyllus; and at the Catholicon or Cathedral is the inscription of one more early than that of Lysicrates by ten years. Another inscription, which we did not see, is published by Spon, and refers to the first year of the cxiiith Olympiad[2]. Themistocles and Aristides dedicated Tripods with similar inscriptions, cited, but imperfectly, by Plutarch. These were in Attic characters. The choragic monument of Aristides, with the inscription and Tripods, remained, when Plutarch wrote; as did also that of the famous Nicias. Another belonged to Lysias, who, in an oration still extant, relates, that when Glaucippus was archon[3], he provided a chorus of men for the Dionysia, and gained the victory; and that he expended on the chorus and the consecration of his

[1] Before Christ, 402. [2] Before Christ, 426. [3] Before Christ, 408.

Tripod the fum of five thoufand drachms, which has been computed at 208 *l*. 6 *s*. 8 *d*. fterling[1].

THE Dionyfium, or antient temple of Bacchus, is often ftyled the temple *in Limnis*, that portion of the city being fo named. It was kept fhut, like the church now on or near its fite, except at the Dionyfia or feftival of the deity, which was celebrated yearly in the month Anthefterion or February. The facred rites were then performed by women, and *the Queen*, the wife of the archon called *the King*, facrificed for the city.

IT has been already remarked, that Paufanias appears to have paffed from the theatre of Bacchus to the front of the Acropolis by a way leading behind the Odéum and the portico adjoining to it. The temple of Venus, ftanding by the Agora, was probably lower down than the other temples. That of Ceres was an elegant edifice, as may be collected from a piece of architrave, with an infcription, which once ranged in the front, and recorded the name of the perfon by whom it was dedicated; now fixed in the caftle-wall, within the gate at which the Turkifh guard is ftationed.

AMONG *the other articles*, which Paufanias faw in the Acropolis, was, it is probable, the temple or edifice facred to Pandion father of Erectheus, in which the infcribed marble, mentioned as having rolled down from the Acropolis, was once placed. One ftatue of him was among thofe of the Eponymi or heroes, from whom the tribes had been named; and another, worthy notice, was in the acropolis; probably in this building, which may be fuppofed to have ftood near the eaftern extremity of the rock. A temple likewife was then extant, infcribed, " The People. To the goddefs Rome and to Auguftus Cæfar.
" Pammenes fon of Xeno of Marathon, the prieft of the
" goddefs Rome and of Auguftus the Saviour, in the Acropolis,

[1] Ruins of Athens, p. 30.

" being

"being Strategus or General of the city¹. A daughter of
"Asclepiades of Alæ being priestess of Minerva Polias, the
"most mighty. In the archonship of Areus son of Morio
"a Pæanian." The year in which this person was archon is
not ascertained, but it coincides with the building of the temple, which was posterior to the year of Rome seven hundred
and forty one. The inscription was copied, before Mahomet
the second got possession of Athens, from the vestibule of a
temple in the Acropolis, then a church dedicated to the Panagia or Virgin Mary.

PAUSANIAS, after mentioning Enneacrunus as the only
fountain at Athens, has yet recorded two more; one in the
temple of Æsculapius, the other below the Propyléa. Both
these, it is likely, were unserviceable, except for certain ablutions and purifications. The water of the latter is now conveyed
to the principal mosque in the town for such uses². It may be
conjectured that the fountain stood antiently higher up toward
the cave of Pan; and that the current, since intercepted, was
continued into the temple of Æsculapius. There it disappeared;
but emerged again, after running twenty stadia, or two miles
and a half, underground toward Phalerum. It was first named
Empedo and then Clepsydra.

WE have before remarked, that a writer who lived under
the two emperors named Theodosius, has mentioned the Areopagus as no longer a court of judicature. The first instance of
a trial for murder there was said to have been furnished by
a crime, which Halirrhotius, a son of Neptune, committed
in the temple of Æsculapius, and which provoked Mars to kill
him. Most of the other magistracies were likewise extinct; and

---

¹ Some for πολλας read οπλιτας. See the inscription in *Fabricii Roma*, Gruter
p. cv, 9, and in *Corsini Fast. Att.* t. 1. p. 42. This learned Chronologer places
Areus in the year U. C. 727 or in the following, t. 4. p. 140, but see *Chishull
Antiq. Asiat.* p. 205, p. 207.
² v. Ruins of Athens, p. 15.

in particular, the tribunal called Delphinian, the Heliæan, which was near the Agora, the council of *Five Hundred*, and *the Eleven*; with the Polemarch, the Thefmothetæ and the *annual* Archon.

The proceffion at the Greater Panathenæa attended a peplus or garment, defigned as an offering to Minerva Polias in the Acropolis. This was woven by felect virgins in various colours reprefenting Minerva and Jupiter engaged with the Titans, and the exploits of Athenian Heroes. It was extended as a fail to the veffel, which was moved by machinery. The proceffion formed in the Ceramicus without the city, and entering at Dipylon, paffed between the porticoes, and through the Agora; croffed the Iliffus, and going round the Eleufinium, returned by the Pelafgicon and the temple of Apollo Pythius to the ftation of the veffel, near the Areopagus; from whence, it may be inferred, the offering was carried by men up to the temple, the afcent to the Propyléa being long and fteep. Harmodius and Ariftogiton concealed each a poignard in a myrtle-bough, and waited to affaffinate the tyrants, who regulated this folemnity, in the Ceramicus without the city; but, fearing they were betrayed, rufhed in at Dipylon, and flew Hipparchus by the Leocorium or monument of the daughters of Leo, one of the Eponymi, which was in the middle of the inner Ceramicus. Demetrius a defcendant of the Phaleréan, that his miftrefs Ariftagora, a courtezan of Corinth, might enjoy the fpectacle, erected for her a ftage againft the Mercuries.

CHAP.

CHAP. XXI.

Omiſſions in Pauſanias --- The tower of the Winds --- Dance of the Derviſhes --- A Doric portal --- Suppoſed the entrance of an Agora --- The Athenians given to flattery --- Pauſanias illuſtrated.

WE have now completed the propoſed ſurvey of antient Athens; but two ſtructures yet remain, either omitted or mentioned inexplicitly by Pauſanias. One is the tower of the winds or of Andronicus Cyrrheſtes, which was in or near the ſtreet called *The Tripods*, and bearing ſome reſemblance to the choragic monuments was perhaps overlooked by the author. The other is a Doric portal, ſituated at the foot of the hill of the Acropolis, and once, it is likely, belonging to that Agora, from which the Gymnaſium of Ptolemy was but a little diſtant. Beſides theſe the Pnyx is unnoticed.

THE tower of Andronicus Cyrrheſtes is a ſmall edifice of marble, an octogon, decorated with ſculpture repreſenting the Winds, eight in number; and has ſupported a Triton, which turned as a weathercock, and pointed with a wand to the wind then blowing. On the ſides were ſun-dials to ſhow the hour of the day. It is mentioned by Varro and Vitruvius, and accurately publiſhed in *The Ruins of Athens*. A young Turk explained to me two of the emblems; that of the figure of Cæcias, as ſignifying that he made the olives fall; of Sciron, that he dried up the rivers.

THE tower of the winds is now a *Teckeh* or place of worſhip belonging to a college of Derviſhes. I was preſent, with my companions, at a religious function, which concluded with their wonderful dance. The company was ſeated on goat-ſkins on the floor croſs-legged; forming a large circle. The chief
Derviſh,

Dervifh, a comely man, with a gray beard and of a fine prefence, began the prayers, in which the reft bore a part, all proftrating themfelves, as ufual, and feveral times touching the ground with their foreheads. Of a fudden, they leaped up, threw off their outer garments, and joining hands, moved round flowly, to mufic, fhouting *Alla*, the name of God. The inftruments founding quicker, they kept time, calling out *Alla*. *La illa ill Alla. God. There is no other God, but God.* Other fentences were added to thefe as their motion increafed; and the chief Dervifh, burfting from the ring into the middle, as in a fit of enthufiafm, and letting down his hair behind, began turning about, his body poifed on one of his great toes as on a pivot, without changing place. He was followed by another, who fpun a different way, and then by more, four or five in number. The rapidity with which they whifked round was gradually augmented, and became amazing; their long hair not touching their fhoulders but flying off; and the circle ftill furrounding them, fhouting, and throwing their heads backwards and forwards; the dome re-echoing the wild and loud mufic and the noife, as it were of frantic Bacchanals. At length, fome quitting the ring and fainting, at which time it is believed they are favoured with extatic vifions, the fpectacle ended. We were foon after introduced into a room furnifhed with fkins for fofas, and entertained with pipes and coffee by the chief Dervifh, whom we found, with feveral of his performers, as cool and placid as if he had been only a looker-on.

THE Doric portal may be feen in *The Ruins of Athens*, with its infcriptions. One of thefe informs us, that the people erected the fabric with the donations made to Minerva Archegetis or *the Conductrefs* by the god Julius Cæfar and his fon the god Auguftus, when Nicias was archon. Over the middle of the pediment was a ftatue of Lucius Cæfar, ftiled the fon of the god Auguftus, it is fuppofed, on horfe-back. At each angle was alfo a ftatue; probably of Auguftus and of Julius Cæfar, or M. Agrippa the natural father of Lucius. The goddefs

goddefs Julia, daughter of Auguftus, his mother, had likewife a ftatue; the pedeftal remaining by one of the columns. Minerva was in great repute as a tutelary deity. Auguftus Cæfar afcribed to her guidance his victory at Actium, and honoured her with a temple, in which he dedicated his Egyptian fpoils[1]. She received at Athens a portion of plunder both from him and from Julius as an acknowlegement of her fervices. The Strategus or general of the city-forces, Euclees of Marathon, acted as overfeer of the building for his father Herodes. The great Sophift Tiberius Claudius Atticus Herodes was alfo of Marathon; and in the pavement of the portico of a houfe, which we inhabited for fome months, between the Portal and the remnant of the Gymnafium of Ptolemy, was a pedeftal with an infcription almoft effaced, in which he is ftyled *Pontiff of the Auguftan deities*.

FROM the plan and proportions of the ruin it has been inferred, that the fabric, to which the Portal belonged, was not a temple. An edict of the emperor Hadrian infcribed on the jamb of a door-cafe, regulating the fale of oil and the duties to be levied on it, has been urged in favour of the opinion, that the Portal was the entrance of the inclofure of the Agora or market-place mentioned by Strabo, who lived to about the twelfth year of Tiberius Cæfar, as in a diftrict of the city called Eretria. The Athenians, reduced in number, are fuppofed to have removed it from the Ceramicus, where the blood of the citizens had ftreamed, to a fpot more central and convevenient; and to have employed the donations to their goddefs on a public work of general utility.

THE Athenians were a people ever ready to offer up the incenfe of flattery. A Sophift, a favourite of the emperor Trajan, expoftulates in one of his orations with the Rhodians

---

[1] *Chifhull Antiq. Afiat.* p. 201, p. 193. Lucius was adopted by Auguftus eighteen years before the Chriftian Æra, and died in the fecond year after it.

on the injuftice and abfurdity of their conduct. They freely decreed the honorary ftatue. The prætor felected one out of the great number, which adorned their city. The name was erafed, and it was infcribed to a new owner. The fame method, he adds, was practifed in other places and at Athens, which city deferved cenfure in many articles, and efpecially for its proftitution of public honours. He inftances, the conferring the title Olympius on a noify orator, a Phœnician, a native of an ignoble village; the placing the ftatue of a wretched poet, who had rehearfed at Rhodes, next to Menander; and a ridiculous infcription in compliment of Nicanor, the purchafer of the ifland Salamis. It was his opinion, that the Athenians had difgraced their city, and their predeceffors; and, that the abject ftate of this people rendered Greece, of which it had been the head, an object of compaffion.

PAUSANIAS may be illuftrated from this invective of the Sophift. On entering Athens he obferves near the temple of Ceres an equeftrian ftatue, which reprefented Neptune throwing a fpear at the giant Polybotes; but the infcription gave it then to another, and not to Neptune. The images of Miltiades and Themiftocles in the Prytanéum were changed in the fame manner into a Roman and a Thracian. The author has purpofely concealed their names. The coloffal ftatues of Attalus and Eumenes had been infcribed to Antony, and fubverted by a hurricane. Of thefe he is filent. The ftatue of Menander graced the Theatre of Bacchus; and he informs us in general that the images there were moftly of poets of inferior note. The prefents beftowed by Julius Cæfar and Auguftus did not reconcile the Athenians to their family. A few Triremes, the remains of their navy, had been numbered in the fleet of Pompey. They had honoured Brutus and Caffius, joined Antony, and revolted from Auguftus. Paufanias records the temples of Julius and Auguftus in the Agora of Sparta, but is referved at Athens. In the Parthenon he knew the emperor Hadrian only. He could not for certain fay, whether the equeftrian ftatues

before

before the Acropolis were the fons of Xenophon, or others placed there for ornament. He affirms, that evil having greatly increafed and overfpreading all countries and cities, no perfon, except nominally and from flattery to his fuperior rank, was any longer converted from a man into a God. He did not relifh the human deities. He found at Athens abundant evidence of its antient fplendor, and faw the city re-flourifhing under the aufpices of the emperor Hadrian. He would not revive the memory of its depreffion by enlarging on the monuments of its inconfiftent adulation. He paffes by the temple of Rome and Auguftus in the Acropolis; will not acknowlege the emperor and Agrippa at the entrance; nor defcribe a fabric founded on the munificence of the firft Cæfars, and adorned with all the divinities of the Julian family.

CHAP. XXII.

Athens the feat of philofophy --- The way to the Academy --- Of the Academy --- Of the Colonus Hippius --- Gardens of Philofophers --- The graves and fepulchres levelled --- Site of the Academy. Colonus Hippius --- The river Cephiffus.

ATHENS was the parent of Philofophy as well as of Eloquence. It had three celebrated Gymnafia without the city, the Academy, the Lycéum, and Cynofarges; from which as many fects dated their origin, the Platonic, the Peripatetic, and the Cynic; followers of Plato, of Ariftotle, and Antifthenes. The Stoic philofophy was inftituted by Zeno in the Stoa or Portico named Pœcile, and the garden of Epicurus was in the city.

THE Academy was in the fuburb without Dipylon, and diftant from the gate only fix ftadia or three quarters of a mile.

On the way to it was a small temple of Diana, to which the image of Bacchus Eleutherus was annually borne in procession; then the tomb of Thrasybulus; and a little out of the road, of Pericles, of Chabrias, Phormion, and the citizens who had died in battle serving their country by sea or land. The public solemnized their obsequies, and they were honoured with funeral orations and games. The stelæ or pillars standing on the graves declared the name of each and to what Demos or Borough he belonged. These perished honourably at different periods and in various actions. Some also of the Athenian allies were interred there, and Clisthenes, Conon, Timotheus, the philosophers Zeno and Chrysippus, Nicias an eminent painter, Harmodius and Aristogiton, the orator Ephialtes, and Lycurgus son of Lycophron, with many more of high renown. Not far from the Academy was the monument of Plato, and in this region was shown the tower of Timon, the man-hater. A miraculous tomb not far from Dipylon, on the left hand, is not mentioned by Pausanias. It was of earth, not large, and had on it a short pillar, which was always crowned with garlands. There Toxaris, a Scythian and physician, was buried. He was believed to continue to cure diseases, and was revered as a hero.

THE Academy was once the possession of a private person named Academus, who gave it to the people. Hipparchus, son of Pisistratus, surrounded it with a wall. Cimon drained the low grounds near it. The spot, parched and squalid, was improved and rendered very pleasant. The walks were shaded with tall plane-trees, and cooled by running water. Before the entrance was an altar of Love; and, besides others, one of Prometheus, from which the race called Lampadophoria began. The winner was he who first reached the city with his lamp unextinguished. Plato commenced teaching at the Academy, then reputed unwholsome. Afterwards he preferred a small garden by the Colonus Hippius, his own property. The Lacedæmonians spared the Academy, when they ravaged Attica; but Sylla, wanting timber for machines, cut down the grove there

and

and at the Lycéum. The succeffors of Plato enjoyed a confiderable revenue, which, in the subfequent ages, was greatly augmented by legacies from perfons defirous of contributing to the leifure and tranquillity of the philofophic life.

COLONUS Hippius *the Equeſtrian hill* was beyond the Academy and diftant ten ftadia, a mile and a quarter, from the city. There was an altar of *Equeſtrian* Neptune and Minerva, with an heroum or monument of Pirithous and Thefeus, of Œdipus, and of Adraftus. It was affirmed, that the unhappy Theban, an exile and fuppliant, had refted there in the facred portion of the Furies; but Paufanias preferred the authority of Homer. The grove and temple of Neptune had been burned by Antigonus. Sophocles was born and lived at the Colonus, and there were the copper mines.

THE little garden of Epicurus in the city was on the fide toward Dipylon and by the road to the Academy. The teacher of eafe, it is recorded, was the firft who introduced that fpecies of gratification, the enjoyment of the country in town. The garden of the philofopher Melanthius was oppofite to the ftatue of Minerva Pæonia, which is mentioned as the firft in *the Mercuries*. It was in the way to the Academy; for Lycurgus fon of Lycophron, with fome of his defcendants, was buried in it at the public expenfe. On the graves were placed flat flabs with infcriptions. The Lacydéum or garden of Lacydes was in the Academy.

BY the deftruction of Dipylon and the City-wall we are deprived of the antient boundaries of Athens; and the town, befides being reduced in its extent, furnifhes a variety of avenues to the plain. Moreover, the manfions of the illuftrious dead, like the bodies which they covered, are confumed, and have difappeared. Time, violence, and the plough have levelled all, without diftinction; equally inattentive to the meritorious ftatefman, the patriot, the orator, and philofopher, the foldier, the

artift,

artiſt, and phyſician. Atticus is deſcribed by Cicero as pleaſed with recollecting where the renowned Athenians had lived, or been accuſtomed to ſit or diſpute; and as ſtudiouſly contemplating even their ſepulchres. The traveller will regret, that deſolation interferes, and by the uncertainty it has produced, deprives him of the like ſatisfaction; but, in the ſtyle of the antients, to omit the reſearch would merit the anger of the Muſes.

It has been obſerved, that, without Dipylon, the road branched off toward the Piræus and Eleuſis as well as the Academy. The road to the haven and to Eleuſis divides now not far from the temple of Theſeus, and is nearly in the ſame direction as formerly. On the right hand of the Eleuſinian road is a way, which leads to the ſite of the Academy. Achmet Aga had lately erected a houſe on or near it, with a large garden, and a plentiful fountain by the road-ſide, ſupplied, it is likely, by the channels which conduced to the coolneſs and verdure of the old ſuburb. Farther on is a rocky knoll, which was the Colonus Hippius. Some maſſive fragments of brick-wall occur there, with a ſolitary church or two.

In the plain beyond the *Equeſtrian hill* is the Cephiſſus[1], a muddy rivulet, turning ſome over-ſhot mills in its courſe through a rich and fertile tract covered with gardens, olive-trees, and vineyards. The ſtream antiently croſſed the *Long-walls* in its way to the Phaleric ſhore, which alſo received the Iliſſus. Theſe waters, it is likely, formed the marſh. The Cephiſſus was very inconſiderable in the ſummer. It is now commonly abſorbed, before it reaches the coaſt; except after melting ſnow or heavy rain ruſhing down from the mountains.

[1] Κηφισσος εκ Τρινεμεων αρχας ιχων. Strabo.

CHAP.

CHAP. XXIII.

The Lycéum --- Cynofarges --- Mention of them in Plato --- The fite.

WE proceed now to the Gymnafia on the other fide of Athens, the Lycéum and Cynofarges.

THE Lycéum was facred to Apollo Lycius, a proper patron, as an antient author has remarked, the god of health beftowing the ability to excel in gymnic exercifes. The image reprefented him as refting after fatigue, with a bow in his left hand, his right arm bending over his head. The Gymnafium was erected by Lycurgus fon of Lycophron. The militia of Athens paraded there, and were inftructed in the management of their horfes, fhields and fpears, in forming the phalanx and in all the eftablifhed modes of attack and defence. Behind the Lycéum was a monument of Nifus. The Lycéum was long noted for a plane-tree of uncommon fize, which is defcribed by Pliny, and was near a fountain by the road-fide.

CYNOSARGES was but a little without the city-gate. There was a temple of Hercules. They related, that when Diomus was facrificing to the Hero, a white bitch had feized part of the victim, and carried it to this fpot, where the altar was erected in obedience to an oracle, which had foretold that incident. On a fummit near was the tomb of Ifocrates. Philip who reduced the city to require aid from the Romans, encamped by Cynofarges, and fet fire both to that place and the Lycéum.

THESE Gymnafia were near the Iliffus, which river flowed from the region beyond Agræ, the Lycéum, and the fountain celebrated by Plato [1] ; the bed making a curve near the junction with the Eridanus. Phædrus has been defcribed as going from a houfe by the temple of Jupiter Olympius toward the Lycéum,

[1] Strabo, p. 400. Hence Statius, *Amfractu riparum incurvus Iliffus.* Theb. l. IV. v. 52.

as turning out of the way with Socrates, and fitting down by Enneacrunus and the Iliſſus, above the croſſing over to the temple of Diana Agræa. In the dialogue entitled Lyſis, Socrates paſſing from the Academy to the Lycéum by the way without the wall, and coming to the gate, where was the fountain of Panops, diſcovers over againſt the wall an incloſure with an open gate, which was a palæſtra or place for exerciſes lately built. This probably belonged to Cynoſarges. In another dialogue, going out of the city to Cynoſarges, and approaching the Iliſſus, he ſees Clinias running toward Calirhoe, turns out of the way to meet him, and accompanies him, the way by the wall, to a houſe near the Itonian gate [1].

The Lycéum was beyond the Iliſſus, and the croſſing over is below that which led to the temple of Diana Agræa. The ſite is now marked by a well and a church, and many large ſtones ſcattered about. Cynoſarges was not far from the Lycéum, and perhaps on the ſame ſide of the Iliſſus as the city, where is now a garden near this bed, and by the road. The artificial currents of water having ceaſed, the environs of Athens are become, except near Enneacrunus, more bare and naked than they were even after the devaſtations of Philip and Sylla.

[1] The Itonian gate was by the pillar of the Amazon. In an account of the battle of Theſeus with the Amazons it is related, that the left wing of their army was toward the Amazonéum ; and the right toward Pnyx (πρὸς τὴν Πνυκα κατὰ τὴν Χρυσαν ἥκει ;) that on this ſide, the Athenians, who engaged from the Muſéum were repulſed, and that the tombs of the ſlain were by the broad-way leading to Dipylon, probably from the Agora; but that thoſe who attacked from the Palladium, Ardettus, and the Lycéum drove the enemy to their camp; and that the pillar by the temple of Tellus Olympia was placed over the Amazon, who lived with Theſeus, and is generally called Antiope. Pauſanias informs us, that the goddeſs ſurnamed Olympia had a ſacred portion within the wall of the Olympiéum; that the monument of Antiope was by the entrance of the city from Phalerum; and that the Athenians had alſo a tomb of Molpadia, another Amazon, by whom ſhe was ſlain.

The monument by the City-gate coming from the Piræus, of which Pauſanias ſays, that he did not know to whom it belonged, was probably the heroum of Chalcodon, for that is mentioned as near the Piræan gate. Ægeus, father of Theſeus, eſpouſed his daughter. *Meurſius Att. Lect. p.* 1773. *De regibus Ath.* p. 1108.

C H A P.

CHAP. XXIV.

Of the University of Athens --- The Professors --- Degrees --- Dresses --- Manner of entrance --- Character and extinction of the Philosophers --- Ruin of the University.

ATHENS maintained under the Romans its reputation for philosophy and eloquence, and continued, though subdued, the metropolis of learning, the school of art, the centre of taste and genius. The Gymnasia and the gardens of the Philosophers were decorated with the capital works of eminent masters, and still frequented. The fierce warrior was captivated by Greece and Science, and Athens humanized and polished the conquerors of the world. But Sylla greatly injured the city, by transporting to Rome the public Library, which had been founded by Pisistratus, carefully augmented by the people, removed by Xerxes into Persia, and restored long after by Seleucus Nicanor. The spirit of learning drooped on the loss; and the Roman youth, under Tiberius, were sent to study at Marseilles, instead of Athens. Even there the barbarous Gauls joined in the pursuit of Eloquence and Philosophy. The Sophist, as well as the Physician, was hired to settle among them; and the nation was civilized by the Greek city.

THE emperor Hadrian embellished Athens with a noble library and a new Gymnasium, and restored science to its antient seat. Lollianus, an Ephesian, was first raised to the high dignity of the sophistical throne, which was afterwards filled by Atticus Herodes, and by other eminent and illustrious persons. The number of professors was increased by Antoninus the philosopher, who had studied under Herodes. His establishment consisted of thirteen; two Platonists, as many Peripatetics, Stoics, and Epicureans, with two Rhetoricians and Civilians;

Civilians; and a Prefident ftyled *Præfect of the Youth*. The ftudent proceeded from the philofopher to the rhetorician, and then to the civilian. A yearly falary of fix hundred *Aurei* or pieces of gold [1] was annexed to each of the philofophical chairs; and one of a talent to thofe of the civilians. The profeffors, unlefs appointed by the emperors, were elected after folemn examination by the principal magiftrates.

EDUCATION now flourifhed in all its branches at Athens. The Roman world reforted to its fchools, and reputation and riches awaited the able preceptor. The tender mind was duly prepared for the manly ftudies of philofophy and eloquence. Age and proficiency were followed by promotion. The youth was advanced into the higher claffes, enrolled with the philofophers, and admitted to their habit. The title of Sophift was conferred on him, when mature in years and erudition; and this was an honour fo much affected, that the attainment of it almoft furnifhed an apology for infolent pride and extravagant elation. It was a cuftom of the mafters to infcribe on marble the names of their fcholars, thofe of Attica ranged under their refpective tribes; and alfo to what demos or borough each belonged. Some fpecimens of thefe regifters are preferved in the Oxford collection, and many fragments are yet extant at Athens.

AT this period Athens abounded in philofophers. It fwarmed, according to Lucian, with clokes and ftaves and fatchels; you beheld every where a long beard, a book in the left hand, and the walks full of companies, difcourfing and reafoning. The cloke or Tribonium was the habit of all the orders. The general colour was dark, but the Cynic wore white, and, with the Stoic, had the folds doubled. One fhoulder was bare; the hair hanging down; the beard unfhaven. The Cynic, with

[1] About 468 *l*. See W. Wotton's Hiftory of Rome. London 1701. p. 106, with the *Errata* and p. 169.

the

the Stoic and Pythagorean, was flovenly and negligent, his cloke in tatters, his nails long, and his feet naked. The Cynic was armed with a ftaff, as a defence from dogs or the rabble. The Sophift was adorned with purple, and commonly polifhed as well in drefs and perfon as in manners and language. It behoved the profeffor, as Lucian affirms, to be handfomely clothed, to be fleek and comely, and above all to have a flowing beard infpiring thofe who approached him with veneration, and fuitable to the falary he received from the emperor.

A learned father[1], who was contemporary with Julian at Athens, has defcribed the manner in which the Novice was treated on his arrival there, with the ceremony of initiation. He was firft furrounded by the pupils and partizans of the different Sophifts, all eager to recommend their favourite mafter. He was hofpitably entertained; and afterwards the ftudents were allowed to attack him with rude or ingenuous difputation, as each was difpofed. This, the relater has furmifed, was intended to mortify conceit, and to render him tractable. He was next to be invefted with the habit. A proceffion in pairs, at equal diftances, conducted him through the Agora to a public bath, probably that without Dipylon by the monument of Anthemocritus. An oppofition was feigned on their approach to the door, fome calling out and forbidding his admiffion, fome urging on and knocking. Thefe prevailed. He was introduced into a warm cell, wafhed, and then clothed with the Tribonium. He was faluted as an equal on his coming out, and re-conducted. No one was fuffered to appear in that drefs at Athens without the permiffion of the Sophifts and this ceremony, which was attended with confiderable expenfe.

THE Philofophers were long as diftinguifhed by their averfion to Chriftianity as by their garment. It is recorded of Juftin Martyr, that he preached in the Tribonium, to which

[1] Gregorius Nazianzen. Orat. xx.

he had been admitted before his converfion. Some Monks alfo, whom the Gentiles termed impoftors, aſſumed it, uniting with fpiritual pride and confummate vanity, an affectation of fingular humility and of indifference to worldly fhow. But the emperor Jovian commanding the temples to be fhut, and prohibiting facrifice, the prudent philofopher then concealed his profeffion, and relinquifhed his cloke for the common drefs. The order was treated with feverity by Valens his fucceffor, becaufe fome of them, to animate their party, had foretold that the next Emperor would be a Gentile. They were addicted to divination and magic, and it was pretended, had partly difcovered his name. The habit was not wholly laid afide. In the next reign, a fedition happened at Alexandria, when Olympius a Philofopher, wearing the cloke, was exceedingly active, urging the Gentiles to repell the Reformers, and not to remit of their zeal or be difheartened becaufe they were difpoffeffed of their idols; for the powers, which had inhabited them, were, he afferted, flown away into heaven. The Heathen philofophers gradually difappeared; but the Chriftian, their fucceffors are not yet extinct, ftill flourifhing in Catholic countries, and differing not lefs than the antient fects, in drefs, tenets, and rules of living.

The decline of Philofophy muft have deeply affected the profperity of Athens. A gradual defertion of the place followed. Minerva could no longer protect her city. Its beauty was violated by the Proconful, who ftripped Pœcile of its pretious paintings. It was forfaken by good fortune, and would have lingered in decay, but the Barbarians interpofed, and fuddenly completed its downfall. When the Goths were in poffeffion of it in the time of Claudius, two hundred and fixty nine years after Chrift, they amaffed all the books, intending, it is related, to burn them; but defifted, on a reprefentation that the Greeks were diverted by the amufements of ftudy from military purfuits. Alaric, under Arcadius and Honorius, was not afraid of
their

TRAVELS IN GREECE. 117

their becoming foldiers. The city was pillaged, and the libraries were confumed. Devaftation then reigned within, and folitude without its walls. The fweet firens, the vocal nightingales, as the Sophifts are fondly ftyled, were heard no more. Philofophy and Eloquence were exiled, and their antient feat occupied by ignorant honey-factors of mount Hymettus.

CHAP. XXV.

Of the people of Athens --- The Turkifh government --- The Turks --- The Greeks --- The Albanians --- The Archbifhop --- Character of the Athenians.

ATHENS, after it was abandoned by the Goths, continued, it is likely, for ages to preferve the race of its remaining inhabitants unchanged, and uniform in language and manners. Hiftory is filent of its fuffering from later incurfions, from wars, and maffacres. Plenty and the profpect of advantage produces new fettlers; but, where no trade exifts, employment will be wanting, and Attica was never celebrated for fertility. The plague has not been, as at Smyrna, a frequent vifitant; becaufe the intercourfe fubfifting with the iflands and other places has been fmall, and the port is at a diftance. The plague defcribed by Thucydides began in the Piræus, and the Athenians at firft believed that the enemy had poifoned the wells. If, from inadvertency, the infection be now admitted into the town, the Turks as well as the Greeks have the prudence to retire to their houfes in the country or to the monafteries, and it feldom prevails either fo long or fo terribly as in cities on the coaft.

A colony of new proprietors was introduced into Athens by Mahomet the fecond; but the people fecured fome privileges by their capitulation, and have fince obtained more by addrefs or money.

money. The Turk has favoured the spot, and bestowed on it a milder tyranny. The Kislar Aga or chief of the black Eunuchs at Constantinople is their patron; and by him the Turkish magistrates are appointed. The Vaiwode purchases his government yearly, but circumspection and moderation are requisite in exacting the revenue, and the usual concomitants of his station are uneasiness, apprehension, and danger. The impatience of oppression, when general, begets public vengeance. The Turks and their vassals have united, seized and cut their tyrants in pieces, or forced them to seek refuge in the mountains or in the Acropolis. An insurrection had happened not many years before we arrived, and the distress, which followed from want of water in the fortress, was described to us as extreme.

THE Turks of Athens are in general more polite, social, and affable, than is common in that stately race; living on more equal terms with their fellow-citizens, and partaking, in some degree, of the Greek character. The same intermixture, which has softened their austerity, has corrupted their temperance; and many have foregone the national abstinence from wine, drinking freely, except during their Ramazan or Lent. Some too after a long lapse have re-assumed, and rigidly adhere to it, as suiting the gravity of a beard, and the decorum of paternal authority. Several of the families date their settlement from the taking of the city. They are reckoned at about three hundred. Their number, though comparatively small, is more than sufficient to keep the Christians fully sensible of their mastery. The Turks possess from their childhood an habitual superiority, and awe with a look the loftiest vassal. Their deportment is often stern and haughty. Many in private life are distinguished by strict honour, by punctuality, and uprightness in their dealings; and almost all by external sanctity of manners. If they are narrow minded in the extreme, it is the result of a confined education; and an avaritious temper is a natural consequence of their rapacious government.

THE

TRAVELS IN GREECE.

The Greeks may be regarded as the reprefentatives of the old Athenians. We have related, that, on our arrival in the Piræus, an Archon came from the city to receive us. The learned reader was perhaps touched by that refpectable title, and annexed to it fome portion of its claffical importance; but the Archons are now mere names, except a tall fur-cap, and a fuller and better drefs than is worn by the inferior claffes. Some have fhops in the Bazar, fome are merchants, or farmers of the public revenue. The families, ftyled Archontic, are eight or ten in number; moftly on the decline. The perfon, who met us, was of one reckoned very antient, which, by his account, had been fettled at Athens about three hundred years, or after Mahomet the fecond. His patrimony had fuffered from the extortions of a tyrannical Vaiwode, but he had repaired the lofs by trade and by renting petty governments. The ordinary habit of the meaner citizens is a red fkull-cap, a jacket, and a fafh round the middle, loofe breeches or trowfers, which tie with a large knot before, and a long veft, which they hang on their fhoulders, lined with wool or fur for cold weather. By following the lower occupations, they procure, not without difficulty, a pittance of profit to fubfift them, to pay their tribute-money, and to purchafe garments for the feftivals, when they mutually vie in appearing well-clothed, their pride even exceeding their poverty.

The lordly Turk and lively Greek neglecting pafturage and agriculture, that province, which in Afia Minor is occupied by the Turcomans, has been obtained in Europe by the Albanians or Albanefe. Thefe are a people remote from their original country, which was by the Cafpian fea, fpreading over and cultivating alien lands, and, as of old, addicted to univerfal hufbandry and to migration. It is chiefly their bufinefs to plough, fow, and reap; dig, fence, plant, and prune the vineyard; attend the watering of the olive-tree; and'gather in the harveft; going forth before the dawn of day, and returning joyous on the clofe of their labour. If fhepherds, they live on the mountains, in the vale, or the plain, as the varying feafons require, under arbours or fheds covered with boughs, tending their flocks abroad, or milking the ewes and fhe-goats at the fold, and making cheefe and butter to fupply the city. Inured early to fatigue and the fun, they are hardy and robuft, of manly carriage, very different from that of the fawning obfequious Greek, and of defperate bravery under every difadvantage, when compelled by neceffity or oppreffion, to unite and endeavour to extort redrefs. Their habit is fimple and fuccinct, reaching to the knees. They have a national language, and are members of the Greek communion.

THE Chriftians, both Greeks and Albanians, are more immediately fuperintended by the Archbifhop, and by the two Epitropi or curators, who are chofen from among the principal men, and venerable for their long beards. Thefe endeavour to quiet all difputes, and prevent the parties from recurring to the fevere tribunal of the Cadi or Turkifh judge, watching over the commonweal, and regulating its internal polity, which ftill retains fome faint and obfcure traces of the antient popular form, though without dignity or importance. The fee was now poffeffed by Bartholemew, a Walachian, who had lately purchafed it at Conftantinople. He was abfent when we arrived; but on his return to Athens, fent us a prefent of fine fruit and of honey from M. Hymettus; and came to vifit us at the convent, on horfeback, attended by a virger and fome of his clergy on foot. He was a comely and portly man, with a black thick beard.

A TRADITIONAL ftory was related to us at Smyrna and afterwards at Athens, to illuftrate the native quicknefs of apprehenfion, which, as if tranfmiffive and the property of the foil, is inherited even by the lower claffes of the people. A perfon made trial of a poor fhepherd, whom he met with his flock, demanding, απο πȣ; και πȣ; και πως; και ποτα. *From whence? and where? and how? and how many?* He was anfwered without

out hefitation, and with equal brevity, απ' Αθηνας, ως Ληβαδια, Θεοδωρος, και πεντακοσια. *From Athens, to Livadia, Theodore, and five hundred.* In the citizens this aptitude not being duly cultivated, inftead of producing genius, degenerates into cunning. They are juftly reputed a moft crafty, fubtle, and acute race. It has been jocofely affirmed, that no Jew can live among them, becaufe he will be continually out-witted. They are confcious of their fubjection to the Turk, and as fupple as depreffed, from the memory of the blows on the feet and indignities, which they have experienced or feen inflicted, and from the terror of the penalty annexed to refiftance, which is the forfeiture of the hand uplifted: but their difpofition, as antiently, is unquiet; their repofe difturbed by factious intrigues and private animofities; the body politic weakened by divifion, and often impelled in a direction oppofite to its true intereft. They have two fchools, one of which poffeffes a fmall collection of books, and is entitled to an annual payment from Venice, the endowment of a charitable Athenian, but the money is not regularly remitted.

CHAP. XXVI.

Care of the female fex at Athens --- Drefs of the Turkifh women abroad --- Of the Greek --- Of the Albanian --- Drefs of the Greek at home --- Manner of colouring the fockets of their eyes --- Their education.

THE liberty of the fair fex at Athens is almoft equally abridged by the Turks and Greeks. Their houfes are fecured with high walls, and the windows turned from the ftreet, and latticed, or boarded up, fo as to preclude all intercourfe, even of the eyes. The harám, or apartment of the Turkifh women, is not only impenetrable, but muft not be regarded on the outfide with any degree of attention. To approach them, when abroad, will give offence; and in the town, if they cannot be

R avoided,

avoided, it is the cuſtom to turn to the wall and ſtand ſtill, without looking toward them, while they paſs. This mode of carriage is good breeding at Athens.

The Turkiſh women claim an exemption from their confinement on one day only in the week, when they viſit their relations, and are ſeen going in companies to the baths or ſitting in the burying-grounds on the graves of their friends, their children, huſbands, or parents. They are then enwrapped and beclothed in ſuch a manner, it is impoſſible to diſcern whether they are young or old, handſome or ugly. Their heads, as low as the eye-brows, are covered with white linen, and alſo their faces beneath; the prominency of the noſe and mouth giving them nearly the viſages of mummies. They draw down a veil of black gauſe over their eyes, the moment a man or boy comes in view. They wear ſhort looſe boots of leather, red or yellow, with a large ſheet over their common garments, and appear very bulky.

The dreſs of the Greek matrons is a garment of red or blue cloth, the waiſt very ſhort, the long petticoat falling in folds to the ground. A thin flowing veil of muſlin, with a golden rim or border, is thrown over the head and ſhoulders. The attire of the virgins is a long red veſt, with a ſquare cape of yellow ſattin hanging down behind. They walk with their hands concealed in the pocket-holes at the ſides, and their faces are muffled. Sometimes they aſſume the Turkiſh garb. Neither prudence nor modeſty ſuffers a maiden to be ſeen by the men before ſhe is married. Her beauty might inflame the Turk, who can take her legally, by force, to his bed, on a ſentence of the Cadi or judge; and the Greek, if ſhe revealed her face to him even unwillingly, would reject her as criminal and with diſdain.

The Albanian women are inured early to hard living, labour, and the ſun. Their features are injured by penury, and their
complexions

complexions by the air. Their drefs is coarfe and fimple; a fhift reaching to the ancle, a thick fafh about the waift, and a fhort loofe woollen veft. Their hair is platted in two divifions, and the ends faftened to a red filken ftring, which, with a taffel, is pendant to their heels, and frequently laden with pieces of filver coin, of various fizes, diminifhing gradually to the bottom. Among thefe the antiquarian may often difcover medals of value. They are feen carrying water on their backs, in earthen jars, with handles; wafhing by the fountains, or affembled by the Iliffus after rain, with the female flaves of the Mahometans and other fervants; treading their linen, or beating it with a piece of heavy wood, fpreading it on the ground or bufhes to dry, and conveying it to and fro in panniers or wicker-bafkets on an afs. Their legs and feet are generally bare; and their heads hooded, as it were, with a long towel, which encircles the neck, one extremity hanging down before and the other behind. The girls wear a red fkull-cap plated with peraus or Turkifh pennies of filver perforated, and ranged like the fcales of fifh.

The Greek will fometimes admit a traveller into his gynecæum or the apartment of his women. Thefe within doors, are as it were uncafed, and each a contraft of the figure fhe made when abroad. There the girl, like Thetis, treading on a foft carpet, has her white and delicate feet naked; the nails tinged with red. Her trowfers, which in winter are of red cloth, and in fummer of fine callico or thin gaufe, defcend from the hip to the ancle, hanging loofely about her limbs; the lower portion embroidered with flowers, and appearing beneath the fhift, which has the fleeves wide and open, and the feams and edges curioufly adorned with needle-work. Her veft is of filk, exaftly fitted to the form of the bofom and the fhape of the body, which it rather covers than conceals, and is fhorter than the fhift. The fleeves button occafionally to the hand, and are lined with red or yellow fattin. A rich zone encompaffes her waift, and is faftened before by clafps of filver gilded, or of gold

gold fet with pretious ftones. Over the veft is a robe, in fummer lined with ermine, and in cold weather with fur. The head-drefs is a fkull-cap, red or green, with pearls; a ftay under the chin, and a yellow forehead-cloth. She has bracelets of gold on her wrifts; and, like Aurora, is rofy-fingered, the tips being ftained. Her necklace is a ftring of Zechins, a fpecies of gold coin, or of the pieces called Byzantines. At her cheeks is a lock of hair made to curl toward the face; and down her back falls a profufion of treffes, fpreading over her fhoulders. Much time is confumed in combing and braiding the hair after bathing, and, at the greater feftivals, in enriching and powdering it with fmall bits of filver gilded, refembling a violin in fhape, and woven in at regular diftances. She is painted blue round the eyes; and the infides of the fockets, with the edges on which the lafhes grow, are tinged with black. The Turkifh ladies wear nearly the fame attire, and ufe fimilar arts to heighten their natural beauty.

For colouring the lafhes and focket of the eye, they throw incenfe or gum of Labdanum on fome coals of fire, intercept the fmoke, which afcends, with a plate, and collect the foot. This I faw applied. A girl, fitting crofs-legged as ufual, on a fofa, and clofing one of her eyes, took the two lafhes between the forefinger and thumb of her left hand, pulled them forward, and then thrufting in, at the external corner, a bodkin, which had been immerfed in the foot, and extracting it again, the particles before adhering to it, remained within, and were prefently ranged round the organ; ferving as a foil to its luftre, befides contributing, as they fay, to its health, and increafing its apparent magnitude.

The improvement of the mind and morals is not confidered as a momentous part of female education at Athens. The girls are taught to dance, to play on the Turkifh guittar and the tympanum or timbrel, and to embroider, an art in which they generally excel. A woman fkilled in reading and writing is

spoken

spoken of as a prodigy of capacity and learning. The mother of Ofman Aga, a Turk who frequented our houfe, was of this rare number, and, as he often told us, fo terrible for her knowlege, that even Achmet Aga her kinfman had been feen to tremble, when he received her annual vifit. In common life the woman waits on her hufband, and after dreffing the provifions, which he purchafed, eats perhaps with a female flave; the ftately lord feeding alone or in company with men.

C H A P. XXVII.

Of the territory of Athens --- The olive-groves --- Bees --- Provifions --- Birds --- Hare-calling --- Wild beafts --- The horned owl --- A water-fpout --- Antient prognoftics of weather --- Sting of a Scorpion.

THE territory of Athens was antiently well peopled. The demi or boroughs were in number one hundred and feventy four; fcattered, except fome conftituting the city, about the country. Frequent traces of them are found; and feveral ftill exift, but moftly reduced to very inconfiderable villages. Many wells alfo occur on Lycabettus, at the Piræus, in the plain, and all over Attica. Some are feen in the vineyards and gardens nearly in their priftine ftate; a circular rim of marble, about a yard high, ftanding on a fquare pavement; adorned, not inelegantly, with wreathed flutings on the outfide; or plain, with mouldings at the top and bottom; the inner furface deep-worn by the friction of ropes. The bucket is a kettle, a jar, or the fkin of a goat or kid diftended; and clofe by is commonly a trough or hollow ftone, into which they pour water for the cattle. The city was fupplied with corn from Sicily and Africa; and the regard of the emperors and kings, its patrons, was difplayed in largeffes of wheat and barley to be diftributed, generally in the Odéum. At prefent, Attica is thinly inhabited, and probably produces

grain

grain sufficient for the natives; but the edicts prohibiting exportation are continually eluded, and public distress bordering on famine ensues almost yearly.

The olive-groves are now, as antiently, a principal source of the riches of Athens. The wood of these trees, watered by the Cephissus, about three miles from the city, has been computed at least six miles long. The mills for pressing and grinding the olives are in the town. The oil is deposited in large earthen jars sunk in the ground in the areas before the houses. The crops had failed for five years successively when we arrived. The cause assigned was a northerly wind called Greco Tramontano, which destroyed the flower. The fruit is set in about a fortnight, when the apprehension from this unpropitious quarter ceases. The bloom in the following year was unhurt, and we had the pleasure of leaving the Athenians happy in the prospect of a plentiful harvest. By a law of Solon no tree could be planted less than five feet, nor an olive or fig-tree less than nine feet from one of another proprietor.

The honey, as well as the oil of Attica, was antiently in high repute. Many encomiums are extant on that of Hymettus, in particular, and it deserves them all. Flies are remarked to buzz about it, without settling, which has been attributed to the odour it derived from thyme. The race of bees was said to have been originally produced in Hymettus, and to have swarmed from thence in numerous colonies to people other regions. The mountain furnishes a succession of aromatic plants, herbs and flowers peculiarly adapted to maintain them both in summer and winter. The hives are set on the ground in rows inclosed within a low wall. Their form, and management, and the method of taking the comb without destroying the insects, has been described [1]. By a law of Solon no person was allowed to place a stand within three hundred yards of one before established.

[1] Wheler, p. 411.

Provisions of all kinds are good and cheap at Athens. The frequent and severe fasts imposed by the Greek church have an influence on the market. The Christians are often confined to vegetables or to things without blood; such as snails, which they gather from the shrubs, the cutle-fish, or the sea-polypus. The latter called by the Greeks octopodes, from the number of its feet, is beaten to make it tender; and, when boiled, is white, like the tail of lobster, but has not much flavour. Hares, game, and fowl, may be purchased for little more than the value of the powder and shot. Oranges, lemons, and citrons grow in the gardens. The grapes and melons are excellent, and the figs were celebrated of old. The wines are wholsome, but the pitch, infused to preserve them, communicates a taste, to which strangers are not presently reconciled.

When the figs ripen, a very small bird, called by the Italians beccafigo, by the Greeks sycophas, appears, and is continually settling on the branches of the tree and pecking the fruit. If frightened away, they return almost immediately, and a person sitting in the corn or concealed by a thicket may fire with little intermission. They are eaten roasted entire each in a vine-leaf, and are a delicacy. When the olives blacken, vast flights of doves, pigeons, thrushes and other birds repair to the groves for food. Wild turkies are not rare. The red-legged partridge, with her numerous brood, basks in the sun or seeks shade among the mastic-bushes. They are fond of the berries in the season, and have then a strong but not disagreeable taste. In winter, woodcocks abound; descending, after snow on the mountains, into the plain, especially on the side of the Cephissus, and as suddenly retiring. If the weather continue severe, and the ground be frozen, they enter the gardens of the town in great distress, rather than cross the sea; and are sometimes taken with the hand. Snipes, teal, widgeon, ducks, and the like, are also found in plenty. A horse or ass is com-

monly

monly provided by fportfmen, who go in a party, to bring home what they kill.

HARES are exceedingly numerous. Calling is practifed in ftill weather from the latter end of May to about the middle of Auguft. Three or four men in a company ftand filent and concealed in a thicket, with guns pointed in different directions. When all are ready, the caller applies two of his fingers to his lips, and fucking them, at firft flowly and then fafter, produces a fqueaking found; when the hares, within hearing, rufh to the fpot. In this manner many are flaughtered in a day. One of my companions, with Lombardi, a Turk and Greek or two, who were adepts, killed eleven; among which was a female big with young. Thefe animals are faid to affemble together, to leap and play, at the full of the moon; and, it is likely the fhepherds, who live much abroad, obferving and liftening to them, learned to imitate their voices, to deceive, and make them thus foolifhly abet their own deftruction.

THE wild beafts, which find fhelter in the mountains, greatly annoy the fhepherds; and their folds are conftantly guarded by feveral large fierce dogs. The perfon, who killed a wolf, was entitled by a law of Solon to a reward; if a female to one drachm, about feven-pence half-penny; if a male, to five drachms. Afterwards a talent, or one hundred and eighty pounds fterling was paid for a young wolf; and double that fum for one full grown. The peafant now produces the fkin in the Bazar or market, and is recompenfed by voluntary contribution. Parnes, the mountain toward the Cephiffus, is haunted, befides wolves, by deer and foxes, as it formerly was by wild boars and bears. The fportfmen lie in ambufh by the fprings, which they frequent, waiting their approach in the dufk of evening. Pliny[1] mentions the deer bred about Parnes and Brileffus, as remarkable for four kidneys, and the hares as hav-

[1] l. 11. c. 37.

ing two livers[1]. The latter peculiarity in some, which we purchased, was much noticed by our Swiss, who once brought the two livers for my inspection on a plate. The youth of Athens were antiently trained to hunting as a manly and useful exercise.

THE favourite bird of Minerva was the large horned owl. The Athenians stamped its effigy on their coin, and placed it as her companion in her temple in the Acropolis. We had not been long at the convent before a peasant brought us one alive, with the wing broken. This recovered, and was much visited during our stay, as a novelty. Afterwards I saw another, flying, in the day-time. They are as ravenous as eagles, and, if pressed by hunger, will attack lambs and hares. On leaving Athens, we set our venerable and voracious prisoner at liberty, not without fear that, after so long confinement, he would be unable to procure food, or, being unweildy, to escape the wild beasts, which prowl nightly in quest of prey.

ABOUT the middle of October, while we resided at the convent, I had the satisfaction of seeing distinctly the phænomenon called a water-spout from the window of my apartment, which looked toward the sea. The weather had changed from settled and pleasant, and clouds resided on the mountains, black and awful, particularly on Hymettus, whose side and tops were covered. About seven in the morning, when I rose, a cloud tapering to a point had descended in the gulf between the islands Ægina and Salamis. Round it at the bottom was a shining mist. After a minute or more, it began gradually to contract itself, and retired very leisurely up again into the sky. We had little rain this day, but at night pale lightning flashed at short intervals, and thunder, bursting over our heads, exceedingly loud, rolled tremendously, and it poured down as from open sluices. The quantity of water, which fell, was answerable to the long and visible preparation, but seasonable; seed time approaching.

[1] The partridges in Paphlagonia were found to have two hearts, and the hares in Bisaltia two livers. A. Gellius, p. 906.

ATHENS has on the weft fide of the plain the mountains Ægaleos and Parnes, now called Daphne-vouni and Cafha; on the north, Brileffus or Nozea; on the north-eaft about fix miles diftant, Pentele; and next the Ægean fea, Hymettus or Telo-vouni. The latter has a gap in it, dividing the greater from the leffer mountain, which is toward the fouth and was formerly called Anydrus, from its being deftitute of water. The clouds attracted by fome of thefe mountains antiently furnifhed a variety of prognoftics of the weather. A fmall cloud in the hollow of Anydrus, or white clouds in fummer above the greater or leffer mountain and on the fide of Hymettus, portended rain. If in the night a long white cloud girded it beneath the top, the rain generally continued for fome days. A long cloud refting on Hymettus in winter pre-fignified a violent ftorm. At the fetting of the feven ftars called Vergiliæ, lightning about Parnes, Brileffus, and Hymettus, if all were comprehended, denoted a great ftorm; if two, a leffer; but if Parnes alone, ferene weather. A ftorm enfued, if clouds enveloped that portion of Parnes, which was toward Zephyrus or the weft. It was obferved alfo, that a cloud refting on Ægina and above the temple of Jupiter Panhellenius there, was commonly followed by rain.

A DAY or two after the ftorm before-mentioned, the capuchin, as we were converfing by the window of his apartment, put his hand incautioufly on the frame, and, fuddenly withdrawing it, complained of a painful puncture. A Turk, who was with us, on examining the wall, found a fcorpion of a pale green colour, and near three inches long, which he crufhed with his foot, and bound on the part affected, as an antidote to its own poifon. The fmart became inconfiderable after the remedy was applied; and as no inflammation followed, foon ceafed. The fting, if neglected, produces acute pain attended with a fever and other fymptoms for feveral hours, until the paroxyfm is over, when, the malignancy of the virus as it were

decaying,

decaying, the patient is left gradually free. Some preferve fcorpions in oil in a vial, to be ufed if that which commits the hoftility fhould efcape; though it feldom happens but on turning up a log or ftone another may be found to fupply its place. This was the only one I ever faw at Athens, within doors. We fuppofed it had entered at the window for fhelter, and to avoid the danger of being drowned by the flood.

CHAP. XXVIII.

We remove from the Convent --- A Turk defcribed --- The Athenians civil to us --- A Turkifh foot-race and wreftling-match --- Dance of the Arabian women --- Greek dances --- Marriages of the Turks --- Of the Greeks --- Of the Albanians --- Funeral ceremonies --- No learning --- Credulity and fuperftition.

WE were inftructed by the committee of DILETTANTI not to interfere at Athens with the labours of Meff^{rs}. Stuart and Revett, but folely to attend to thofe articles, which they had either omitted or not completed. With this reftriction, we foon perceived, that we had matter to detain us much longer than had been expected. After fome weeks the profpect of a fpeedy conclufion continuing diftant, we removed from the convent to a large and commodious houfe, belonging to one of the archons. It had many trap-doors and hiding-places, and, ftanding detached, was called (νησί) *the ifland.*

A PLACE where the fair fex bears no part in fociety will be juftly fuppofed dull and uniform. Indeed, a Turk is generally a folemn, folitary Being; with few vifible enjoyments except his pipe and coffee. The former is his conftant companion. It is his folace on the fofa; and when fquatting on his hams, as he is sometimes seen, in the shade by the door of his house; or in a group, looking on, while the horses, which are staked down with a rope, feed in the season on the green corn. When he is walking or riding, it is carried in his hand or by an attendant. The tube is of wood perforated, commonly long and pliant, and sometimes hung with small silver crescents and chains, with a mouth-piece of amber. The bole is earthen, and a bit of aloe-wood put into it, while he is smoking, augments his pleasure, yielding a grateful perfume. A silken embroidered bag is usually tucked in at his sash, by his side, and contains tobacco. His horse, his arms, and harám are the other chief objects of his attention. He is grave, sententious, and steady, but fond of narrations and not difficult to be overcome by a story.

The Turks, observing that we did not use the sign of the cross, and being informed that we disapproved of the worshipping of pictures or images, conceived a favourable opinion of us. Their abhorrence of hog-flesh is unfeigned, and we derived some popularity from a report, which we did not contradict, that we held it in equal detestation. Several of them frequented our table. The principal Turks came all to our house at night, while it was Ramazan or Lent when they fast in the day-time; and were entertained by us with sweet-meat, pipes, coffee, and sherbet much to their satisfaction, though distressed by our chairs; some trying to collect their legs under them on the seats, and some squatting down by the sides. When we visited them, we were received with cordiality, and treated with distinction. Sweet gums were burned in the middle of the room, to scent the air; or scattered on coals before us, while sitting on the sofa, to perfume our mustaches and garments; and at the door, on our departure, we were sprinkled with rose-water. The vaiwode at certain seasons sent his musicians to play in our court. The Greeks were not less civil, and at Easter we had the company of the archons in a body. Several of them also eat often with us; and we had daily presents of flowers, sometimes

TRAVELS IN GREECE. 133

times perfumed, of pomgranates, oranges and lemons freſh gathered, paſtry, and other like articles.

THE Turks have few public games or ſports. We were preſent at a foot-race and at a wreſtling-match provided by a rich Turk for the entertainment of his ſon and other boys, who were about to be circumciſed. A train, headed by the vaiwode and principal men on horſes richly capariſoned, attended the boys, who were all neatly dreſſed, their white turbans glittering with tinſel ornaments, to a place without the city, where carpets were ſpread for them on the ground, in the ſhade, and a multitude of ſpectators waited ſilent and reſpectful. The race was ſoon over, and the prizes were diſtributed; to the winner a ſufficient quantity of cloth for an upper garment, to the next a live ſheep, to the third a kid, to the fourth a huge water-melon. The company then removed to a level ſpot near the ruin of the temple of Jupiter Olympius, and formed a large circle. The wreſtlers were naked, except a pair of cloſe drawers, and were anointed all over with oil.

SOME Arabians and black ſlaves, who had obtained their freedom and were ſettled at Athens, had a feaſt on the performance of the rite of circumciſion. The women danced in a ring, with ſticks in their hands, and turning in pairs claſhed them over their heads, at intervals, ſinging wildly to the muſic. A couple then danced with caſtanets; and the other ſwarthy ladies, fitting croſs-legged on a ſofa, began ſmoking.

ATHENS was antiently enlivened by the choruſes ſinging and dancing in the open air, in the front of the temples of the gods and round their altars, at the feſtival of Bacchus and on other holidays. The Greeks are frequently ſeen engaged in the ſame exerciſe, generally in pairs, eſpecially on the anniverſaries of their ſaints, and often in the areas before their churches. Their common muſic is a large tabour and pipe, or a lyre and tympanum or timbrel. Some of their dances are undoubtedly

of

of remote antiquity. One has been supposed [1] that which was called *the crane*, and was said to have been invented by Theseus, after his escape from the labyrinth of Crete. The peasants perform it yearly in the street of the French convent, at the conclusion of the vintage; joining hands, and preceding their mules and asses, which are laden with grapes in panniers, in a very curved and intricate figure; the leader waving a handkerchief, which has been imagined to denote the clew given by Ariadne. A grand circular dance, in which the Albanian women join, is exhibited on certain days near the temple of Theseus; the company holding hands and moving round the musicians, the leader footing and capering until he is tired, when another takes his place. They have also choral dances. I was present at a very laborious single dance of the mimic species, in a field near Sedicui in Asia Minor; a goat-herd assuming, to a tune, all the postures and attitudes of which the human body seemed capable, with a rapidity hardly credible.

MARRIAGES are commonly announced by loud music at the house of the bridegroom. A Turk or Greek neither sees nor speaks to the maiden beforehand, but for an account of her person and disposition relies on his female relations, who have opportunities of seeing her in their visits and at the bath. The Turk, when terms are adjusted with her family, ratifies the contract before the cadi or judge, and sends her presents. If he be rich, a band of musicians precedes a train of peasants, who carry each a sheep, lamb, or kid, with the horns gilded, on their shoulders; and these are followed by servants with covered flaskets on their heads, containing female ornaments, money, and the like, for her use; and by slaves to attend her. Years often intervene before he requires her to be brought to his home. The streets through which she is to pass are then left free; and she is conducted to his house, under a large canopy,

[1] Le Roy, p. 22.

surrounded

surrounded by a multitude of women, all wrapped in white, with their faces muffled. If a Turk finds a pair of papouches or flippers at the door of his harám, it is a sign that a stranger is within, and he modestly retires. That apartment is even a sanctuary for females flying from the officers of justice.

A PAPAS or priest reads a service at the Greek weddings, the two persons standing and holding each a wax-taper lighted. A ring and gilded wreath or crown is used; and, at the end of the ceremony, a little boy or girl, as previously agreed on, is led to the bride, and kisses her hand. She is then as it were enthroned in a chair, and the husband remains at a respectful distance, with his hands crossed, silent and looking at her; until the women enter and take her away, when the men carouse in a separate apartment. Her face and hands are grossly daubed over with paint; and one, which I saw, had her forehead and cheeks bedecked with leaf-gold.

THE Albanians convey the bride to the house of her husband in procession, on horseback, with a child astride behind her, a loose veil or canopy concealing her head and face, her fingers laden with silver rings, and her hands painted red and blue in streaks. Their dress is a red jacket handsomely embroidered, with a coloured Turban. I was present at one of their entertainments, which consisted of a great variety of dishes, chiefly pastry, ranged under a long low arbour made with boughs; the company sitting on the ground. When the bride is to be removed to a place at a distance, some women dance before her to the end of the town.

THE wife of a Turk, who lived near us, dying, we were alarmed on a sudden with a terrible shriek of women and with the loud expostulations of the husband. She was carried to the grave at day-break. The Greeks bury in their churches, on a bier. The bones, when room is wanting, are washed with wine in the presence of the nearest male relation, and then
removed.

removed. I was at a funeral entertainment provided by one of the archons, whofe daughter had been recently interred. The proceffion fet out from his houfe, before fun-rife, headed by a papas or prieft and fome deacons, with lighted candles; the women, who were left behind, fcreaming and howling. One man bore a large wax-taper painted with flowers and with the portrait of the deceafed in her ufual attire, and hung round with a handkerchief of her embroidering, in gathers. Two followed, carrying on their heads each a great diſh of parboiled wheat; the furface, blanched almonds difpofed in the figure of a dove, with gilding and a border of raifins and pomgranate-kernels. Thefe, on our arrival at the church, were depofited over the body. The matins ended with a fervice appropriated to this ceremony, and read by the prieft near the fpot. The diſhes were then brought round, and each perfon in his place took a portion, and was afterwards helped in turn to a fmall glafs of white brandy called rakí or of wine. The wax-taper, with the handkerchief, was fufpended from the ceiling, as a memorial of the girl reprefented on it; and fome peraus or filver pennies were diftributed to the poor, who attended.

THE Turks are a people never yet illuminated by fcience. They are more ignorant than can eafily be conceived. Athens now claims no pre-eminence in learning. The leifure of the Greeks is chiefly employed in reading legendary ftories of their faints tranflated into the vulgar tongue. This and their nation they ftyle *the Roman*. It has a clofe affinity with the antient language, which they call the Hellenic; but the grammar and fyntax are much corrupted. They fpeak rapidly, and curtail many of their words, which are farther depraved by incorrect fpelling. Their pronunciation differs widely from the Englifh. They have no knowlege of the old quantity of fyllables, but adhere to the accents, and compofe verfes in rhyme with great facility. I enquired for manufcripts, and was told of fome belonging to the monaftery of St. Cyriani on mount Hymettus. Thefe were ſhown me, with feveral books printed by Aldus, negligently

negligently scattered on the floor in a loft at Athens, where the hegumenos or abbot resided. I wished to purchase the manuscripts, but the consent of the archbishop and of some of his brethen was necessary; and unfortunately the former, who had been forced to fly, was not re-instated in his see before we left the place.

CREDULITY and superstition prevail at Athens and all over the East. The traveller may still hear of Medeas, women possessed of magic powers, and expert in various modes of incantation. Amulets or charms are commonly worn to repel any malignant influence. Children are seen with crosses or thin flat bits of gold, called phylacteries, hanging about their necks or on their foreheads, The Turks inscribe words from the Koran. The Greeks confide in holy water, which is sprinkled on their houses yearly by a priest, to purify them and to drive away any dæmon, who may have obtained entrance. The insides of several of their churches are covered with representations of the exploits of their saints, painted on the walls; extravagant, ridiculous, and absurd beyond imagination. The old Athenian had a multitude of deities, but relied chiefly on Minerva; the modern has a similar troop headed by his favourite Panagía. He listens with devout humility to fanciful tales of nightly visions, and of miracles vouchsafed on the most trivial occasions. The report is propagated, and if, on examination, the forgery be detected on the spot, the remoter devotee continues in his conviction, and exults in the contemplation of the solid basis, on which he conceives his faith to be founded. In the first year of our residence in the Levant, a rumour was current, that a cross of shining light had been seen at Constantinople pendant in the air over the grand mosque once a church dedicated to St. Sophia; and that the Turks were in consternation at the prodigy, and had endeavoured in vain to dissipate the vapour. The sign was interpreted to portend the exaltation of the Christians above the Mahometans; and this many surmised was speedily to be effected; disgust and jealousy then subsisting between the Ruffians and the Porte, and the Georgians contending with fuccefs againſt the Turkiſh armies. By ſuch arts as theſe are the wretched Greeks preſerved from deſpondency, rouſed to expectation, and confoled beneath the yoke of bondage. The traveller, who is verſed in antiquity, may be agreeably and uſefully employed in ſtudying the people of Athens.

CHAP. XXIX.

We continue at Athens --- Account of Lombardi --- The archbiſhop forced to fly --- Diſtreſs from want of corn --- Intrigues of Lombardi.

OUR ſtay at Athens was prolonged by unforeſeen obſtacles, which were to be ſurmounted, as they aroſe, before our buſineſs could be completed. Some buildings required ladders ſo long and ſtrong, it was difficult to procure fit materials, or even a workman capable of making them. Several figures could be drawn only from a particular terrace or the window of a houſe, and a churliſh or rapacious owner was to be ſatisfied. The Ramazan or Lent of the Turks, and the Bairam or holidays, interfered. We encountered many a vexatious delay, and our reſidence became irkſome as well from the continual apprehenſion of ſome untoward accident or enſnaring treachery, as from our deteſtation of Lombardi, who haunted our houſe, and, by his hateful preſence and by diſcourſe, which was impure, indelicate, and impious in the higheſt degree, polluted and poiſoned every enjoyment.

LOMBARDI was ſaid to have been a prieſt, and to have robbed the altars of the church. He had fled from his country, it was certain, to avoid the puniſhment of ſome crime of a moſt atrocious nature. He was acquainted with the Latin language, had

had some knowlege of medicine, and had lived with several
Bashas and great Turkish officers as their physician. He had
signalized his courage and conduct in dangerous expeditions
against banditti and insurgents; which services had been rewarded with money, horses, and garments lined with skins.
He possessed uncommon addrefs, eloquence, profligacy, hypo-
crify. He had been a pretended proselyte to the Greek communion, and had written a book in Italian, entitled " *Truth the*
" *Judge. By Father Bentzoni, a Jesuit and Convert to the true*
" *Oriental Church;*" of which a translation into the vulgar
Greek, with ludicrous cuts, was printed at Johannina, a city of
Epirus, and dispersed over Turkey. The malignancy of this
lampoon on Christianity was so concealed, that for some time
the author was reputed a champion for the pure faith of the
Greeks. He had also composed a long and bitter invective
against an archbishop of Larissa in Thessaly. He had been im-
prisoned at Athens, and had obtained his release with difficulty,
by tears, intreaties, and the interposition of the Turks. This
usage, however deserved, had made him outrageous, and revenge
was his highest gratification. He had employed the most un-
justifiable means to compass the downfall, and even the deaths,
of his principal enemies. He was recently returned from Constantinople, and boasted, that, by his intrigues there, he had
levelled some proud archons at Athens, who had lately hoisted
flags as consuls to European powers; a privilege from which the
subjects of the Porte were excluded by an edict, which had been
enforced during our residence at Smyrna. He talked unconcern-
edly of the death of his elder and favourite son, whom he had taken
with him, and sent home in a vessel, in which the plague afterwards appeared. The young man sickened in the Piræus, and
was removed to a monastery; and a another passenger dying of it
suddenly was thrown into a well by the shore, with a large
stone to cover the body. Before our departure, he formally
repudiated his wife, who was an Athenian; and renounced her
children, a son and two daughters, who refused to relinquish
Christianity. The Turks were offended at his want of natural
affection,

affection, and pleaded in their behalf. He had espoused a young Albanian in the presence of the Cadi or Turkish Judge, and now co-habited with her; but a plurality of wives ranked among the least criminal of his various enormities.

A GENERAL disquiet of the people likewise contributed to render our situation not agreeable. Some exactions of the archbishop, who was eager to pay the money borrowed for the purchase of his see, made him unpopular. He had incurred also the displeasure of the vaiwode, and an open quarrel ensued on his applying for leave to rebuild or repair a church, and remonstrating that the sum demanded was unreasonable. The vaiwode lifted his pipe to strike him, and, in their altercation, averred he was neither deacon, priest, or bishop. An explanation was asked, when he replied with a proverb, (Γαιδαρος αει γαι-δαρος) *The ass is always an ass.* The difference was compromised, but soon broke out again. The Greek clergy joined the vaiwode, and the archbishop was expelled Athens.

THE scarcity of corn increased as winter advanced, until the distress of the people was so great, that an insurrection was apprehended daily, and Achmet Aga, to appease the clamour, opened his granaries. Yet the vaiwode, to raise money for the purchase of his post for the ensuing year, sold a large portion of the future grain by contract to M^r. Keyrac, a French merchant, who resided at Nauplia or Napoli in the Morea. The basha of Negropont would have interfered, but the Athenians claim immunity from his jurisdiction. The officers, whom he commissioned to enquire into the abuse, could scarcely procure a lodging on their arrival, and they soon left the town. Achmet Aga refused them admittance at his house, from a dislike of their errand; and the Greeks pleaded a *barát* or charter exempting them from such burdens. Some Turks at another time had required Isosime, who was epitropos or curator, to provide for them a *conac* or place of refreshment, but he would not comply; and, on their threatening to pistol him or to cut off his head

with

with their fabres, had bared his breaſt and extended his neck, declaring, the privilege ſhould not be loſt by want of courage in him to preſerve it. The jealouſy of the Athenians fruſtrated the purpoſe of the baſha, but their murmuring did not ceaſe. The oppreſſion and extortion of the vaiwode were complained of as unprecedented.

LOMBARDI fomented the public diſcord, working in private like a mole underground. His zeal in perſecuting the archbiſhop gave him influence with his enemies and with the vaiwode. He ſpirited up a mob to ſhout, *Barabbas, Barabbas*, on his coming from a church, in which the clergy had been aſſembled; and he uſed every method, which the moſt diabolical malice could ſuggeſt, to blacken his character. He laboured alſo to accompliſh the ruin of other perſons, at whom he had taken offence. One of theſe was a native of Corfu, a practitioner in phyſic, countenanced by M^r. Keyrac; whoſe agent, a Frenchman, urged the vaiwode to do him no injury, and at laſt obtained a promiſe, which was ratified by his putting his hand on the head of his ſon, and ſaying, *So may Iſmaël live.*

CHAP. XXX.

Journey to mount Hymettus --- An antient well --- Veſtiges of Alopece --- Arrive at ſome bee-ſtands --- Alarmed in the night --- Turkiſh rigour --- A well --- The ſhaft of a mine --- Dinner --- At Dragoniſi --- A ſpeckled owl --- The monaſtery of St. Cyriani.

WHILE we reſided at the French convent, we were informed of certain ſubterraneous wonders ſaid to exiſt in the bowels of mount Hymettus. The report of an eye-witneſs, though of a nature not to be entirely credited, ſeemed to merit ſome attention. Our ſervants provided ropes, wax-tapers, and other

other neceffaries; and we fet out on the fifth of October, after the heat of noon, accompanied by Lombardi. We had alfo fome dogs and falcons belonging to the vaiwode.

WE croffed the Iliffus and paffed by the fite of the Lycéum. After a fhort ride with the greater Hymettus on our left, the road winding toward the fea, we came near a village called Dragonifi, confifting of a ruined tower and a very few houfes, on a fmall eminence in the plain. We alighted beneath a fhady tree by an antient well fhaped like a parallellogram, and divided in the middle by five tranfverfe marble beams, one above another. Here a leather bucket was procured, a fire kindled, and coffee made.

GOING on, we foon came to a fpot over-run with bufhes, among which are feveral wells moftly choked with foil and rubbifh. Many of the demi or antient boroughs were unimportant places, and, from their want of character, can never be afcertained. Some too of more confequence are almoft equally unknown, the information concerning them not being fufficiently explicit. This is one of the few to which a name may be affigned. On the fide of Athens next the Heracléum and Cynofarges was Alopece, the place to which Socrates belonged. A farm at Alopece is on record as only eleven or twelve ftadia, about a mile and a half, from the city-wall.

WE now turned to the left, and entered the gap between the greater and leffer Hymettus. Here, on our fpringing a partridge, the Falconer unhooded and let his hawk fly, but the bird, inftead of purfuing his quarry, foared high up in the air, making toward Athens; the Greek his keeper looking at and running after him, until he funk again and was recovered. We penetrated into the receffes of the mountain, and about funfet halted by fome bee-ftands, and fupped on the provifions we had brought from Athens.

NIGHT

NIGHT approaching, we lay down to sleep among the thickets, each on a small carpet, and wrapped in a *pellice* or garment lined with skins; the whole company forming a circle round our horses and other animals, which were fastened to the bushes. About midnight we were disturbed by a sudden kicking and confusion among the horses, which was followed with a cry of *lycos lycos, a wolf, a wolf.* In an instant all were up, with guns ready to fire, but the moon shining, the occasion of our alarm was presently discovered to be an ass, which from love of society, hope of food, or some other motive, had been induced to intrude on us, and now retired precipitately, braying.

AT the dawn of day we ascended an acclivity of the mountain, the track rough and narrow, and on the margin of a water-course; leaving our baggage behind us, heaped in a thicket. We were told it was secure amid these uninhabited solitudes, though unguarded; for, such is the rigour of the Turkish polity, if a pilferer be not detected, the vaiwode on complaint levies far more than the value of what is lost on the district; rejoicing in the opportunity of uniting his private gain with public justice and the satisfaction of the party defrauded.

WE were now brought by the Greek, our guide, to a circular well sunk in the rock many fathom deep, the mouth above forty feet wide. This was the place to be examined. A stout piece of wood was cut, and fixed so as to project over the brim. The Greek then got astride a stick tied to a rope, by which he held; another rope was fastened about his body; and he was let gently down to the bottom. Our Swifs was lowered next in like manner, and both disappeared; two narrow passages in the well leading, in opposite directions, under the mountain. The Swifs fired a pistol, but the report did not reach us. On their return, they conveyed up to us, by a rope, some specimens of the concretions formed on the roof and sides, as usual in caverns.

The-

The shape, which a portion of this substance had chanced to assume, proved the occasion of our journey. The Greek had received from it a lively idea of a human figure, and, filled with admiration, had represented it as the image of a caloyer or monk with a venerable beard and of a striking aspect. We re-hoisted our two adventurers, and mounting our horses went back to our baggage by the way we came.

The mountains on this side of Athens were once noted for silver. The mines were private property, and were worked for the benefit of individuals, to the time of Themistocles. By his advice, the republic took possession of them, and applied the profits to the building of triremes to be employed in the war with Ægina. Demetrius the Phaleréan said, that the Athenians laboured on them as eagerly as if they hoped to dig up Plutus himself, the god of riches. The produce, which at first was plentiful, failing, they re-melted the old scum and dross, and found ore, which, from want of skill, had not been extracted. The well, to which we were conducted, was probably a shaft. The honey of Attica esteemed most exquisite was taken near the mines.

On our arrival at the thicket where our baggage lay, a couple of Greeks climbed the mountain to search for wild honey; and our servants began to prepare dinner, striking fire, and hewing down bushes with their sabres. The fold of Mustapha Bey, a friendly Turk of Athens, supplied us with a sheep fed on the fragrant herbage of Hymettus, They embowelled the carcase, and fixed it whole and warm on a wooden spit; which was turned by one of them sitting on the ground. They cut in pieces the heart, liver, and the like, and mingled them on a skewer, to be dressed on the coals. Some boughs of green mastic served us at once for tablecloth and dish. We fell to with knives or fingers, for the latter are principally used; and a Greek, kneeling by us, circulated wine, pouring it

into

into a shell. Our men feasted in their turn, and made merry, until the heat of noon overpowered them.

After sleeping, some in a shallow watercourse beneath the scanty shade under which we had dined, and some among the thickets at a distance, we mounted and returned back to Dragonisi, where a hospitable Albanian received us, sweeping the ground, and spreading a mat for us, before the door of his house. We supped on fowls, cheese, salted olives, eggs, and such articles as could be procured. The evening was concluded with wild singing and rustic dancing. We passed the night round a fire, having no mountain as before to shelter us, and the air getting cold.

In the morning the falconer, after placing a piece of raw meat in a tree at a distance, unhooded and dismissed a hawk, which immediately flew toward it; but, stooping mid-way, seized a small speckled owl lurking among the few green tufts scattered on the surface of the soil. The ravenous bird was easily deceived by a bit of flesh, which the falconer substituted, as usual, in the room of his prey, and loosed the owl alive from his talons. We likewise saw a partridge chased, taken on the wing, and carried into a thicket.

The purple hills of Hymettus were the scene of the famous story of Cephalus and Procris[1]. The fatal mistake of the husband was said to have happened among some thickets near a sacred spring or fountain. This seems the spot called Pera, where was a temple of Venus, and a water, which was believed to conduce to pregnancy and to an easy delivery. The fame, it is probable, is now occupied by the monastery of Cyriani. In many instances the temple or its site, with the consecrated portion, have changed their owners, and the deity been dispossessed by the saint. The convent is an old irregular building

---

[1] Ovid. de Arte Amandi, l. 3, v. 687.

on the side of the greater Hymettus, in view from Athens, encompassed by a wall with battlements, and entered by a low iron door. The Greek women repair to it at particular seasons, and near it is a fountain much extolled for its virtues. The papas or priest affirmed, that a dove is seen to fly down from heaven to drink of it yearly, at the feast of Pentecost. I ascended to the top of the mountain, where I enjoyed a fine prospect of the country and of the islands in the Ægean sea, near the coast of Attica.

CHAP. XXXI.

Towns between Phalerum and Sunium --- Capes and islands --- Barrows by Alopece --- Vestiges of Æxone and Anagyrus --- Entertained by a Greek Abbot --- A Panéum or sacred cave --- Wheler's rout from Sunium to Athens --- Remarks.

THE towns on the coast, going from Phalerum toward Sunium, were Alimus, Æxone, Alæ of Æxone, Anagyrus, Thoræ, Lampra, Ægilia, Anaphlystus, Azenia. Alimus was at the same distance as Phalerum from Athens, and had a temple of Ceres and Proserpine. Lampra was the place to which Cranaus the successor of Cecrops fled from Amphictyon. His monument remained in the time of Pausanias, above sixteen hundred years after his death, and, if a barrow, is perhaps still extant.

THE long promontory, the first after Æxone, was named Zoster, because, it was said, Latona had loosed her zone there in her way to Delos, whither she was conducted by Minerva. On the shore was an altar. After Thoræ was Astypalæa. Before one of the capes was the island Phaura; before the other, Eleusa; and opposite to Æxone, Hydrusa. Toward Anaphlystus

tus' was a Panéum or cave of Pan, and the temple of Venus Colias. The weft wind fcattered the wrecks of the Perfian fleet, after the battle of Salamis, along the fhore as far as Colias. Before thefe places lay Belbina, at no great diftance, and the foffe of Patroclus, but moft of the iflands were defert. Paufanias mentions cape Colias, with the image of Venus, as twenty ftadia or two miles and a half from Phalerum. Colias was famous for earthen ware, tinged with vermilion.

SOME information, received foon after our return from mount Hymettus, induced us to go in the following month to Vary, a metochi or farm belonging to a Greek monaftery at Athens, on the fea-coaft, and diftant about four hours. The road led us, as before, to the veftiges of Alopece, beyond which we faw feveral fmall barrows, the foil poor and ftony. Their origin may be deduced from early hiftory. The Lacedæmonians fent an army under Anchimolius to free Athens from the tyranny of the fons of Pififtratus. He landed at Phalerum, encamped, was attacked, and killed with many of his men. Their graves or barrows, fays Herodotus, are by Alopece[2].

ON our approach to the fhore, fome veftiges occurred, it is likely, of Æxone. We then turned, and travelled toward Sunium, through a gap in mount Hymettus, which running out forms the promontory once called Zofter. Within the gap, near the end, we came to the fite of a confiderable town, fome terrace walls of the fpecies called Incertum remaining. Beyond thefe is a church. We found fome fragments of infcriptions fixed in the wall; and one of my companions afterwards copied a fepulchral marble recording a perfon of Anagyrus, which, it is probable, was the name of the place. The terrace perhaps was the fite of the temple of the mother of the gods.

THE convent ftands on a knoll above the fea, with Lampra, the promontories Sunium and Scyllæum, and the foffe of Patro-

---

[1] πρὸς δὲ Ἀναφλυστῳ---Strabo p. 398. There was a temple of Ceres.
[2] l. v. c. 6. Pififtratus died in the year before Chrift, 528.

clus, Belbina, and other iſlands, in view. We found there the hegumenos or abbot, who was come from Athens to receive us, and two or three caloyers or monks, who manage the farm. We were entertained with boiled fowls, olives, cheeſe, and the like fare. The ſky, as uſual, was our canopy; and after ſun-ſet, we lay down to ſleep, ſome under a ſhed, ſome in the court, and one of my companions in a tree, where a man had watched the Alóni or corn-floor, which was cloſe by, during the harveſt.

We aſcended early in the morning to a cave or grotto, which was the object of our journey, diſtant about three quarters of an hour, inland, in the mountain. This, which appears to be the Panéum mentioned by Strabo, will be the ſubject of the following chapter. It affords ſhelter to the goatherds in winter, and is frequented at all ſeaſons for water by thoſe who have their occupation on the mountain. Our men made a fire in it to purify the air, and we tarried all day, dining again on a ſheep roaſted whole.

An abſtract of the journey of Sir George Wheler from Sunium to Athens will illuſtrate this portion of the geography of Attica. He directed his courſe along the ſhore of the Saronic gulf and paſſed the night with ſome ſhepherds near Metropis a town on a hill. Ten or twelve miles farther on, he came to ruins on a rock, near a bay. Theſe were called Enneapyrgæ, *the Nine Towers.* From Lampra, three or four miles more inland, he travelled north-weſtward in a cultivated plain to a very few houſes called Fillia. He then turned more north-weſtward into the way to Athens, and entered between two ridges of mount Hymettus, one called Lampra-vouni, the other Telo-vouni. This deſcended with a ſharp point into the ſea, making a promontory named Halikes, before which are four ſmall iſlands or rocks called Camboniſia, *the Button Iſlands.* He then arrived in the plain of Athens.

Of theſe places, Metropis may have been, as he ſuppoſes, Azenia. Enneapyrgæ was Anaphlyſtus. The next village was

upper

upper Lampra; and Fillia perhaps was that of which the people were once called Philaidæ. Halikes, with the Cambonifia, was Zoſter with the iſlets about it. Lampra-vouni was on his left hand. He appears to have quitted the coaſt, and to have entered the plain of Athens through the gap dividing the greater from the leſſer Hymettus.

CHAP. XXXII.

Diſtinct provinces of the heathen gods --- Their characters and places of worſhip --- A Panéum or Nymphæum, with inſcriptions --- Of Archidamus and the age when he lived --- Of the Nymphs --- Of Nympholepſy --- Of ſacred caves --- Of a cave in Ithaca --- In Paphlagonia --- Of the two entrances --- The offerings --- Deſign of the cave.

THE pious Athenian was antiently furniſhed with patron-gods for every occupation, ſituation, and purſuit. He who ventured to ſea firſt propitiated Neptune, Amphitrite, and the Nereïds. The artiſt ſacrificed to Minerva and Vulcan; the ſtudent to the Muſes, Apollo their leader, Memory, and Mercury; the lover to Venus and Cupid, Perſuaſion, and the Graces; the huſbandman to Ceres and her ſon Bacchus; and the ſportſman to Diana the huntreſs, Apollo, Pan, the Nymphs, and the deities of the mountains.

THE characters of the gods of Greece were as diſtinct as the provinces over which they were ſuppoſed to preſide. Apollo, with the Muſes about him, was a moſt accompliſhed deity; Pan a very ruſtic. Some were of a ſocial turn and gods of pleaſure; wh le others preferred retirement, and lived ſequeſtered in the country. The city Bacchus was preſent in the theatres; the Nymphs were diſcovered by ſprings and fountains.

tains. Their offerings alfo had commonly a relation to their nature, office, and ideal fuperintendency. Their altars differed in height, fhape, or ornaments. The fubterraneous gods had their trenches; the terreftrial and the Heroes their hearths. The tenants of Olympus were worfhipped in temples; the Nymphs with Pan and the rural clafs in caves.

The Panéum or Nymphæum by Vary is a fingular curiofity, of a fpecies, it is apprehended, not defcribed by any traveller. It is found in the mountain-fide, near a brow. You defcend through a fmall mouth; the forked trunk of a tree, with branches faftened acrofs, ferving as a ladder. At the landing-place is a Greek infcription very difficult to be read. It is cut on the rock firft fmoothed, and informs us, that Archidamus of Pheræ made the cave for the Nymphs, by whom he was *poffeffed*. Oppofite is a fmall niche or cavity; with fome letters, part of a word, fignifying that the offering for fruits, perhaps a fmall piece of money, was to be placed there. From the landing-place two ways lead into the cavern. Going down by the narrow ftairs cut in the rock, on the left hand is infcribed in very antient characters, " Archidamus the Pheræan." When you are down and face the ftairs, at the extremity on the right hand is an ithyphallus, the fymbol of Bacchus; and near it is Ifis, the Egyptian Ceres. The Athenians had early an intercourfe with Egypt, and fome writers have afferted were originally a colony from that country. Under fmall niches, in two places, is infcribed, " Of Pan." On the other fide of the ftairs are two more niches, and beneath each, " Of Apollo. " Offer." Beyond thefe is a very rude figure of the fculptor reprefented with his tools, as working, and by it his name, Archidamus, twice repeated, the letters irregular and badly cut. On removing fome mould we difcovered that his feet are both turned inward. Near the image of Ifis lay a ftone, with two fides infcribed, once fet up fo that both might be vifible. From one I copied " Archidamus the Pheræan and Cholliden-
" fian made this dwelling for the Nymphs;" from the other,
" Archidamus

"Archidamus the Pheræan planted the garden for the Nymphs." The stairs, which are continued along by the side of the rock below the figure of Archidamus, are covered with soil formed by leaves or washed in by rain from above; and the descent to the lower grotto, to which they led, is become steep and slippery. That is entered by a narrow passage left in the partition, which has been rendered picturesque by petrifactions. It is of a circular form, the sides adorned with fantastic incrustation, and the roof with sparry icicles. Of these several are growing up, pointed, from beneath; and some have already met and united with those pendant from above. At the bottom is a well of very clear and cold water. On the left hand, going up again, near the landing-place, is a square horizontal cavity; and farther on is an inscription on the rough rock, not legible. The cavity probably contained the garden of the Nymphs before mentioned, consisting of a little soil set with such herbs and flowers as were reputed grateful to them. If a small trench be deemed unworthy of the appellation, it may be noted, that gardens were planted for Adonis not equal in magnitude even to this plat, each being a shell or pot with earth, in which certain vegetables thrived awhile and then withered. Such were the flower-gardens in the hall called by his name in the palace of Domitian at Rome.

ARCHIDAMUS was sollicitous, as may be inferred from his figure, to transmit a knowlege of his person to future ages. He was a native of Pheræ, a city of Thessaly, who had settled in Attica and was admitted to his freedom in Chollis, one of the borough-towns. The inscriptions, as may be collected from the diversity in the characters and in their powers, are of different dates. That at the landing-place was added, it is likely, long after his decease, as a memorial of his labour and its cause; which was nympholepsy. From those which appear to be contemporary with the sculptor it may be argued that he lived when the Attic or Cadmean and Palamedean alphabet, consisting of sixteen letters, was in use; or before the Atheni-

ans

ans were prevailed on[1] to adopt the Ionic alphabet, in which the number was twenty-four. The figure of Archidamus, so unshapely and unsightly, will coincide with a period, when *design* was in its infancy and not commonly professed. It is certainly among the oldest specimens extant of the beginnings of the art; furnishing an example of the rough out-line and proportionless sketch, from which it gradually rose to correctness, precision, and sublime expression; animating marble, and giving to statues a perfection of form unequalled by nature, and a dignity of aspect superior to human.

THE Nymphs were supposed to enjoy longevity, but not to be immortal. They were believed to delight in springs and fountains. They are described as sleepless, and as dreaded by the country people. They were susceptible of passion. The Argonauts, it is related, landing on the shore of the Propontis to dine in their way to Cholcos, sent Hylas, a boy, for water, who discovered a lonely fountain, in which the nymphs Eunica, Malis, and Nycheia were preparing to dance; and these, seeing him, were enamoured and seizing him by the hand, as he was filling his vase, pulled him in. The deities, their co-partners in the cave, are such as presided with them over rural and pastoral affairs. If Priapus be substituted in the place of Bacchus, he also was honoured where goats and sheep fed and where bee-hives stood.

THE old Athenians were ever ready to cry out, a god! or a goddess! The tyrant Pisistratus entered the city in a chariot with a tall woman dressed in armour to resemble Minerva, and regained the Acropolis, which he had been forced to abandon, by this stratagem; the people worshipping and believing her to be the deity, whom she represented. The Nymphs, it was the popular persuasion, occasionally appeared; and nympholepsy is characterized as a frenzy, which arose from having beheld

[1] In the fourth year of Olympiad XCIV; or, before Christ 399 years.

them.

them. Superstition disposed the mind to adopt delusion for reality, and gave to a fancied vision the efficacy of full conviction. The foundation was perhaps no more than an indirect, partial, or obscure view of some harmless girl, which had approached the fountain on a like errand with Hylas, or was retiring after she had filled her earthen pitcher.

AMONG the sacred caves on record, one on mount Ida in Crete was the property of Jupiter, and one by Lebadea in Bœotia of Trophonius. Both these were oracular, and the latter bore some resemblance to that we have described. It was formed by art, and the mouth surrounded with a wall. The descent to the landing-place was by a light and narrow ladder, occasionally applied and removed. It was situated on a mountain above a grove; and they related, that a swarm of bees conducted the person by whom it was first discovered. But the common owners of caves were the Nymphs, and these were sometimes local. On Cithæron in Bœotia, many of the inhabitants were *possessed* by Nymphs called Sphragitides, whose cave, once also oracular, was on a summit of the mountain. Their dwellings had generally a well or spring of water; the former often a collection of moisture condensed or exsuding from the roof and sides; and this, in many instances, being pregnant with stony particles, concreted, and marked its passage by incrustation, the ground-work in all ages and countries of idle tales framed or adopted by superstitious and credulous people [1].

[1] Intus aquæ dulces, *vivoque* sedilia saxo,
Nympharumque domus. Virg.
See Theocritus ζ' v. 136, and Strabo, p. 343. Philostratus, p. 411, mentions a Nymphæum by the sea near Puteoli, in which was a well, with a rim of white stone. The interpreter has mistranslated the passage. The author, p. 764, describes likewise a picture, in which a cave of Achelous and the Nymphs was represented, he observes, properly; the images seeming of bad stone and workmanship, as injured by time, and cut by the young thoughtless boys of the herdsmen and shepherds.

THE defcription of a cave of this fpecies in the Odyffey has been underftood as fymbolical, and furnifhed, contrary to all natural interpretation, with myftic meaning, by Porphyry, a philofopher, who flourifhed in the third century [1]. This cave was fituated near the head of a port in Ithaca. It was obfcure within, but remarkable for perennial water, and ftone bowls and veffels, bees depofiting honey, and long ftone looms, with nymphs weaving purple garments wonderful to behold. The poet here records real and imaginary refemblances, probably traced and reported by the iflanders, and which perhaps he had likewife feen with admiration. It may be furmifed, that ideal perfonages and reprefentations were antiently found alfo in the Attic cave.

A CAVE in Paphlagonia was facred to the Nymphs, who inhabited the mountains about Heraclea. It was long and wide, and pervaded by cold water, clear as chryftal. There alfo were feen bowls of ftone, and nymphs, and their webs, and diftaffs, and curious work, exciting admiration. The poet [2], who has defcribed this grotto, deferves not to be regarded as fervilely copying Homer. He may juftly claim to rank as an original topographer.

THE caves of Ithaca and Heraclea had each two entrances, one toward the north, the other toward the fouth. At Ithaca, men defcended only by the northern aperture, the fouthern being accounted holy and the way of the gods. In the fecond cave was alfo a track referved for fuperior Beings, and this is defcribed as both difficult and dangerous, lying on the brink of a deep pit. The fame diftinction, it is likely, prevailed in the Attic cave. The perfons, who prefided occafionally and were benefited by the religion of the place found perhaps a paffage appropriated to their ufe both convenient and neceffary, and

[1] See Pope's Odyffey, the notes on v. 124 and v. 134 of the thirteenth book.
[2] Q. Smyrnæus, l. 6. v. 470.

obtained

obtained an exclusive right by establishing an idea of its sanctity.

The countryman and shepherd, as well as the sportsman, has often repaired, it is likely, to this cave, to render the deities propitious by sacrificing a she-goat or lamb, by gifts of cakes or fruit, and by libations of milk, oil, and honey; simply believing, that this attention was pleasing to them, that they were present though unseen, and partook without diminishing the offering; their appetites as well as passions, caprices, and employments resembling the human. At noon-day the pipe was silent on the mountains, lest it might happen to awake Pan, then reposing after the exercise of hunting, tired and peevish.

It is related, where druidism prevailed, the houses were decked with evergreens in December, that the sylvan Spirits might repair to them, and remain unnipped with frost and cold winds, until a milder season had renewed the foliage of their darling abodes. The gods of Greece, at least the inferior class, were conceived liable to like sufferings. They were capable of dissolving with heat and shivering with cold. Among the punishments imprecated on Pan[t], if he should prove unkind, are these; that in mid winter he might be exposed on the bleak mountains of Thrace, and during summer in the torrid regions of Æthiopia. The piety of Archidamus furnished a retreat for the Nymphs, where they might find shelter and provision, if distressed; whether the sun parched up their trees, or Jupiter enthroned in clouds upon the mountain-top scared them with his red lightening and terrible thunder, pouring down a deluge of rain, or brightening the summits with his snow.

[t] Theocritus, Id. ζ.

CHAP. XXXIII.

Towns on the eastern coast of Attica --- Of Thoricus --- Of Potamus Of Prasiæ --- Of the port of Prasiæ or port Raphti --- The road to it from Athens --- Extract from Wheler continued.

ATTICA has the Ægæan sea on the east. The course, coasting from Sunium, is to the north, inclining to the west. The towns on this side were Thoricus, Potamus, Prasiæ, Stiria, Brauron, Alæ of Araphen, Myrrhinus, Probalinthus, Marathon, Tricorythus, Rhamnus, and, on the confines of Attica and Bœotia, Oropus. The land at first lies between two seas, and is narrow. Farther on, it widens. The coast, toward Oropus, was gibbous or rounded like a moon.

THORICUS was once a place of importance. It was fortified in the first year of the ninety third Olympiad[1]. Xenophon was of opinion, that the workmen might continue their employment at the silver-mines in time of war, as this fortress was near them by the sea on the north, and Anaphlystus on the south; each distant from the other only about sixty stadia or seven miles and a half; but recommended the eminence of Besa, which was mid-way between them, as a proper spot for a third fortress, where all might assemble on an alarm; though he did not apprehend the mines would be attacked, because the enemy, advancing either from Megara, which city was much above five hundred stadia or sixty two miles and a half distant, or from Thebes, which exceeded six hundred stadia or seventy five miles, must pass Athens and leave their own country exposed. The failure of the mines was probably followed by the ruin both of Thoricus and Anaphlystus. Pausanias is silent

[1] In the year before Christ, 406.

concerning

concerning them; and Mela, who wrote under Claudius Cæſar, mentions the former as then but a name; which, however, is not yet difuſed. The ſhip, in which Mr. Le Roy failed in 1754, was forced into the port by contrary winds. He deſcribes it as oppoſite to *Long Iſland*, fix miles north-weſt of Sunium, and near a large plain ſurrounded with hills, which on the ſouth are overtopped by a mountain ſtretching toward the entrance of the gulf. This, he ſuppoſes, was Laurium. Among the thickets he diſcovered ſome ruins of a very antient temple. Helene or *Long Iſland* extended along the coaſt from Thoricus as far as Sunium.

AT Potamus was the monument of Ion, from whom the Ionians were named. The Athenians, when they provided a huſband for a grandaughter of Ariſtogiton, who had lived in poverty and obſcurity at Lemnos, gave a farm there as her dowry.

AT Praſiæ was a temple of Apollo. The ſhip named Theoris failed from thence annually to Delos with an unknown offering packed in wheat-ſtraw and tranſmitted from the Hyperboreans, a remote people. The monument of Eryſichthon, who died on that voyage, was ſhown there. Some ruins of the town were ſeen by Sir George Wheler, upon the ſhore near the haven, now called port Raphti.

THE port of Praſiæ or port Raphti is deſcribed as a moſt ſafe, commodious, and delightful harbour, almoſt encompaſſed with charming vales riſing gradually and terminating in lofty mountains; the ſlopes covered with pine-trees and verdure. A ſharp point of land, running out into the middle, divides the bay; and toward the mouth are two little iſlands or rocks. One of theſe, on the right hand ſailing in, is high and ſteep, the ſhape exactly conical, the baſe about a mile in circumference. On the ſummit is a white marble coloſſal ſtatue, the poſture ſedent, the head and arms broken off. It is ſuppoſed to have been twelve

feet

feet high, when unmutilated; and is placed on a pedeftal near eight feet high. On the other ifland, which is farther in, is feen a maimed marble ftatue of a female[1]. Thefe images perhaps reprefented Apollo and Diana, and were placed as feamarks, or, holding lights, ferved each as a Pharos to affift veffels in finding the port in the night-time.

WHELER vifited port Raphti from Athens. The road lay directly eaftward. He paffed by the mountain called St. George about a mile, and made toward the end of Hymettus, which he left on the right hand, about four miles from Athens. In about two miles more he faw on his left a village called Agopi, where the plain, which is between Hymettus and the Sunian promontory, begins. He dined at a *metochi* or farm belonging to the convent of St. Cyriani, and continuing his journey arrived at the port, which is reckoned eighteen miles from the city. A beautiful image of a marble lion, the body and neck and head entire and three yards long, was feen not many years ago at the door of a church ftanding about midway, a mile on the left of the road from the port. The diftant view of Athens on this fide muft prevent the moft infenfible traveller from approaching with indifference.

TURNING from port Raphti a little to the right, and riding about fix miles, Wheler arrived at Marcopoli, a fmall village by ruins of an antient town, it feems, of Potamus. In three hours more he came to a folitary church, by which were olive-trees and the biggeft lentifcus he ever faw, with tears of maftic iffuing from feveral places of the body. He went on an hour and a half, fouthward, to Kerateia, probably Thoricus, which he defcribes as an antient place, with fome remains. It had been deftroyed by Corfairs. In three long hours he reached Sunium, the track very rocky and bad. About midway he paffed over a little mountain, where cinders in abundance lay

---

[1] See Perry's view of the Levant, p. 487; and Wheler's Travels, p. 447.

fcattered

scattered up and down. It then afforded some copper, and he was told that silver was secretly extracted from the ore. The harbour for boats by the sea-side was that in which we moored on our first arrival in Attica. This coast was part of the region called Paralos.

CHAP. XXXIV.

Road to Marathon---Of Cephisia---An Inscription at Oxford brought from thence---Another inscription---Journey continued---Of Brauron---Of Marathon---Funeral of Atticus Herodes---Pass the night on Pentele.

MARATHON was distant only eighty stadia or ten miles from Athens. I was desirous of seeing the plain, and on the fifth of May, after the heat of noon was over, set out attended by a couple of Greeks. The elder brother was acquainted with the road, possessing a share in a stand of goats and sheep in that neighbourhood. We left the two Ionic columns of the reservoir of *new Athens* on our right; passing by a huge single rock, which is split; and by one, on which are inscriptions mostly illegible. The mountain of *St. George*, called antiently, it is supposed, Anchesmus, was on our right hand. It is a naked range, reaching from near Pentele, with a church of the saint ' standing on the lofty summit above the columns and visible afar.

WE soon arrived at Cephisia, a village situated on an eminence by a stream near the western extremity of mount Pentele. It was once noted for plenty of clear water and for pleasant shade suited to mitigate the heat of summer. It has a mosque, and is still frequented, chiefly by Turks of Athens, who retire at

See the View. Ruins of Athens, p. 37.

that

that feafon to their houfes in the country. The famous comic poet Menander was of this place. Atticus Herodes, after his enemies accufed him to the emperor Marcus Aurelius as guilty of oppreffion, refided here and at Marathon; the youth in general following him for the benefit of his inftruction. Among his pupils was Paufanias of Cæfarea, the author, it has been affirmed, of the defcription of Greece.

ATTICUS Herodes had three favourites, whofe lofs he lamented, as if they had been his children. He placed ftatues of them in the drefs of hunters, in the fields and woods, by the fountains, and beneath the plane-trees; adding execrations, if any perfon fhould ever prefume to mutilate or remove them. One of the hermæ or *Mercuries* was found in a ruinous church at Cephifia, and is among the marbles given by Mr. Dawkins to the univerfity of Oxford. This reprefented Pollux, but the head is wanting. It is infcribed with an affectionate addrefs to him; after which the poffeffor of the fpot is required, as he refpects the gods and heroes, to protect from violation and to preferve clean and entire, the images and their bafes; and if he failed, fevere vengeance is imprecated on him, that the earth might prove barren to him, the fea not navigable, and that perdition might overtake both him and his offspring; but if he complied, that every bleffing might await him and his pofterity. Another ftone with a like formulary, was feen there by Mr. Wood; and a third near Marathon.

WE difmounted about funfet at a place almoft deferted, called Stamati; and after fupper lay down to fleep beneath a fpreading vine before the cottage of an Albanian. Early in the morning, I proceeded, with a guide, to examine an infcription of which a peafant had given me information; quitting the ftrait road to Marathon, between which place and Athens was once a town named Pallene. We foon entered between two mountains, Pentele ranging on our right; and on the left, one of Diacria the region extending acrofs from mount

Parnes

Parnes to Brauron. Tarrying to water our horses near some houses, I was presented by an Albanian with a handful of white roses fresh gathered. We penetrated into a lonely recess, and came to a small ruined church of St. Dionysius standing on the marble heap of a trophy or monument erected for some victory obtained by three persons named Ænias, Xanthippus, and Xanthides. The inscription is on a long stone lying near.

THE two mountains are divided by a wide and deep watercourse, the bed of a river or torrent antiently named Erasinus. The track is on the margin, rugged and narrow, shaded with oleander, flowering shrubs, and evergreens. A tree had fallen across, but we passed under it, and entered the plain of Marathon at the corner next to Athens; Pentele continuing in the same direction toward the sea, which, with a lofty barrow not far from the shore, was now in view. The watercourse, after winding before a few Albanian cottages, intersects part of the plain and then ceases. This village is corruptly called Vronna. The old name was Brauron. Here we procured, not without difficulty, a live fowl, which was boiled for breakfast, and some eggs, to be fried in oil. We eat under an olive-tree, then laden with pale yellow flowers. A strong breeze from the sea scattered the bloom, and incommoded us, but the spot afforded no shelter more eligible.

BRAURON was noted for a temple of Diana, in which was an antient image of the goddess. Iphigenia, the daughter of Agamemnon, was said to have left there the idol, which she conveyed from Scythia Taurica. That had been carried to Susa by Xerxes, and given by Seleucus to the Laodiceans of Syria, who continued in possession of it in the time of Pausanias. Beyond the watercourse is a large barrow; and by it, toward Pentele, are three smaller; with one, a little out of the line, which had been opened for a furnace or lime-kiln. The cenotaph of Iphigenia is probably among them. Some stones

Y lie

lie about. The lofty barrow, mentioned before, is diftinct, in the plain, nearer the fea, and vifible all around.

QUITTING the olive-tree by Brauron, we rode along the edge of the plain, with Pentele behind us; paffed a folitary church, and, after a few minutes, turned into a narrow vale on the left hand. We then croffed a mountainous ridge, the track rough and ftony, and came into the road, which leads directly from Athens to Marathon. This place has retained its antient name, is well watered but very inconfiderable, confifting only of a few houfes and gardens. It was equidiftant from Caryftus in Euboea and from Athens.

ATTICUS Herodes directed his freedmen to bury him at Marathon, where he died at the age of feventy fix; but the Ephebi or young men of Athens tranfported his body on their fhoulders to the city, a multitude meeting the bier and weeping like children for the lofs of a parent. The funeral obfequies were performed in the ftadium, which was chofen for the place of fepulture. The epitaph of this diftinguifhed perfon was a fingle diftich.

WE returned toward Brauron along the edge of the plain, and paffed fome cottages and a church or two, on the fite perhaps of Oenoe, which town was near Marathon. We afterwards flanted off to the lofty barrow by the fea. The evening approaching, we repaired to a goat-ftand on the fide of Pentele, not far from Brauron. The peafants killed and roafted a kid for my fupper, after which I lay down to fleep in the lee of a huge bare rock. This region abounds in wolves. Several large and fierce dogs guarded us, and at intervals barked vehemently and ran together, in a troop, as it were to an attack, or to repel fome wild beaft from their charge. Thefe dogs render it very dangerous for a ftranger to go near their ftation even in the daytime, unlefs accompanied by one of their keepers; and then likewife I have feen them not eafily pacified, and prevailed on to retire.

CHAP.

CHAP. XXXV.

Of the plain of Marathon --- Extract from Wheler --- Of Rhamnus --- The battle of Marathon --- Description from Pausanias --- The large barrow.

THE plain of Marathon is long and narrow. Oppofite to the range of mountains, by which the village ftands, is the fea. Pentele, with a lake at the extremity, as I noted from one of the fummits, is the fouthern boundary. At the other end is alfo a ridge, the ifthmus of a confiderable promontory once named Cynofura. This is beyond a marfh or lake, from which a ftream iffued; the water at the head fit for cattle, but falt near the mouth and full of fea-fifh. Many aquatic birds, fuch as we faw by the Gygæan lake, were flying about. The foil is reputed exceedingly fertile. We rode through fome very thick corn of moft luxuriant growth, and the barley of this tract was antiently named Achilléan, perhaps from its tallnefs.

WHELER, travelling on in the plain, paffed by Marathon, and croffed a river, which defcends from the mountains near it, and enters the fea. Soon after he came to a fountain, of which the water feemed prefently to ftagnate into a lake or rather a marfh or bog, at times almoft dry; then covered with rufhes and weeds. Some caloyers or monks of the convent of Pentele attend the fifhery, which furnifhes very large eels, and look after the buffaloes, which are fond of feeding and wallowing in the mire. By the fountain was a ruined town and a church, where he fuppofes Tricorythus ftood. About a mile farther on was a little village called Chouli, inhabited by Albanians, who had another village of the fame name on the mountains; the cold forcing them to defcend with their cattle in winter, and the drought, with the flies fwarming from the lake, to return in fummer. He proceeded three or four miles northward, and came to the fea-fhore oppofite to Eubœa, and to a ruined town fituated in the ifthmus, and called Tauro-caftro or Hebræo-caftro, antiently Rhamnus. The mountain ends here in unpaffable rocks and precipices.

RHAMNUS was fixty ftadia or feven miles and a half from Marathon, in the road going from thence to Oropus by fea. It was famous for a temple of Nemefis, now reduced to a heap lying on a hill in the middle of the ifthmus. The ftatue was exceedingly celebrated, and ten cubits or fifteen feet high. It was made by Phidias out of a block of marble, which the Barbarians, intending to erect a trophy in Attica, had tranfported from Paros. The ruins, confifting of white marble, are vifible afar off. I wifhed to examine the fpot, but was too flightly attended to advance farther on that fide, the Turks of Eubœa bearing a very bad character.

THE Barbarians croffed from Ionia under Datis and Artaphernes, with a fleet of fix hundred triremes. They reduced Caryftus and Eretria, and fet the flaves taken at the latter town on fhore on Ægileia, an ifland belonging to Styra near Caryftus. They were conducted by Hippias to the plain of Marathon, as a place fuited to their cavalry. The Athenian army did not exceed nine thoufand, reckoning the old men and the flaves. A thoufand Platæenfians, who joined it while drawn up in the Heracleum or facred portion of Hercules at Marathon, were placed in the left wing. The line was of equal extent with that of the enemy, and the diftance between them not lefs than a mile. The Barbarians broke the centre, which was thin and weak, and purfued the routed troops up the country; but the wings, which conquered, uniting to receive them on their return, they alfo were beaten, and the flaughter reached to the fhips, of which feven were feized. Many of the fugitives, from confufion and ignorance, took toward the marfh, and, crouding one on on another, were driven into it. Six thousand and four hundred were slain. The loss of the Athenians amounted only to one hundred and ninety two. It had been usual to inter the citizens who perished in war, at the public expense, in the Ceramicus without the city; but the death of these was deemed uncommonly meritorious. They were buried, and a barrow was made for them, where their bravery had been manifested. The Athenians continued to commemorate this victory, which was obtained in the first year of the seventy second Olympiad[1], in the time of Plutarch.

PAUSANIAS examined the field of battle about six hundred years after this event. His account of it is as follows. " The " barrow of the Athenians is in the plain, and on it are pillars " containing the names of the dead under those of the tribes " to which they belonged; and there is another for the Platæ-" ensians and slaves; and a distinct monument of Miltiades, " the commander, who survived this exploit. There may be " perceived nightly the neighing of horses and the clashing of " arms. No person has derived any good from waiting on " purpose to behold the spectres; but their anger does not fall " on any one, who happens to see them without design. The " Marathonians worship those who were slain in the battle, " styling them heroes.---A trophy also of white marble has " been erected. The Athenians say the Medes were buried, " religion requiring that the corpse of a man be covered with " earth; though I was not able to find any place of sepulture; " for there is no barrow or other sign visible, but they " threw them promiscuously into a pit.---Above the lake " are the marble-mangers of the horses of Artaphernes, with " marks of a tent on the rocks."

MANY centuries have elapsed since the age of Pausanias, but the principal barrow, it is likely, that of the gallant Athenians,

[1] Before Christ, 491.

still

ftill towers above the level of the plain. It is of light fine earth, and has a bufh or two growing on it. I enjoyed a pleafing and fatisfactory view from the fummit, and looked, but in vain, for the pillars on which the names were recorded, lamenting that fuch memorials fhould ever be removed. At a fmall diftance northward is a fquare bafement of white marble, perhaps part of the trophy. A Greek church has ftood near it; and fome ftones and rubbifh, difpofed fo as to form an open place of worfhip, remain. The other barrows mentioned by Paufanias are, it is probable, among thofe extant near Brauron.

CHAP. XXXVI.

A cave and the goat-ftand of Pan near Marathon --- Story of the woman of Nonoï --- Way to the cave --- Account of it --- Remarks.

" A LITTLE farther from the plain than Marathon, fays
" Paufanias, is the mountain of Pan, and a cave worth fee-
" ing. The entrance into it is narrow. Paffing it, there are
" houfes and fonts or wafhing-places; with the goat-ftand of
" Pan, as it is called, being rocks, which have been likened
" chiefly to goats. On this fide is Brauron."

I ENQUIRED for this cave of a peafant, who came to me, while I tarried beneath the olive-tree. He affirmed it was not much out of my way to Marathon, and undertook to conduct me to it. In the vale, which we entered, near the veftiges of a fmall building, probably a fepulchre, was a headlefs ftatue of a woman fedent, lying on the ground. This, my companions informed me, was once endued with life, being an aged lady poffeffed of a numerous flock, which was folded near that fpot. Her riches were great, and her profperity was uninterrupted.

She

She was elated by her good fortune. The winter was gone by, and even the rude month of March had fpared her fheep and goats. She now defied Heaven, as unapprehenfive for the future, and as fecure from all mifhap. But Providence, to correct her impiety and ingratitude, commanded a fierce and penetrating froſt to be its avenging miniſter; and ſhe, her fold, and flocks were hardened into ſtone. This ſtory, which is current, was alſo related to me at Athens. The grave Turk cites the woman of Nonoï, for fo the tract is called, to check arrogance, and enforce the wifdom of a devout and humble difpoſition. I regretted afterwards my inattention to it on the ſpot; for I was aſſured that the rocky craggs afford at a certain point of view the fimilitude of fheep and goats within an incloſure or fold.

The road from Athens defcending toward Marathon is rough and narrow. By the fide at the foot of the hill is a tall tower; and below, a rivulet called Catakephalari. In the ſtream were veſtiges of antient building, probably of the fonts or places where the women waſhed linen. We paſſed by them to a ſhallow river, which we croſſed in view of Marathon. Our guide led us up the ſtream to a fmall arched cave near the brow of the rock above the current, ufed perhaps by ſhepherds, while their flocks are browfing or drinking below. This place not correſponding with the defcription in Pauſanias, I re-mounted, intending to enquire at Marathon. On the way we came to a mill, in which fix or feven Albanians were fitting in a circle on the floor at dinner. One of them declared the grotto was near, and that on fome occaſion he had been in it. We tarried while they difpatched their homely fare, of which they invited me to partake, and then returned with five of them to the rivulet; and quitting our horſes, afcended the mountain-fide, which is ſteep, with the tower on our left hand.

The cave has two mouths diſtant only a few feet from each other. The rock before them is flat and fmooth; and, above them,

them, is cut down perpendicularly. The entrances are low and narrow. That oppofite to the left hand is leaft commodious. By this, two of the favages with a light, creeping on their bellies, got in, not without difficulty, the aperture barely admitting the body. I followed, and foon arrived in a chamber, where I could ftand on my feet. The roof and fides were incrufted with fpar. We proceeded into fimilar chambers, in one of which was water; often ftooping and creeping; my conductors with their piftols cocked, fearing fome lurking wolf or wild beaft. I made my egrefs at the avenue intended for mortals, or that moft eafy; very dirty, but pleafed with what I had feen, as well as glad to revifit day, and to regain a purer atmofphere, with freedom of refpiration; the moift air confined within being faturated, as it were, with the fmoke of our waxtapers and cedar torches. We difmiffed the Albanians, and proceeded to Marathon.

THE reader will recollect the account we have given of the god Pan, and his prowefs at the battle of Marathon. It is likely, the mountain owed its name and the cave to his fuppofed merit in that tranfaction. He became a favourite deity, and, it feems, was provided with a habitation near the fpot, where he had acquired fo much renown. But now Pan with his terrors is forgotten. His goat-ftand is poffeffed by an ideal woman; and the old fable concerning it, whatever it was, is fupplanted by a modern fiction, ingenious as capable of moral application. Both tales, it may be remarked, have been engrafted on the fame ftock; and each, as in the metamorphofis of Niobe, has appealed to the judgement of the eye, and reclined in fome meafure for fupport on the evidence of appearances, which exift.

CHAP.

CHAP. XXXVII.

Afcend mount Pentele --- The Quarries --- Chapels, &c. --- The Monaftery of Pentele --- Return to Athens --- Numerous Churches, &c.

I LEFT the goat-ftand by Brauron early in the morning, followed by the good wifhes of my ruftic hoft, and began to afcend Pentele; chufing to crofs the mountain, rather than return to Athens by the way, which we came. The track, as we advanced, became fo rough and fteep, and fo full of hazard from precipices, that I had frequent occafion to be difpleafed with this preference. At length, however, we attained nearly to the fummit, and alighted to refrefh on a green fpot by a fpring.

DESCENDING on the oppofite fide, we difcovered a caloyer or monk tending his flock, and were directed by him to the quarries, which lay out of the beaten track, on a root of the mountain. The upper quarry is open to the fky, with the rock cut down perpendicularly; the lower is remarkable for vaft humid caverns. In thefe the wide roof extends awfully over head, and is adorned with hollow pendant tubes, like icicles, each having a drop of clear water quivering at the end, and by its fall about to add to the fpars growing up beneath. Within the entrance, on the right hand, a fmall tranfparent petrifying ftream trickles down the fide of the rock; fpreading with many curious ramifications, as if congealed by froft; and forming bowls and bafins, from which it overflows. A well is funk deep in the mountain, with a narrow way down to the water, which is exceedingly cold. We faw chippings of marble; and were fhown at Athens a chryftal found in this quarry.

THE marble of Pentele was efteemed both by the ftatuary and architect. Athens owed many of its fplendid edifices to the vicinity of that mountain and of Hymettus, where alfo is a quarry in view from the town. After its decline, the ruins furnifhed plenty of materials for fuch buildings as were wanted. The lower quarry has, within the mouth, fome ruined chapels, the walls painted with portraits of faints. Without it, high up, is a fmall fquare building or room, with a window, projecting from the fteep fide of the rock, which has been cut down perpendicularly, except a narrow ridge refembling a buttrefs. This is covered with thick and antient ivy, and terminates fome feet below, leaving the place inacceffible without a ladder, which, it is likely, was placed there and occafionally removed. I fhould fuppofe it the cell of fome hermit, but it feems to have been planned and erected, when the quarry was worked. It was defigned perhaps for a centinel, to look out and regulate by fignals the approach of the men and teams employed in conveying marble to the city.

WE defcended by a very bad track to the monaftery of Pentele, a large and ordinary edifice, with the church in the middle of the quadrangle. The monks here were fummoned to prayers by a tune, which is played on a piece of iron hoop fufpended. They are numerous, but were now difperfed, having each his particular province or occupation. I was courteoufly received by the few who were refident; and enjoyed there the luxury of fhade under fome trees by a clear ftream, with good wine, water, and provifions. My carpet was fpread in the area of the quadrangle, near a gate-way, under which we flept at night. I enquired for the manufcripts, which were fhown to Sir George Wheler in 1676, but found no perfon who had knowlege of them. The monaftery is one of the moft capital in Greece, and enjoys a confiderable revenue from bees, fheep, goats, and cattle, arable land, vineyards, and olive-trees. The
protection

TRAVELS IN GREECE. 171

protection of the Porte is purchased yearly, as the custom is, and at a price not inferior to its ability.

THE next evening we descended from Pentele into the plain, and passed by Callandri, a village among olive-trees, to Angele-kipos or *Angele-gardens*. This place is frequented in summer by the Greeks of Athens, who have their houses situated in a wood of olives, of cypresses, and of orange and lemon-trees, with vineyards intermixed. The old name was Angele; and, it is related [1], the people of Pallene would not intermarry with the inhabitants because of some treachery which they had experienced in the time of Theseus. We rode on, leaving the road to port Raphti on our left; and, keeping the range of Anchesmus on our right, came near a monastery called Hagios Asomatos, standing among olive-trees not far from the junction of the two rivers, the Eridanus and Ilissus. The place, where water is collected to be conveyed in chanels to the town, is at no great distance. From the monastery of Pentele to Athens is reckoned a journey of two hours.

THE old Athenians sanctified even their mountains. Minerva had a statue at Pentele; Jupiter, on Anchesmus, which is mentioned as not a large mountain; and also on Hymettus, and on Parnes. The latter was made of brass. On Hymettus were altars likewise, of the *showery* Jupiter, and of Apollo *the presager*; and on Parnes was an altar of Jupiter *the signifier*, with one on which they sacrificed to him under different titles, styling him *showery* or *innocent* as directed by the weather. The later citizen has equalled, if not surpassed, the piety of his heathen predecessor, and has scattered churches and convents over the whole country. They occur in the fields, and olive-groves, in the nooks and the recesses of the mountains.

[1] Wheler, p. 450.

CHAP. XXXVIII.

The northern boundary of Attica --- Wheler's rout from Marathon to Oropus --- Eleutheræ --- Deceleia --- Phyle --- Harma --- Wheler's rout from Thebes to Athens.

ATTICA was feparated from Bœotia on the north by a range of mountains, many-named, extending weftward from Oropus to the Megaris or country of Megara. On the confines were Panactos, Hyfiæ fituated by the Afopus under mount Cithæron, and Oenoe by Eleutheræ. Oropus was forty four miles from Athens, thirty fix from Thebes, and twenty four from Chalcis in Eubœa [1].

WHELER, leaving Marathon, afcended the mountain now called Nozea, and travelled by the river, which has its courfe to the plain interrupted by little cataracts or water-falls. After an hour and a half he paffed a ruined village, called Kalingi, on the fide of the mountain; and, riding as long in the plain on the top, Capandritti or Capodritti, famous for good wine. He proceeded an hour farther, by an eafy afcent, to the higheft point of the mountain. He then defcended an hour and more along a torrent, and arrived at a town on the fide called Marcopoli, where he faw fome antient fragments. Lower down he came to the fhore of Euripus, and, after riding by it two hours and a half, to the mouth of the Afopus, which river was then fwelled by rain from mount Parnes and not fordable on horfeback. He travelled along the banks to Oropus, a town two or three miles from the fea.

THE territory of Platæa was contiguous with Attica more weftward or on the fide of Eleufis, and mount Cithæron was the

[1] Antonine Itinerary.

boundary

boundary of Bœotia; Eleutheræ having furrendered to Athens not from compulfion but voluntarily, from a defire to be under its government and from hatred of the Thebans. Ruins of the wall and of houfes remained at Eleutheræ in the time of Paufanias. In the plain before it was a temple and ftatue of Bacchus; and more remote, a fmall cave with a fountain of cold water; where, it was related, the twin brothers Zethus and Amphion were expofed by Antiope their mother, and found by a fhepherd.

DECELEIA, a town vifible from Athens, was toward Oropus. It was one hundred and twenty ftadia or fifteen miles from the city, and equidiftant from Bœotia. This place was refpected by the Lacedæmonians, becaufe when Caftor and Pollux were in queft of their fifter Helen, Decelus informed them, fhe was concealed by Thefeus at Aphidna. They fortified it with a wall in the nineteenth year of the Peloponnefian war. It was the burying-place of Sophocles and his anceftors. When the poet died, it was faid, Bacchus appeared to Lyfander in his fleep, and bade him permit the body to be put into the fepulchre.

PHYLE was a caftle toward Bœotia, one hundred ftadia or twelve miles and a half from Athens. It was reckoned impregnable, and was the place to which Thrafybulus fled from the thirty tyrants. It is now called Bigla-caftro, the *Watch-caftle*. The antient fortrefs is almoft entire', ftanding on a high rock in the way from Thebes, the top not half a mile in circumference, the walls of hewn ftone well cemented. Athens may be feen from it.

AN oracle had directed, that the victims, which the Athenians were accuftomed to fend to Delphi, fhould not depart until it lightened at Harma, a place on mount Parnes, by

' Wheler, p. 334. Pococke, p. 160.

174   TRAVELS IN GREECE.

Phyle; and this fignal was expected during three months, certain priefts watching in each three days and nights. Their ftation was at the hearth of the *lightning* Jupiter, on the wall between the temple of Apollo Pythius and the Olympiéum at Athens.

WHELER, with his companion, travelled foutheaftward from Thebes along the ftream Ifmenus, and afcending came to the fource, a very large, and clear fpring. He continued to mount a mile or two, and then defcending croffed a bridge over the Afopus. He paffed the top of a rocky hill, the way bad, to Vlachi a village of Albanians, where he obferved fome antient walls, and caves underground. On a fummit was a little tower, from which Thebes might be feen. This was on a ridge of Cithæron, which runs eaftward toward Oropus. He went on two hours and a half in a plain, and faw feveral ponds[1] with plenty of wild ducks and teal, and many low oaks, of the fpecies which produces the large acorns. He then afcended Parnes, a great and high mountain almoft covered with pine-trees, now called Cafha, from a village on the fide in the way down toward Attica. He paffed the night in a ruined khan by a very curious fountain, reforted to by wolves, and bears, and wild boars, which abound. Phyle was juft by this place. From the eminence he looked down, as he relates, with unfpeakable pleafure and content on the celebrated Athens, and the noble plains fo famous in antient ftory. A narrow dangerous track led by Cafha to the foot of the mountain; and a level road from thence to Athens; paffing by a wood of olive-trees, with feveral pleafant villages in it, watered by a river. Every fhepherd they met here bade them welcome, and wifhed them a good journey.

[1] See Strabo, p. 406.

CHAP.

CHAP. XXXIX.

Excursions by sea---The straits of Salamis---Manner of fishing with a light---Mode of living---Arrive at Eleusis.

I VISITED the principal places of the Saronic gulf in two excursions by sea from Athens. One was in a caicque or wherry, with Lombardi and a couple of fishermen. We were off Ægina on the twenty ninth of March, O. S, and observed about sunset a staff of light near the horizon, in the south-west, which appeared again the next evening. We returned sooner than was intended, finding our little boat too much incumbered with provisions and necessaries to proceed with comfort or safety. Another wherry with two men was hired to carry luggage and an Albanian servant; and in the evening, April the seventh, we left Athens on horseback, passing by some cotton-grounds to the sea shore.

THE creek, in which our wherries waited, is to the west of the Piræus, and was antiently named port Phoron or *Thieves' port.* By the coast is a low naked range of mountains, once called, with a town, Corydallus. The partridges between it and the city were observed to have a different note from those beyond[1]. Farther on was Ægaleos a woody mountain, and a ferry over to the island of Salamis, by which stood antiently an Heracléum or temple of Hercules. Amphiale was a root running out into the sea, with a quarry above it. Two rocky islets near the cape were named Pharmacusæ, and on the greater was shown the burying-place of Circe, perhaps a barrow. After Amphiale was the town named Thria, the Thriasian coast and plain, and Eleusis; beyond which are the two mountains

---

[1] Toward the city κακκαβιζυσιν. Beyond the mountain τιτυβιζυσιν.

Kerata

Kerata or *The horns*, which divided Attica from Megaris. The ifland Salamis, now called Coluri, is oppofite; and a long, narrow, rocky point called antiently Cynofura or *The dog's tail* extends toward port Phoron. The chanel in feveral places is narrow and intricate. It is land-locked by Amphiale and the oppofite cape. The width at the ferry was only two ftadia or a quarter of a mile.

AFTER fupping on a turkey, which our men roafted on the fhore, we lay down to fleep among the bare rocks, waiting until the moon was fet. We embarked with a rougher fea than was pleafing, and rowed out in the dark toward the ifland, intending to fifh. We joined our two feines; and the boats parted, moving each a different way, a man letting the net gently down into the water. We met again in the centre, when fome embers, which had been hidden, were blown up and expofed on an iron grate. The flame was fed with cedar dipped in oil; which, blazing in the wind, brightened over the deep; the red coals hiffing as they fell and were extinguifhed. At the fame time we began to clatter with wooden hammers on the fides and feats of the wherries, to dafh with a pole, and to throw ftones; difturbing and driving the fifh, and darting a trident or fpear if any appeared at the top, dazzled by the light; fprinkling oil to render the furface tranquil and the water pellucid [1]. The men drew up the net with caution, fearing the fins of fome poifonous fifh, particularly the fcorpion, which is killed with a blow on the head, while entangled, when the danger ceafes. The boats meeting again, they untie the feines, and throwing the fiery brands into the fea, proceed in the dark to fome other place. This is the common method of fifhing in thefe feas. It is of antient origin, and not unnoticed by the

---

[1] The antients knew this property of oil. Pliny tells us, " Mare omne oleo tranquillari; et ob id urinantes ore fpargere, quoniam mitigat naturam afperam lucemque deportet." v. 2. p. 122. See alfo Plutarch.

Greek poets[1]. Many fires are seen on the water nightly about the mouth of the gulf of Smyrna.

WE continued tossing and toiling on the waves until the morning dawned, when we had taken a considerable quantity of mullet, with some cuttle-fish, and a sea-spider or two. We then landed, and made a fire with pieces of dry wood, and brands collected along the shore. Some red mullets were dressed on the coals for breakfast, and the nets spread in the sun to dry. When the moon was down we resumed our watry occupation. We continued near a week in the straits. The men in the day-time were employed in salting fish, or in rowing along the coast, and looking for the echinus or sea-chesnut, cockles, oysters, and the like; sprinkling oil on the surface, when necessary; and taking them up with iron instruments fastened in long poles. The sea polypus lurks at the bottom of the water. We found the penis marinus with the pointed ends of the two shells fixed in the mud, and the fan or broad part open. The fish is like a muscle, and occupies only the lower portion; but each has guards, a kind of shrimp, generally two or three in number, which live in the vacant space, and give it notice to shut up on the approach of danger. We slept on shore, often in scanty shade; and rambled on the mountains, which are covered with low bushes of lentiscus or mastic. We killed some partridges, and I was assured, that in this region they are heard to sing, and sometimes are seen perching. It was amusing to view the waves raging, and to listen to the roar about the headlands and promontories; while in the lee it was stark calm. The experienced mariner judges of the storm unfelt and unseen, and is directed by the noise to launch forth or to tarry in the portlet.

WE landed by the ferry, where some passengers waited the return of the boat; but I found no vestiges of a temple. We

---

[1] See Oppian. Cyneg. l. 4. and a beautiful simile in Q. Smyrnæus, l. 7. v. 568.

viſited a monaſtery oppoſite to it in the iſland. This is a recent ſtructure, pleaſantly ſituated, not far from the ſea. We repleniſhed our ſkins and veſſels there with wine, and dined under a tree. We touched alſo on the Pharmacuſæ, now called Megala Kira and Micra Kira. A ruinous church on one of them afforded us ſhelter from the ſun. We eoaſted the level Thriaſian plain, then green with corn, and entered the port of Eleuſis. We left our wherries, and paſſed through corn to the village, which is at ſome diſtance. A reſpite from fiſh, ſea-weed fried in batter, and the like fare, was not unacceptable.

CHAP. XL.

Of the Eleuſinian Myſteries --- Of Eleuſis --- Of the myſtic temple and the miniſters --- Of the ſecreſy obſerved by the initiated --- An hypotheſis concerning the deſign of the myſteries --- Account of the ceremony of initiation --- The foundation of the myſteries.

" CERES, ſays an Athenian orator, wandering in queſt of
" her daughter Proſerpine, came into Attica, where ſome good
" offices were done her, which it is unlawful for thoſe, who
" are not initiated, to hear. In return ſhe conferred two un-
" parallelled benefits; to wit, the knowlege of agriculture, by
" which the human race is raiſed above the brute creation, and
" the myſteries, from which the partakers derive ſweeter hopes
" than other men enjoy, both as to the preſent life and to
" eternity." It was the popular opinion, that the Eleuſinian goddeſſes ſuggeſted prudent counſel to their votaries, and influenced their conduct; that theſe were reſpected in the infernal regions, and had precedence in the aſſemblies of the bleſſed; while the unhallowed were in utter darkneſs, wallowing in mire, or labouring to fill a leaky veſſel. The Athenians were ſollicitous to ſecure theſe advantages to their children, by having them

initiated

initiated as soon as was allowed. Diogenes the Cynic was more sensible. He asserted it was ridiculous to imagine that Agesilaus and Epaminondas were existing in filth, or that any person from the sole merit of initiation would obtain a place in the islands of the happy.

Ceres was supposed to be particularly partial to Eleusis and its vicinity. There were the memorials of her presence and of her bounty; the well named Callichorus, by which she had rested, in the reign of Erectheus; the stone, on which she sate, named *the sorrowful*; the Rharian plain, where barley was first sown; and the threshing-floor and altar of Triptolemus, a herdsman, whom she instructed in the culture of that grain, the use of which succeeded to acorns. There also the grand mysteries were celebrated. This exhibition enriched Eleusis, which had increased to a city. The Athenians reduced it to the rank of their demi or towns, but still the reputation of the goddess was unsullied. Her mysteries continued to possess a pre-eminence in holiness, and to be accounted as much superior to all other religious festivals as the Gods were to the Heroes. Even the garments worn at the solemnity were supposed to partake of their efficacy, and to be endued with signal virtues. It was usual to retain them until they were perishing, and then to dedicate them in the temple, or to reserve them for the purpose of enwrapping new-born children.

The mystic temple, as it was called, provided by Pericles for the solemnity, created such awe by its sanctity as could be equalled only by the effect of its beauty and magnitude, which excited astonishment in every beholder. The profane or uninitiated were forbidden to enter it on any pretence. Two young Acarnanians happened inadvertently to mix with the croud at the season of the mysteries, and to go in; but the questions suggested by their ignorance presently betrayed them, and their intrusion was punished with death. The chief priest, hierophant, or myſtagogue, was taken from the Eumolpidæ, a holy family flouriſhing at Athens, and deſcended from Eumolpus, a ſhepherd and favourite of Ceres. He was enjoined celibacy, and wore a ſtole or long garment, his hair, and a wreath of myrtle. The grand requiſites in his character were ſtrength and melody of voice, ſolemnity of deportment, magnificence, and great decorum. Under him, beſides many of inferior ſtation, was the Daduchus or *torch bearer*, who had likewiſe his hair, with a fillet; the prieſt, who officiated at the altar; and the Hiero-ceryx or *ſacred herald*; all very important perſonages. The latter was of a family which claimed the god Mercury and Aglauros the daughter of Cecrops for its anceſtors.

THE ſecrecy, in which the myſteries were enveloped, ſerved to enhance the idea of their conſequence, and to increaſe the deſire of participation. It was ſo particular, that no perſon was allowed even to name the hierophant by whom he had been initiated. Public abhorrence and deteſtation awaited the babbler, and the law directed he ſhould die. Auguſtus Cæſar diſmiſſed his council and all the aſſembly, when a cauſe reſpecting the privileges of the prieſts of Ceres came before his tribunal at Rome. Pauſanias declares, he was forbidden by a dream to deſcribe what was contained within the ſacred wall; and adds, that as it was unlawful for the profane to be preſent, ſo it was for them even to hear the myſteries revealed. The violating this inveterate taciturnity, and the removing of the barrier, was reſerved to a later age, when uniformity in religion had ceaſed, and the civil power was weak or divided by jarring parties; the various ſectaries ſtriving to procure or retain their proſelytes, and mutually ſtruggling for ſuperiority. The dark tranſactions of that once impenetrable rite were then diſcloſed; and the information which has reached us, if it be not ſufficient to gratify a minute curioſity, yet contains more than is well worth knowing.

IT

It has been afferted that the myfteries were defigned to be a vehicle of fublime knowlege, and reprefented in a kind of drama of the hiftory of Ceres " the rife and eftablifhment of " civil fociety, the doctrine of a future ftate of rewards and " punifhments, the error of Polytheifm, and the principle of " unity, which laft article was their famous fecret." But this weighty fuperftructure is not reared on the folid bafis of antiquity. It is certain, that the ftory of Ceres, which was the ground-work of the myfteries, befides its abfurdities, was both ludicrous and indecent. Let Orpheus and Baubo filence the advocate for their dignity and purity[1]. But the author of this hypothefis perhaps intended his differtation on the fixth book of the Æneis as a piece of folemn irony; and probably has laughed at its fuccefs.

The grand myfteries were quinquennial. When the feafon approached, the myftæ, or perfons who had been initiated only in the leffer myfteries, repaired to Eleufis to be inftructed in the ceremonial. The fervice for the opening of the temple, with morning facrifice, was performed. The ritual was then produced from the fanctuary. It was enveloped in fymbolical figures of animals, which fuggefted words compendioufly, in letters with ligatures, implicated, the tops huddled together, or difpofed circularly like a wheel; the whole utterly inexplicable to the profane. The cafe, which was called Petroma, confifted of two ftones exactly fitted. The myfterious record was replaced after the reading, and clofed up until a future feftival. The folemnity began on the fifteenth of the month Boedromion, and ended on the twenty third. The principal rite was nocturnal, and confined to the temple and its environs. The myftæ waited without, with impatience and apprehenfion. Lamentations and ftrange noifes were heard. It thundered. Flafhes of light and of fire rendered the deep fucceeding darknefs more terrible. They were beaten, and perceived not the

---

[1] See a treatife of the learned Meurfius entitled *Eleufinia*, p. 137 in the collection of Grævius, and his *Atticæ Lectiones*, p. 1786.

hand.

hand. They beheld frightful apparitions, monſters, and phantoms of a canine form. They were filled with terror, became perplexed and unable to ſtir. The ſcene then ſuddenly changed to brilliant and agreeable. The Propylæa or veſtibules of the temple were opened, the curtains withdrawn, the hidden things diſplayed. They were introduced by the hierophant and daduchus, and the former ſhowed them the myſteries. The ſplendor of illumination, the glory of the temple and of the images, the ſinging and dancing which accompanied the exhibition, all contributed to ſooth the mind after its late agitation, and to render the wondering devotee tranquil and ſelf-ſatisfied. After this inſpection or, as it was called, the Autopſia, they retired, and others advanced. The ſucceeding days were employed in ſacrifice, in pompous proceſſions, and ſpectacles, at which they aſſiſted, wearing myrtle-crowns. On the twenty third, two vaſes were filled, and placed toward the eaſt and weſt. Some myſtic words¹ were pronounced, the vaſes were overturned, and the feſtival ended. The archon ſtyled *The king* ſacrificed and repeated the prayer for the people of Athens, and took cognizance of any irregularity, impiety, or act of injuſtice committed during the feſtival. The language of the myſteries², like the letters of the ritual, was incomprehenſible to the profane. The paſs-port to initiation was an occult formulary not to be acquired but at the leſſer myſteries; and the acclamation³ at the concluſion, if the words had any ſignification, was intelligible only to the aſſembly.

The ſtory of Ceres and Proſerpine, the foundation of the Eleuſinian myſteries, was partly local. It was both verbally delivered, and repreſented in allegorical ſhow. Proſerpine was gathering flowers when ſhe was ſtolen by Pluto. Hence the proceſſion of the holy baſket, which was placed on a car dragged along by oxen and followed by a train of females, ſome

¹ Ὕε. Τοκυιι.
² The myſtic name of the goddeſs was Αχθηκ.
³ Κογξ. Ὀμπαξ.

carrying

TRAVELS IN GREECE. 183

carrying the myftic chefts, fhouting, *Hail Ceres*. At night a proceffion was made with lighted torches to commemorate the goddefs fearching for her daughter. A meafure of barley, the grain which, it was believed, fhe had given, was the reward of the victors in the gymnic exercifes; and the tranfaction at the temple had a reference to the legend. A knowlege of thefe things and places, from which the profane were excluded, was the amount of initiation; and the mode of it, which had been devifed by craft, was fkillfully adapted to the reigning fuperftitions. The operation was forcible, and the effect in proportion. The priefthood flourifhed as piety increafed. The difpenfation was corrupt, but its tendency not malignant. It produced fanctity of manners and an attention to the focial duties; a defire to be as diftinguifhed by what was deemed virtue as by filence.

CHAP. XLI.

The proceffion of Iacchus from Athens --- The facred way to the mountains --- The monaftery of Daphne, &c. --- The facred way beyond, to Eleufis --- The Rhiti or falt-ftreams, &c. --- An Infcription --- Incurfions of the Lacedæmonians into Attica.

THE fixth day of the Eleufinian myfteries was called Iacchus from a fon of Jupiter, who was faid to have accompanied his mother Ceres when feeking Proferpine. An image of him, crowned with myrtle and bearing a torch, was carried from the inner Ceramicus at Athens in folemn proceffion to Eleufis, as it were to vifit Ceres and his fifter; attended by a vaft multitude, fome with victims, fhouting, finging and dancing, and playing on cymbals, tabors, and other mufical inftruments. The way, on which he paffed with his retinue, was called *the facred*. It was exactly defcribed by Polemo *the guide*.

Eleufis

Eleufis is reckoned about four hours from Athens. In the Antonine Itinerary the diftance is thirteen miles.

THE *facred way* was one of the roads which branched off without the gate called Dipylon. On it was the pillar of Anthemocritus; and beyond, a tomb; and a place called Scirum from Scirus a prophet of Dodona, who was buried there by the torrent-bed. A monument ftood near it. Farther on were two; with the facred portion of the hero Lacias, the town called Laciadas, a monument, an altar of Zephyrus, and a temple of Ceres and her daughter, with whom Minerva and Neptune were jointly worfhipped. Here Phytalus, it was faid, received the goddefs into his houfe, who requited him, as the infcription on his tomb teftified, by difcovering to him the culture of the fig. The proceffion refted at the *facred fig-tree* on its return to Athens. Nearer the Cephiffus was a monument; and on the bank, a ftatue of a woman, and of her fon cutting off his hair in honour of the river. Beyond the Cephiffus was the altar of *the mild* Jupiter, at which Thefeus was purified; with two tombs. By the road was a fmall temple of Cyamites or *the bean-giver*. This was an epithet of Bacchus, but Paufanias was uncertain whether he was intended or fome hero; for the invention of beans, from which the myftæ were directed to abftain, was not to be referred to Ceres. He adds, " Who-
" ever has been initiated at Eleufis or has read the Orphica
" knows what I mean." The monument of a Rhodian was remarkable for its magnitude and beauty; as alfo one erected by Harpalus the Macedonian for a courtezan, whom he married at Athens. This portion of the *facred way*, it is believed, extended to the mountains which bound the plain of Athens toward Eleufis. The prefent road is nearly in the fame direction, leading to the olive-groves and the Cephiffus. Inftead of the fepulchres, altars, and temples, now occur folitary churches, and a few traces fuggefting unfatisfactory conjecture. The Cephiffus was formidable as a torrent. A bridge was erected, that Iacchus might pafs without delay. An epigram which

was

was infcribed on it is, preferved under the name of Simonides. It is an addrefs to the myftæ, bidding them to proceed to the temple of Ceres without fear of wintry floods; for Xenocles of Lindus, a city of Rhodes, had provided for their fafety in paffing the broad ftream. I faw fome piers remaining not far from the place where travellers crofs.

A GAP in the mountains beyond the river, vifible from Athens, feparates Ægaleos on the left hand from Parnes on the right. The entrance on the road through it was termed *the myftic*. About mid-way to Eleufis in the mountain is a monaftery called Daphne Farther on is a heap of ruins, and part of a wall, of the mafonry termed the Incertum; the remnants of a temple of Venus, and of a wall of rough ftones in the front mentioned by Paufanias as worth feeing. The rock on the right hand is cut down perpendicularly, with grooves as for the reception of tablets, and perhaps was that called Pœcilon or *the painted*. At the foot lies a marble fragment or two; we fuppofed, of an alcove. On the way to that temple was antiently one of Apollo, in which was placed a ftatue of Ceres, of Proferpine, and of Minerva. Riding on to the end of the gap, you have the fea, the Thriafian plain, and Eleufis in view.

THE monaftery of Daphne is a mean and barbarous edifice, inclofed within a high wall. Before the gate is a well of excellent water. The church is large and lofty, and reputed the moft antient in Attica. The infide of the dome is adorned with a figure of Chrift in Mofaic, much injured. In one of the chapels is a marble farcophagus. The Turks are frequent and unwelcome vifitants in their way to and from the Morea. The corfairs formerly infefted it from the fea, and it was almoft deferted. I found there a prieft with a monk or two. It probably occupies the fite of the temple of Apollo. Some ftanding columns are immured in a wall by the church; and in the court is a long ftone with a Latin infcription, which records the confecration of fomething, it is likely of the temple, by the

B b emperors

emperors Arcadius and Honorius, when Eusebius was procurator of the province of Achaia. Arcadius commanded that the temples should be destroyed[1], and the bridges, high-ways, aquæducts, and city-walls be repaired with their materials; but spared some to be converted into churches at the request of bishops and eminent persons.

PAUSANIAS from the temple of Venus proceeds to the currents called Rhiti. These were streams of salt-water. " One " may believe, says he, that they flow from the Euripus of " Chalcis, falling from the land into the lower sea." They were sacred to Ceres and Proserpine, and the priests only had the privilege of fishing. Beyond the Rhiti was a tract called the kingdom of Crocon; with the monument of Eumolpus; of Hippothoon, from whom one of the tribes was named; and of Zarex, who was said to have been instructed in music by Apollo. Pausanias then mentions the Eleusinian Cephissus. This river was more violent than the former. By it Theseus slew Procrustes; and, as they related, Pluto descended into hell with Proserpine. A flood happening while the emperor Hadrian was at Athens, he ordered the building of a bridge for passengers.

WHELER came to the sea-side in less than half an hour from the monastery, and to a small salt lake running into the bay by a little stream. A town, perhaps Thria, had stood on a hill to the north of it[2]. Soon after he passed another little stream. He travelled over a plain, seven or eight miles long westward, and three or four broad from the sea northward. It was then, in the month of February, beautified with anemonies. The causey was paved with large stones. Along it were many ruins of churches or temples; one with a pannel of wall standing, of a grayish stone. The two streams were the Rhiti, but he has called the latter the Cephissus. The water was confined, when

[1] In the year of Christ, 399.
[2] At Thria was a temple of Venus Phile erected by the flatterers of king Demetrius in honour of his mother, whose name was Phile. The place was called Philæum.

I saw

I faw it, by a low wall intended to make a head fufficient to turn a mill. The Cephiffus, it is probable, was an occafional torrent from the mountains. Pococke did not obferve any river in the way to Eleufis.

In the plain beyond the Rhiti, an hour from the village, is a fmall heap of ruins, probably of one of the fepulchres feen by Paufanias, on which a church has been erected; fome traces remaining. A long piece of marble, fixed as a fide jamb for the door-way of the latter edifice, is infcribed in large characters, and informs us, that the lofty monument belonged to an hierophant exceedingly renowned for his wifdom; who, by his intrepidity, had preferved the myftic rites from hoftile violence, an exploit, for which he had been honoured with a crown by the people. The hierophants were greatly revered, and ftyled divine, and god-like.

A way led from Eleufis into Bœotia and the Platæis or territory of Platæa. The Lacedæmonians in the Peloponnefian war made an incurfion into Attica from this quarter at the feafon of the harveft. They endeavoured to reduce Oenoe on the confines, marched to Eleufis, laid wafte the Thriafian plain, defeated a party of horfemen near the Rhiti, and proceeded, with Ægaleos on their right hand, through Cecropia as far as Acharnæ, the moft confiderable town of Attica and diftant only fixty ftadia or feven miles and a half from Athens, which it fupplied with charcoal. The city-gate toward it was called the Acharnenfian. After tarrying there, they deftroyed fome towns between Parnes and Brileffus, and paffing by Oropus re-entered Bœotia. The fame enemy diftreffed Athens by fortifying and keeping a garrifon in Deceleia. The pomp of Iacchus was then tranfported to Eleufis by fea, with many omiffions in the ceremony; but, one year, Alcibiades refolved to conduct it by land. He communicated his defign to the Eumolpidæ and heralds, placed fpies on the eminences, furrounded the priefts, the myftæ, and myftagogues with foldiers, and conveyed them along the facred way with filence and regularity;

larity; exhibiting a religious fpectacle fingularly ftriking and folemn. It is remarkable, that the celebration of the myfteries was only once interrupted during the very long period of their exiftence. Alexander the Great took Thebes on the fixth day, and the Athenians then defifted, that their acclamations to Iacchus might not re-echo to the cries of the captives.

CHAP. XLII.

Extinction of the Eleufinian myfteries --- Of Eleufis --- Of the myftic temple, &c. --- Other remains --- Road to Megara.

A PRINCIPAL ingredient in the character of the Athenians was piety in the extreme. This, as it difpofed them readily to admit the knowlege of any unknown god, fo it preferved them in general unalienated from old opinions, and rigid obfervers of eftablifhed ceremonials. Though St. Paul had preached and an Areopagite been converted, the perfume of incenfe afcended, as before, to the idol; the victim was offered; the proceffion made; and the public attention engaged in fulfilling the ritual of Ceres and Proferpine, Minerva, and Bacchus, and the like divinities. Eleufis ftill maintained an extenfive reputation, and appeared the common property of all nations; fo many pilgrims from various and remote parts of the world continued to vifit it at the feafon of the myfteries. The fectaries increafing, the old formulary " Begone ye profane" was changed; and the herald proclaimed, " If any Atheift, or " Chriftian, or Epicuréan is come a fpy on the Orgies, let him " inftantly retire; but let thofe who believe be initiated, with " good Fortune." The Chriftians, while the emperor Hadrian refided at Athens, were perfecuted[1]; and Quadratus, a difciple

[1] In the year of Chrift, 125.

of

of the apoſtles, and the third biſhop, preſented to him an apology for their profeſſion. At length a law prohibiting nocturnal rites was publiſhed by Valentinian [1]; but Prætextatus, whom Julian had conſtituted governor of Achaia, prevailed on him to revoke it, urging, that the lives of the Greeks would be rendered utterly inſupportable, if he deprived them of this moſt holy and comprehenſive feſtival. Its extinction was reſerved for a foreign foe; and the fatal æra now approached. Alaric with his hoſt ruſhed ſuddenly through the ſtrait of Thermopylæ, and a general ruin of univerſal Greece accompanied the cataſtrophe of Ceres and Eleuſis.

ELEUSIS, on the overthrow of its goddeſs and the ceſſation of its gainful traffic, probably became ſoon an obſcure place, without character or riches. For ſome ages, however, it was not entirely forſaken, as is evident from the vaſt conſumption of the antient materials, and from the preſent remains. The port was ſmall and of a circular form. The ſtones of one pier are ſeen above water, and the correſponding ſide may be traced. About half a mile from the ſhore is a long hill, which divides the plain. In the ſide next the ſea are traces of a theatre, and on the top are ciſterns cut in the rock. In the way to it, ſome maſſes of wall and rubbiſh, partly antient, are ſtanding; with ruined churches; and beyond, a long broken aquæduct croſſes to the mountains. The Chriſtian pirates had infeſted the place ſo much, that in 1676 it was abandoned. It is now a ſmall village at the eaſtern extremity of the rocky brow, on which was once a caſtle; and is inhabited by a few Albanian families, employed in the culture of the plain, and ſuperintended by a Turk, who reſides in an old ſquare tower. The proprietor was Achmet Aga, the primate or principal perſon of Athens.

THE myſtic temple at Eleuſis was planned by Ictinus, the architect of the Parthenon. Pericles was overſeer of the build-

[1] In the year of Chriſt, 364.

ing. It was of the Doric order, the cell fo large as to admit the company of a theatre. The columns on the pavement within, and their capitals, were raifed by Coræbus. Metagenes of Xypete added the architraves and the pillars above them, which fuftained the roof. Another completed the edifice. This was a temple *in antis*, or without exterior columns, which would have occupied the room required for the victims. The afpect was changed to *Proftylos* under Demetrius the Phaleréan; Philo a famous architect erecting a portico, which gave dignity to the fabric and rendered the entrance more commodious. The fite was beneath the brow, at the eaft end, and encompaffed by the fortrefs. Some marbles, which are uncommonly maffive, and fome pieces of the columns remain on the fpot. The breadth of the cell is about one hundred and fifty feet; the length, including the Pronaos and portico, is two hundred and fixteen feet; the diameter of the columns, which are fluted fix inches from the bottom of the fhafts, is fix feet and more than fix inches. The temple was a Decaftyle or had ten columns in the front, which was to the eaft. The peribolus or inclofure, which furrounded it on the north-eaft and on the fouth fide, meafures three hundred and eighty feven feet in length from north to fouth, and three hundred twenty eight feet in breadth from eaft to weft. On the weft fide it joined the angles of the weft end of the temple in a ftraight line. Between the weft wall of the inclofure and temple and the wall of the citadel was a paffage forty two feet fix inches wide, which led to the fummit of a high rock at the north-weft angle of the inclofure, on which are vifible the traces of a temple *in antis*, in length feventy four feet fix inches from north to fouth, and in breadth from the eaft to the wall of the citadel, to which it joined on the weft, fifty four feet. It was perhaps that facred to Triptolemus. This fpot commands a very extenfive view of the plain and bay. About three fourths of the cottages are within the precincts of the myftic temple, and the fquare tower ftands on the ruined wall of the inclofure.

AT

AT a small distance from the north end of the inclosure is a heap of marble consisting of fragments of the Doric and Ionic orders, remains, it is likely, of the temples of Diana Propyléa and of Neptune, and of the Propyléum or gateway. Wheler saw some large stones carved with wheat-ears and bundles of poppy. Near it is the bust of a colossal statue of excellent workmanship, maimed, and the face disfigured; the breadth at the shoulders, as measured by Pococke, five feet and a half; and the basket on the head above two feet deep. It probably represented Proserpine. In the heap are two or three inscribed pedestals; and on one are a couple of torches, crossed. We saw another fixed in the stone stairs, which lead up to the square tower on the outside. It belonged to the statue of a lady, who was hierophant or priestess of Proserpine and had covered the altar of the goddess with silver. A well in the village was perhaps that called Callichorus, where the women of Eleusis were accustomed to dance in honour of Ceres. A tradition prevails, that if the broken statue be removed, the fertility of the land will cease. Achmet Aga was fully possessed with this superstition, and declined permitting us to dig or measure there, until I had overcome his scruples by a present of a handsome snuff-box containing several Zechins or pieces of gold.

A ROAD led from Eleusis into the Megaris. On it was a well called *The flowery*, where Ceres was said to have rested; and a little farther, a temple; and after that, the tombs of the Argives, whose bodies were recovered from the Thebans by Theseus; and then a monument, near which was a spot called in the time of Pausanias the Palæstra or *wrestling-place* of Cercyon. Wheler rode about a mile under the north side of the hill; the way covered with anemonies of several colours, wonderfully beautiful; and turning to the left arrived at the *flowery well*, a spring in a cultivated vale, two or three miles in compass, which he supposes the Rharian plain. Soon after he began to ascend Kerata or Gerata. Two piked rocks on the top show like horns, and on one was a tower. The way over the

mountain

mountain was very bad. He then travelled about an hour in a plain, and arrived at Megara. The diſtance of this place from Eleuſis in the Antonine Itinerary is thirteen miles.

CHAP. XLIII.

Proceed to Megara --- Of the port and town Niſæa --- Of Megara --- The ſtone --- An inſcription --- Dread of Corſairs --- Of the Megaris --- Our lodging, &c.

WE were prevented from tarrying at Eleuſis by the arrival of certain Agas or rich Turks, in their way from Corinth to Athens. Lombardi, who knew them, haſtened to the tower, and appeared full of joy; kneeling before them, fawning, and kiſſing their beards. His tone changed as ſoon as he was out of their preſence, and he poured forth execrations on them very liberally. We proceeded ſlowly as before, toward Megara; and, landing to dine, aſcended the ridge by the ſea, behind which is a conſiderable valley, part of the plain of Eleuſis. We approached the port, and, the wind not permitting us to turn the point of a ſmall rocky promontory once called Minoa, went aſhore, and after ſome ſtay croſſed it on foot; leaving men to convey the boats round into the bay. Megara, like Athens, was ſituated at a diſtance from the ſea.

THE port of Megara was called Niſæa from Niſus ſon of Pandion the ſecond, who obtained the Megaris for his portion, when the kingdom of Athens was divided into four lots by his father. He founded the town, which was eighteen ſtadia or two miles and a quarter from the city, but united with it, as the Piræus with Athens, by long walls. It had a temple of Ceres. " The roof, ſays Pauſanias, may be ſuppoſed to have " fallen through age." The ſite is now covered with rubbiſh, among which are ſtanding ſome ruinous churches. The place has

has been named from them Dodeca Ecclefiáis *The Twelve Churches*, but the number is reduced to feven. The acropolis or citadel, called alfo Nifæa, was on a rock by the fea-fide. Some pieces of the wall remain, and a modern fortrefs has been erected on it; and alfo on a leffer rock near it. An iflet before Nifæa was now green. It is one of five, which, as Strabo relates, occurred in failing from that port toward Attica. There Minos ftationed the Cretan fleet in his war with Nifus.

WE had a hot walk to the village of Megara, which confifts of low mean cottages, pleafantly fituated on the flope of a brow or eminence indented in the middle. On each fide of this vale was an acropolis or citadel; one named Caria, the other from Alcathous, the builder of the wall. They related, that he was affifted by Apollo, who laid his harp afide on a ftone, which, as Paufanias teftifies, if ftruck with a pebble returned a mufical found. An angle of the wall of one citadel is feen by a windmill. The mafonry is of the fpecies called Incertum. In 1676 the city-wall was not entirely demolifhed, but comprehended the two fummits, on which are fome churches, with a portion of the plain toward the fouth. The whole fite, except the hills, was now green with corn and marked by many heaps of ftones, the collected rubbifh of buildings. A few infcriptions are found, with pedeftals fixed in the walls and inverted; and alfo fome maimed or mutilated ftatues. One of the former relates to Atticus Herodes, and is on a pedeftal which fupported a ftatue erected to him, when conful[1], by the council and people of Megara; in return for his benefactions and good will toward the city. In the plain behind the fummits, on one of which was a temple of Minerva, is a large bafin of water, with fcattered fragments of marble, the remains of a bath or of a fountain, which is recorded as in the city and remarkable for its fize and ornaments, and for the number of its columns. The fpring was named from the local Nymphs called Sithnides.

[1] In the year of Chrift, 143.

TRAVELS IN GREECE.

THE stone of Megara was of a kind not discovered any where else in Hellas; very white, uncommonly soft and consisting entirely of cockle-shells. This was chiefly used, and, not being durable, may be reckoned among the causes of the desolation at Megara, which is so complete, that one searches in vain for vestiges of the many public edifices, temples, and sepulchres, which once adorned the city. I observed some of the stone at Athens in the minaret of the Parthenon.

MEGARA was engaged in various wars with Athens and Corinth, and experienced many vicissitudes of fortune. It was the only one of the Greek cities, which did not re-flourish under their common benefactor Hadrian; and the reason assigned is, that the avenging anger of the gods pursued the people for their impiety in killing Anthemocritus, a herald, who had been sent to them in the time of Pericles. The Athenian generals were sworn on his account to invade them twice a year. Hadrian and Atticus were followed by another friend, whose memory is preserved by an inscription on a stone lying near a church in the village. " This too is the work of the most " magnificent count Diogenes son of Archelaus, who regard- " ing the Grecian cities as his own family, has bestowed on " that of the Megarensians one hundred pieces of gold toward " the building of their towers, and also one hundred and fifty " more with two thousand two hundred feet of marble toward " re-edifying the bath; deeming nothing more honourable " than to do good to the Greeks and to restore their cities." This person is not quite unnoticed in history. He was one of the generals employed by the emperor Anastasius on a rebellion in Isauria. He surprized the capital, Claudiopolis, and sustained a siege with great bravery [1].

MEGARA retains its original name. It has been much infested by corsairs, and in 1676 the inhabitants were accustomed, on seeing a boat approach in the day time or hearing their dogs

[1] In the year of Christ, 494.

bark

bark at night, immediately to fecrete their effects and run away. The Vaiwode or Turkish governor, who refided in a forfaken tower above the village, was once carried off. It is no wonder therefore, that Nifæa has been long abandoned. On the fhore, when we croffed the promontory from our boats, fome women who were wafhing linen, perceiving my hat and Lombardi in a ftrange drefs with a gun on his fhoulder, fled precipitately. Our men called after them, but could not prefently perfuade them to lay afide their terror and refume their employment. The place was burned by the Venetians in 1687.

THE Megaris is defcribed as a rough region, like Attica, the Mountain called Oneian or *the Afinine*, now Macriplayi or *the long Mountain*, extending through it toward Bœotia and mount Cithæron. It belonged to Ionia or Attica, until it was taken by the Peloponnefians in the reign of Codrus, when a colony of Dorians fettled in it. The weftern boundary of the plain is a very high mountain called Palæovouni or *the old Mountain*, antiently Gerania. It was covered with a frefh verdure. Megarus, in the deluge which happened under Deucalion, was faid to have efcaped to its fummits. From the hill by the village we could difcern the two tops of Parnaffus, diftinct, and far above the clouds. They are formed by mountains heaped on mountains, and can be feen only at a confiderable diftance.

OUR lodging at Megara was an open fhed adjoining to the houfe of a Greek prieft, a young man of great fimplicity, with a thick black beard. He was Oeconomus or bailiff, no Turk refiding there. In the court were fowls of the rumplefs breed. A woman was fitting with the door of her cottage open, lamenting her dead hufband aloud. Some cavities in the ground near the road from the port feem to have been receptacles of grain. I enquired for medals, and in the evening, when the inhabitants were returned from their labour, notice was given by a crier ftanding on the flat roof of a cottage at the foot of a hill near the center of the village; but very few were produced

duced of any value. The Oeconomus had an Athenian tetradrachm faſtened to his purſe, which he refuſed to part with, regarding it as an amulet or charm.

CHAP. XLIV.

Leave Megara --- Veſtiges of buildings --- Of the Scironian rocks and way --- The preſent road to Corinth --- Paſs the night in a cave --- Coaſt by the Scironian way --- Veſtiges of Cromyon --- Of Sidûs.

WE purchaſed proviſions, with wholſome wine, at Megara; and, after ſome ſtay, I deſcended again to Niſæa, purpoſing to proceed to the iſthmus of Corinth; not without regret on quitting the hoſpitable prieſt and a lodging free from vermin.

THE wind blowing freſh and contrary, we rowed from Niſæa to the ſide of the bay oppoſite to Minoa, and put into a ſmall creek made with ſtones piled to break the waves, by the entrance on the Scironian way, the antient road to Corinth. Near it were heaps of ſtones among corn, as at Megara, the veſtiges of a town or village; a ſarcophagus cut in the rock; the ruin of a ſmall building, the wall faced on the outſide with maſonry of the ſpecies termed Incertum; and by it a lime-kiln, and a piece or two of the entablature not inelegantly carved. This was probably one of the ſepulchres, which Pauſanias deſcribes on the way to Corinth. A torrent-bed, which we croſſed going to Megara from Niſæa, winds to the ſea on this ſide of the plain.

THE Scironian rocks are a termination of the Oneian mountains, waſhed by the ſea. The track over them was ſix miles long, often on the brink of dreadful precipices, with the
mountain

mountain rifing above, lofty and inacceffible. Sciron, while general of the Megarenfians, made it paffable to perfons on foot; and the emperor Hadrian widened it, fo that two chariots might drive one by another. A prominent rock in a narrow part was named Moluris; and from it, as they fabled, Ino threw herfelf into the fea with Melicerte. It was accounted facred to Leucothea and Palæmon, by which names fhe and her fon were enrolled among the marine deities. Beyond Moluris were the *Accurfed Rocks*, where was the abode of Sciron. The infamy of his haunt continued for many ages. On a fummit was a temple of Jupiter; and farther on, a monument of Euryftheus, who was flain there by Iolaus; and defcending, a temple of Apollo; after which were the boundaries of the Megarenfians next the territory of Corinth; where, they related, Hyllus the fon of Hercules contended in fingle combat with an Arcadian. The north-weft wind, blowing from thefe rocks,. was called Sciron at Athens.

The name of the Scironian road is now, the robber being forgotten, Kachè Scála *The bad way*. In 1676 it was as terrible from the ambufcades of the corfairs, as of old from the cruelty of Sciron. It has fince been difufed, and a road made over the mountain, on which the Turks have eftablifhed a dervene or guard, with regulations to prevent the affembling or efcape of robbers and banditti. The diftance from Megara to Corinth, which is now computed at nine hours, was by the Scironian way only fix; but on it the traveller was in continual peril.

We left our boats in the creek and afcended to an arched cave in the rock, black with the fmoke of fires kindled by travellers, who had refted there, or by mariners and fifhermen, who, like us, had declined venturing along fo dangerous a coaft in the night, or waited for favourable weather. We had from it an extenfive view of the turbulent gulf beneath, and

of

of the iflands. We made a fire, and remained in it until morning. It then proved calm, and we re-embarked.

WE coafted by the Scironian rocks, which are exceedingly high, rough, and dreadful. The way is by the edge of perpendicular precipices, narrow, and in many places carried over the breaks and fupported underneath apparently in fo flight a manner, that a fpectator may reafonably fhudder with horror at the idea of crofling. Wheler has mentioned it as the worft road, which he ever travelled. After much time confumed in fcrambling up and down the precipices, he pafled along the fhore, under the mountain, and came to an antient edifice three or four yards high and eight fquare, with feveral large planks of marble lying about it, fome carved in baffo relievo. This, he fuppofes, was the temple of Apollo.

WE landed about noon in the diftrict called antiently Cromyonia lying between the Scironian way and the ifthmus of Corinth. The valley was cultivated, and at fome diftance from the fea were olive-groves with a village named Canetta. Nearer the fhore were many fcattered ftones with a carved fragment or two; veftiges of Cromyon. This town was one hundred and fifty ftadia or eighteen miles and three quarters from Corinth. It once belonged to Megara. There Pityocamptes, who infefted the entrance of the Ifthmus, was educated; and beyond, but near, was the fcene of the exploit of Thefeus. " The " pine, fays Paufanias, has grown until now by the fea-fide." There alfo was an altar of Melicerte. They related that a dolphin had tranfported his body to that fpot; that it was found by Sifyphus, king of Corinth; and that he interred it on the Ifthmus.

SOME green famphire, which we gathered on the Scironian rocks, made part of our repaft at noon, after which we flept in the fhade. We embarked again, and coafted a flat fhore, and
in

in the evening landed about half a mile from a rivulet running into the fea with a fhallow and lively current. There alfo were marble fragments, a deferted church, and among the thickets heaps of ftones, as by Megara ; reliques of the town of Sidûs, which was fituated between Cromyon and the Ifthmus. This region alfo was once a portion of Ionia or Attica. After filling our water-cafks we made a fire among the bufhes, and lay down by it until the moon was fet.

CHAP. XLV.

Land on the ifthmus of Corinth --- At Epidaurus and Methana --- On the iflets in the gulf --- At Ægina --- On the ifland of Salamis.

WE now were near the ifthmus of Corinth. Soon after day-break we landed at the port of Schœnus, and afcended to fome ruins. We met two or three goatherds, who conducted us to their ftation, and protected us from their dogs, which were moft exceedingly fierce. They lamented, that wild beafts often affailed their fold, and rendered a ftrong guard neceffary. They treated us with new cheefe, curdled milk made four, and with ordinary bread toafted on embers. They fpared us fome provifions for our boats, and we felected a fat kid from the flock feeding among the pine-trees and thickets. We faw feveral large lizards or camelions, of a vivid green colour. A low root of mount Oneius extends along the ifthmus, and from the brow I had a view of the two gulfs, the Saronic and the Corinthian ; the latter fhining and placid, and feeming to promife a happy paffage from defolation and barbarifm. The port of Schænus was three hundred and fifty ftadia or forty three miles and three quarters from the Piræus.

ONE

ONE of the goatherds aſſiſted in flaying and roaſting the kid by the ſea-ſide. We retired, after eating, to our boats; and, an hour or two before day-break, began fiſhing. We then ſet ſail, and, leaving the port of Cenchreæ and Corinth on our right, coaſted by a range of lofty mountains reaching into the water to Epidaurus a city of the Peloponneſus, and from thence we croſſed the bay to Methana.

WE paſſed from Methana to the mountainous iſland Anchiſtre, on which are a few cottages of Albanians, who till the ſcanty ſoil. We touched likewiſe on ſeveral of the uninhabited rocks and iſlets in the gulf, as directed by the wind; rowing where the chanel was narrow; often becalmed or waiting for a ſmoother ſea; and ſometimes reduced to a ſmaller allowance of bread, wine, and water, than was agreeable. We ſlept away the heat of noon in the ſhade, and were employed in rambling over our little territory, in ſearching the tranſparent waves along the ſhore for ſhell-fiſh, or in ſpreading our nets during the abſence of the moon. We diſcovered by the light of a cedar-torch, a Muræna, a fiſh ſaid to copulate with ſerpents; reſembling an eel, with bright yellow ſpots. It was in ſhallow water, and was killed by the Albanian, who attacked it with a knife, but cautiouſly, fearing its bite, which is reputed venomous.

AT length a briſk gale ſpringing up wafted us to the iſland of Ægina, and increaſing became very heavy; attended with rain. We had reaſon to rejoice on reaching the ſhore, though it afforded no hoſpitable cave or ſhelter from the weather. We made faſt to ſome rocks in the lee not far from the barrow of Phocus, and ſpreading our ſails on poles, tent-wiſe, over our boats, remained there all night, wet and uncomfortable, toſſed on the waves and incommoded with the ſmoke of our fires, eſpecially while our fiſh were dreſſing. The next day, the gale abating, we ſailed on, and, leaving our boats, aſcended to the town of Ægina, where we tarried two days, the wind continuing ſtrong and contrary.

A CALM enfuing, we re-embarked, intending for the ifland of Salamis, diftant by computation twelve miles from Ægina. The fun was fet, and we had rowed above half way, when we began to hear the hollow-founding fury of the north-weft wind or Sciron reigning afar off. The fea heaved, with the furface lightly dimpled. The fwell increafed gradually, and became very formidable to fmall open wherries; the tempeft ftill raging remote from us. The moon fhined bright, difclofing the head-lands and promontories; the fky blue and ftarry. Our men ftruggled with all their might to get under the lee of the ifland of Salamis; fearing, if the gale overtook us, we fhould be forced out to fea; and, after great labour, fucceeded, much to our fatisfaction in general, and more particularly to that of the young Albanian, who was exceedingly terrified, making his croffes, and calling fervently on the Panagia or Virgin Mary to deliver him from the danger he was in. We lighted a fire and fupped on the fhore, and afterwards lay down to fleep among the maftic-bufhes. A heavy dew fell in the night.

CHAP. XLVI.

Of Salamis --- Iflets --- Fragments on Cynofura --- Trophy for the battle of Salamis --- The city --- Village of Albanians --- Old Salamis --- The flower of Ajax.

THE ifland Salamis is of a very irregular fhape. It was reckoned feventy or eighty ftadia[1] long, reaching weftward as far as the mountains called Kerata or *the Horns*. The Athenians and Megarenfians contended for it with obftinacy; and Solon or Pififtratus interpolated Homer to fhow it had belonged to the Athenians, adding, in the catalogue of the fhips, after " Ajax came from Salamis with twelve veffels," that he ftationed them with the Athenian fquadron. The city

[1] Eight miles and three quarters, or ten miles.

was within Cynofura or *the Dog's Tail,* on the oppofite fide of the bay.

IN the morning we coafted, and, paffing by a church on the fhore of Salamis dedicated to St. Nicholas the patron of fifhermen, came to Cynofura. We touched on Lipfocatalia, a rocky and barren iflet, antiently called Pfyttalia. It was fuppofed to be frequented by the god Pan. There was no image of him formed with art, but only rude reprefentations. Near Pfyttalia was an iflet named Atalante; and toward the Piræus, another, alike rocky and barren.

I LANDED on Cynofura and examined fome remains, confifting of a few ftones with a fragment or two of white marble, while the wherries doubled the cape. We then croffed over to the oppofite coaft of the bay, where are veftiges of the city.

IN Salamis, fays Paufanias, on this fide is a temple of Diana, and on that has ftood a trophy for the victory obtained by Themiftocles, and there is the temple of Cychreus. The trophy was probably a column adorned with arms, which had been thrown down before his time. The remnants on Cynofura, it has been fuppofed, belonged to this monument; and the defeat of the Barbarians, as thofe enemies of Greece were ftyled, may have given rife to the name *Punto Barbaro,* by which the cape is now diftinguifhed. The church of St. Nicholas perhaps occupies the fite of the temple of Cychreus. A ferpent, which was feen in the Athenian fhips while engaging the Medes, was believed, on the authority of Apollo, to have been this hero.

THE city of Salamis was demolifhed by the Athenians, becaufe in the war with Caffander it furrendered to the Macedonians, from difaffection. In the fecond century, when it was vifited by Paufanias, fome ruins of the Agora or *market-place* remained, with a temple and image of Ajax; and not far from the port was fhown a ftone, on which, they related, Telamon

fate

fate to view the Salaminian ships on their departure to join the Grecian fleet at Aulis. The walls may still be traced, and, it has been conjectured, were about four miles in circumference. The level space within them was now covered with green corn. The port is choked with mud, and was partly dry. Among the scattered marbles are some with inscriptions. One is of great antiquity, before the introduction of the Ionic alphabet. On another, near the port, the name of Solon occurs. This renowned law-giver was a native of Salamis, and a statue of him was erected in the market-place, with one hand covered by his vest, the modest attitude in which he was accustomed to address the people of Athens. An inscription on black marble was also copied in 1676 near the ruin of a temple, probably that of Ajax.

THE island of Salamis is now inhabited by a few Albanians, who till the ground. Their village is called Ampelaki, *the Vineyard*, and is at a distance from the port, standing more inland. In the church are marble fragments and some inscriptions, which I copied. Our hotel was a cottage without a chimney. We were almost blinded with the smoke. At night the mud-floor, on which we lay, was covered with men, women, and children; and under the same roof was the poultry and live-stock belonging to the family.

I MOUNTED an ass and went at break of day, with an Albanian on foot, to examine a stone in a ruinous church an hour distant, but found on it only rude sculpture which had been mistaken for letters. Near it were falling cottages, the remains of a deserted village; and farther on, the place where we landed from Ægina. It is likely, there was the site of the more antient city Salamis, which was toward that island and the south. A river was called Bocarus, afterwards Bocalias. It was remarked, that the harvest commenced more early than about Athens.

The botanical traveller may be amufed with fearching for a flower, which, as the Salaminians related, was firft obferved on the death of Ajax. It is defcribed as white, inclining to red, the leaves lefs than in a lily and bearing the letters which are on the hyacinth.

CHAP. XLVII.

An antient oracle --- The battle of Salamis --- Flight of the Perfian fleet.

HERODOTUS has recorded an antient oracle, which was to be fulfilled, when fhips fhould form a bridge between the fea-wafhed Cynofura and the facred fhore of Diana, or acrofs the mouth of the bay of Salamis. This term was believed to have been accomplifhed in the firft year of the feventy fifth Olympiad[1], when that portion of the ftrait became the fcene of the famous battle, which delivered Greece from the incurfions of the Medes.

XERXES, after reducing the citadel of Athens, repaired to Phalerum, where his fleet lay. It was agreed in council to attack the Grecian fleet, which had affembled in the bay of Salamis. The fhips approached the ifland. A report that the Greeks intended to fly toward the Ifthmus was credited, and the Medes determined to prevent their efcape. At midnight the leading fquadron moved filently on, circling in toward Salamis; and the fhips about Ceos, probably the iflet next to the Piræus, and about Cynofura likewife advancing, the whole ftrait was occupied, quite from Munychia. A body of Perfians was

[1] In the year before Chrift, 478.

ftationed

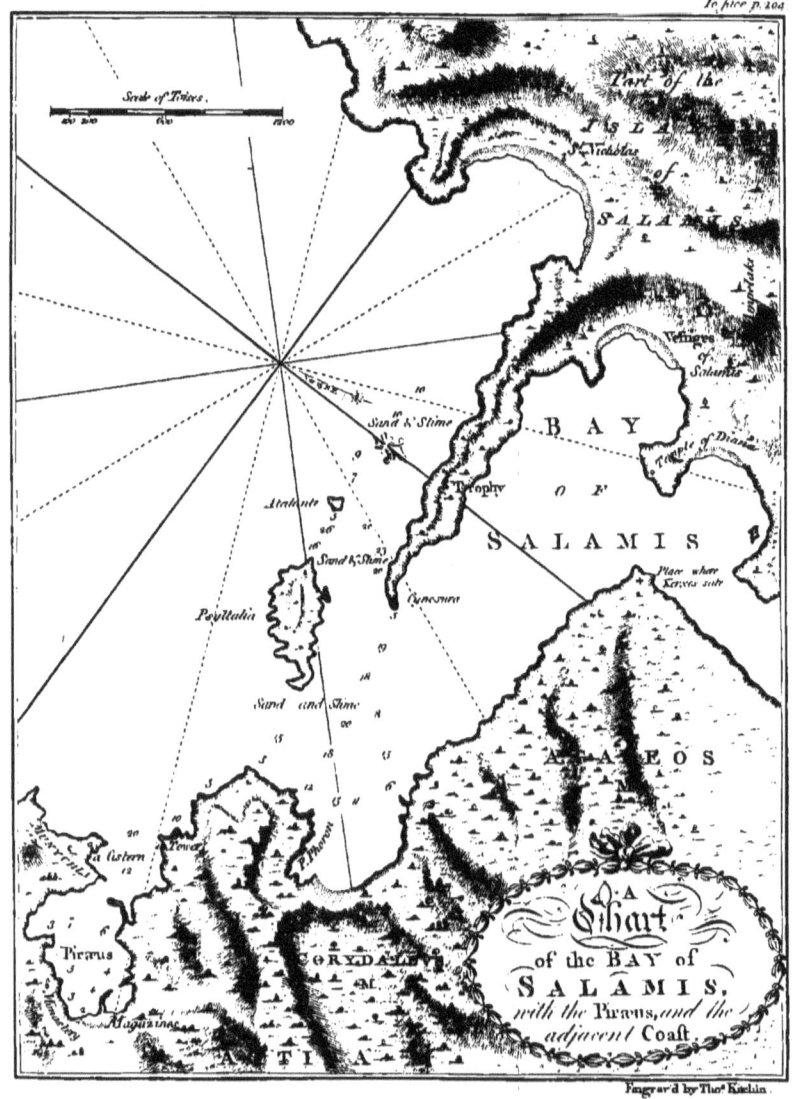

stationed on Pfyttalia to affift the men and difabled veffels, which fhould fwim or float thither, or to deftroy them, if enemies. The morning dawned, and the Greeks advanced from Salamis. The Corinthian admiral, who was irrefolute, failed away with his fquadron as far as the temple of Minerva Sciras, which was in the out-fkirts of Salamis, and returned. The Athenians were oppofite to the Phœnicians, who were on the right of the Perfian line; and the Lacedæmonians to the Ionians, who were on the left[1]. The Barbarians fled toward Phalerum. The Æginetans intercepted them at the mouth of the ftrait, and, during the confufion, a party from Salamis landing on Pfyttalia cut the Perfians there in pieces. The number, according to Paufanias, was four hundred. Xerxes was a fpectator of this action, fitting on mount Ægaleos; and, as one author relates, above the Heracleium. Another has placed him on Kerata, but that mountain is too remote to be even a probable ftation. The filver-footed chair, which he ufed, was preferved for many ages among the Perfian fpoils in the Acropolis.

XERXES, after his defeat, gave orders as if he defigned to renew the fight, and to pafs his army over into the ifland; preparing to join it to the continent by a mole, where the ftrait was only two ftadia wide. His fleet abandoned Phalerum in the night, and haftened back to the Hellefpont to fecure his retreat into Afia. Miftaking the fmall capes and iflets by the promontory Zofter for fhips, it fled with all poffible fpeed.

[1] Diodorus places the Athenians and Lacedæmonians on the left of the Greek line, oppofite to the Phœnicians; the Æginetans and Megarenfians on the right; the other Greeks in the centre, p. 417.

CHAP.

CHAP. XLVIII.

Intended rout from Athens --- Prepare for our departure --- At the Piræus --- Embark --- Land on Munychia --- Pass a haunted rock --- Land on an islet --- On Ægina.

A LETTER from Mr. Fauquier which I received on the twenty fifth of April, dated London February the eleventh 1766, contained directions from the committee of DILETTANTI to return, if it appeared safe and practicable, through the Morea, and by Corfu to Brindisi, and thence through Magna Grecia to Naples.

THE cranes, which returned to Athens in the spring and made their nests on the houses, chimnies, and ruins in the town, had reared their young, and were seen daily as it were exercising before their flight, high in the air, with continued gyrations; when we also began to prepare for our departure. We hired a small felucca of Hydre, with seven men and two boys, which waited for us in the Piræus. The marbles, which I had collected, with our provisions and baggage, were removed on horses to the sea-side, and put on board without being examined at the custom-house. This exemption was proffered to us as a token of regard by the Vaiwode, but Lombardi required of me a number of piasters, which, he pretended, it was necessary to distribute privately among the farmers and officers of the revenue. The Disdar had requested one of our ladders, which were much admired, and we sent it to him in the Acropolis. We restored to the owners some of our furniture, which had been borrowed, and gave the remainder to our friends and domestics.

THE twenty first of June was the day fixed for our removal. Among other civilities at parting, I was presented
with

with a very fine pomgranate, accompanied with a wifh, that I might reach home as found in body and as full of knowlege. We fet out in the evening for the Piræus, attended by Ifofime and a tall Greek named Coletti, who had been in England, and was our neighbour; forming, as ufual, a long and motley cavalcade. A croud, affembled about our gate, followed us with wifhes of a profperous voyage and fpeedy return, believing, as they had been told by Lombardi, that we intended to pafs the winter at Athens. We were joined on the road by Ofman Tyralee Agá, a Turk, who had frequently vifited us. The harveft was then far advanced; the fheaves of corn lying collected in the open air, by the floors; or horfes running in a ring three or four abreaft round a pole to tread out the grain. We repaired to the chamber of the cuftom-houfe, in which we had tarried on our firft arrival in the port, and fupped fitting crofs-legged on a carpet. The archon had provided a gourd of choice wine, and one of our crew excelled on the lyre. It was late at night, when our friends rofe, and bidding us adieu gallopped away toward Athens.

EARLY in the morning we embarked, with two live lambs, George Vandoro a Greek of Patræ our cook, Michaeli a youth of Athens and his brother Conftantine, our Swifs, a Janizary, and Lombardi, who had refolved to accompany us to the borders of Turkey; befides an adventurer of Corfu, whom we indulged with his paffage homeward. This wanderer was a man of a decent and plaufible carriage. He had been diftreffed for money, and imprifoned at Athens, and owed his enlargement to our compaffion, which he repaid with difhonefty and deceit. We rowed by a French veffel, which was waiting in the Piræus to lade with corn; leaving an Albanian youth named Sideri, who had lived with us, crying on the fhore.

THE wind being foutherly, when we got out of the Piræus, we put into a fmall creek of the peninfula on our left, which was once encircled with a wall of excellent mafonry, as appears

from

from the remains, belonging to the fortrefs of Munychia. By the fea-fide is a large fragment of a marble column. The rock was incrufted with falt, white and pure, formerly an article of commerce, and, with the wood, rented of the public. Our men made a tent of the fail and oars to fhelter us from the fun, and collected the low fhrubs and arid herbage to drefs our provifions.

We waited for a wind until the following day, when we failed, three hours after noon, fteering toward the weft end of Ægina. We were becalmed about mid-way, and rowed by a rock or iflet, which the mariners fay is haunted; murmurings and frightful voices being heard on it, perhaps the beating of the waves and the cry of amphibious animals, fuch as the Phocæ or fea-calves, which occafionally repair to land; and nightly goblins ill-treating thofe who are forced to tarry in bad weather.

We went on fhore on an iflet between Ægina and Salamis, where we found plenty of fea-chefnuts. The rock was bare, except a few fhrubs and ftunted trees, but abounded in locufts continually rifing, as we moved through the parched herbage, and fettling again after a fhort flight. The amazing fwarms of thefe infects feen in countries not commonly infefted with them, it is likely, are formed when provifions are fcanty at home; hunger forcing them to affemble to be wafted by the wind to regions of a moifter temperature, where vegetables continue to flourifh. Among the bufhes I difcovered an infect of a fpecies lefs common, refembling the tendril of a vine. It was moving, the colour a lively green. Naturalifts have named it *The walking ſtick*[1]. This, and almoft every rock, has on it a ruinous church. The fun, which was now fetting behind the picturefque iflands and mountains, coloured heaven and earth with a rich variety of exquifite tints. Our crew refted after their labour in the boat, made faft to the fhore, on which we

---

[1] See Edwards, pl. 288, c. 78, part 2d.

lay among cedar-trees and thickets of maſtic. In the night a great dew fell.

EARLY in the morning we had a favourable breeze, of ſhort duration. We had purpoſed to examine again the ſite of Ægina, but on opening the port ſaw in it a large Saité or veſſel at anchor. A Barbary cruiſer had lately appeared off Sunium. Several in the boat were ſeized with panic fear, and called out to the captain to ſteer to the ſhore, which was at a little diſtance. We determined, however, to row on, when the hanging out of a piece of linen to dry ſpread new terror, ſome inſiſting it was a ſignal for us to go on board. We paſſed a rock named Móne, and putting into a bay of Ægina called Perthica dined by a well of cold water, under a thick and wide-ſpreading fig-tree, beneath which we would have ſlept at noon, but our mariners affirmed, the ſhade was bad, that we ſhould riſe heavy and with the head-ach. Our water-caſks were carried to be filled at a better ſpring near a mile diſtant by a metochi or farm, where we procured green almonds, and were informed that the veſſel, which had cauſed our conſternation, was from Crete, manned with Turks, waiting to load with corn. The wind being contrary, we paſſed the night on the rocks near our boat.

CHAP. XLIX.

Sail from Ægina --- The iſland and town of Poro --- The monaſtery --- Way to Calaurea --- Of the city --- The remains --- A goatherd.

IN the morning we ſet ſail from Ægina for Poro, a ſmall iſland near the coaſt of the Morea, diſtant about ſixteen miles. The fair gale ſoon failed, and the land-breeze was heard coming from the peninſula of Methana, making the water foam before it.

it. The sea-breeze was next seen at a distance, and for some minutes we were between both, becalmed. Each then prevailed by turns, and, as it were to decide the conflict, eddies and whirls of wind interposed from the mountains on the coast of the Morea. One moment our sails were to be furled; then to be loosed; now we obeyed this, and presently another gust; turning to and fro as in a labyrinth. The address of the crew in shifting and adjusting the rigging and sails could be exceeded only by the sagacity of our caraboucheri or captain, who foresaw and foretold the changes, though seemingly instantaneous. At length, perplexed and apprehensive of some unlucky accident, as the felucca had been lately overset and was now deep laden, he ordered the men to lower the yards and to row. A fair gale succeeded, and about noon we arrived at Poro.

The island Poro was antiently named Calaurea, and reckoned thirty stadia or three miles and three quarters in circumference. It stretches along before the coast of the Morea in a lower ridge, and is separated from it by a canal only four stadia or half a mile wide. This, which is called Poro or the Ferry, in still weather may be passed on foot, as the water is not deep. It has given its name to the island, and to the town, which consists of about two hundred houses, mean and low, with flat roofs; rising on the slope of a bare disagreeable rock. The inhabitants are supplied with wood for fuel chiefly from the continent. In a church is a Latin inscription, with two in the Italian language, recording a young Venetian, who died of the plague in 1688 and was buried there; and also a surgeon named Altomirus, who was inconsolable for the loss of his friend. In another church is a small round stone in the middle of the floor, the margin inscribed in Latin " Here Altomirus mourned."

After a short stay at Poro, we rowe with a turbulent sea through the strait round a point of land, and, opening the mouth of the gulf, hoisted sail for the monastery of the Panagia or Virgin

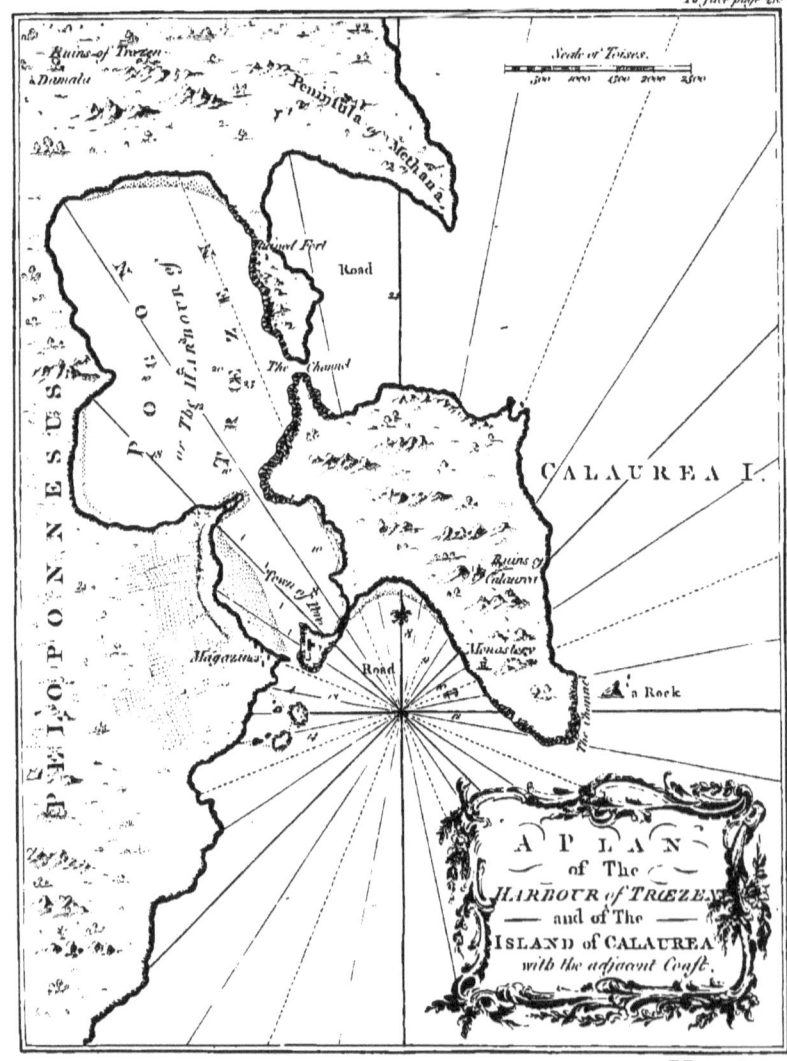

Virgin Mary. The wind was rough, and foon blew off two of our hats. One was recovered by a boy who fwam; the other, with a handkerchief in it to defend the head from the power of the fun, was carried away on the waves. We landed and went to the monaftery, which is at fome diftance from the fea, the fituation high and romantic, near a deep torrent-bed. It was furrounded by green vineyards; thickets of myrtle, orange and lemon-trees, in bloffom; the arbutus with fruit, large but unripe; the oleander or picro-daphne, and the olive, laden with flowers; fweet-fmelling pines and evergreens. Oppofite is a fountain much celebrated. The water is cold, and of a quality very beneficial to perfons indifpofed from drinking a harder and lefs wholfome fluid. We found there a papas or prieft, with fome monks, and were fupplied with good wine and provifions and with plenty of almonds gathered frefh from the trees.

WE fet out from the monaftery for Palatia, *the Palaces,* as the fite of the city Calaurea is now called, at day-break, mounted on mules and affes, refpectable as well as ufeful animals in thefe mountainous regions. We were attended by two or three men on foot, to chide our beafts in a language which they underftood, and to goad them on, when lazy. We had no bridle or halter, but were inftructed to guide them; holding a ftick, if we wanted them to turn, on the oppofite fide of the head; and between the ears, if to ftand ftill. We paffed by a large refervoir or ciftern made at a confiderable expenfe, into which the water of feveral rills is collected to be ufed in agriculture. The track leading to Palatia, diftant about an hour from the fea, is rough and rugged. Beyond that place is a fountain erected by a Turk, the water not inferior to that of the monaftery; and by it a grove of lemon-trees. The fruit was contracted for at feventy peraus or about three fhillings a thoufand.

NEPTUNE was faid to have accepted the ifland of Calaurea from Apollo in exchange for Delos. The city ftood on a high ridge nearly in the middle of the ifland, commanding an extenfive view of the gulf and its coafts. There was his holy temple. The prieftefs was a virgin, who was difmiffed when marriageable. Seven of the cities near the ifland held a congrefs at it, and facrificed jointly to the deity. Athens, Ægina, and Epidaurus were of this number, with Nauplia, for which place Argos contributed. The Macedonians, when they had reduced Greece, were afraid to violate the fanctuary, by forcing from it the fugitives, his fuppliants. Antipater commanded his general to bring away the orators, who had offended him, alive; but Demofthenes could not be prevailed on to furrender. His monument remained in the fecond century, within the inclofure of the temple.

THE city of Calaurea has been long abandoned. Traces of buildings and of antient walls appear, nearly level with the ground; and fome ftones, in their places, each with a feat and back, forming a little circle, once perhaps a bath. The temple, which was of the Doric order, and not large, as may be inferred from the fragments, is reduced to an inconfiderable heap of ruins. The ftone is of a dark colour. We found three pedeftals, of blue veined marble. One, which is infcribed, has fupported a ftatue of king Eumenes, erected by the city as an acknowlegement of his virtues and of his fervices to the God, to the Calaureans, and other Greeks. Many pieces lay ready, cut to the fize which is a load for a mule, to be carried down to the fhore and embarked for the ifland of Hydre, where a monaftery was then building. Our guide was a mafon who had been long employed in deftroying thefe remnants of antiquity.

AMONG the iflanders who repaired to us at the monaftery was a young goatherd, with a fheep from the fold. It happened that one of us pulled out a watch, when he ftared with a face of wonder not to be defcribed. Being afked, if he knew what it was, he replied, he could not tell, unlefs it were a fnuff-box. Perceiving his anfwer occafioned a fmile, he added with
fome

TRAVELS IN GREECE. 213

fome warmth, " How fhould I know? I walk the mountains." We endeavoured in vain to make him comprehend the ufe and nature of that curious and with us common machine.

CHAP. L.

Sail up the harbour of Trœzen --- Land on the peninfula of Methana --- The bay or lake --- Of Trœzen --- The ruins --- The Acropolis --- The water --- Of Damalá --- A proverbial faying.

AFTER waiting fome time for a favourable wind, we left the monaftery, in the morning, and croffed to the oppofite fhore of the Morea. We landed on a fpot called Palæochorio or *old Town*, and found there part of an ordinary Mofaic pavement, a piece or two of marble, fome mean ruins, and a folitary church. About noon the wind, as was expected, became fair, fetting into the canal. We paffed by the town of Poro, and opened the ftrait between the ifland and the peninfula of Methana, through which we had entered. We now failed on, with the main land on our left, up a bay, once named Pogon or *the Beard*. It is fheltered by Calaurea on the eaft, and was the harbour of Trœzen, in which a fquadron of the Grecian fleet affembled before the battle of Salamis.

TRŒZEN was fifteen ftadia or almoft two miles from the fea. A town named Damalá or Thamalá is now near the fite. We purpofed going to this place, but found the water fo fhallow at the top of the bay, that we could not approach the fhore. We moored at fome diftance to a rock by a point of the peninfula. On this fpot a fmall fortrefs had been erected. We could trace the two fide walls running up from the fea, with two round towers at the angles, inland. Thefe remnants are thick, and of the mafonry ftyled Incertum. From an eminence, not far off, a column as it were of fmoke afcended, which we

were

were told was duſt from winnowed corn; the peaſants throwing up the grain and chaff together to be ſeparated and cleanſed by the wind. We could procure no animals to convey us to Damalá before the morning, ſo we lay down to ſleep among the buſhes. The air was filled with noiſome vapours from the dirty ſtagnant bay and its putrefying weeds. Swarms of gnats buzzed about, and preyed on us inceſſantly. Frogs croaked. Dogs barked, and the ſhepherds on the mountains hallooed to encourage them to attack the wild beaſts, which approached their charge.

SARON, one of the early kings of Trœzen, founded a temple of Diana by this ſea. The water was there ſo ſhallow and muddy that it was called the Phœbæan lake. He was addicted to the chace, and following a Doe, which ſwam out into the deep, was drowned. His body was thrown aſhore by the grove, and buried within the incloſure of the temple; and from him the lake was named the Saronian. The fens at this ſeaſon were dry, or much contracted by the power of the ſun. In the morning we croſſed over to that ſhore, and riding through a flat marſhy tract covered with tall ruſhes arrived at Damalá in about an hour. We were then informed, that the ruins, for which we enquired, were a quarter of an hour farther on; and we continued our journey.

TROEZEN was once no ignoble city. It had been called Poſidonia from Neptune. They related, that this deity and Minerva had contended for their country, and, by command of Jupiter, poſſeſſed it jointly; the reaſon, why their money was ſtamped with her head and a trident. Trœzen and Pittheus were ſons of Pelops. Pittheus gave to the city the name of his brother, whom he ſucceeded; but the people were called from him Pittheidæ. He was the maternal grandfather of Theſeus. The place was ſhown, where this hero was born; with the rock, under which Ægeus depoſited his ſword and ſlippers, on the way to Hermione. In the agora or market-place was a

temple

temple of Diana, where, it was faid, Hercules came up from hell with Cerberus. Behind, was the monument of Pittheus; and not far off, a temple of the Mufes, with an antient altar, on which the Trœzenians facrificed to them and to Sleep; affirming, that of all the deities this was the moft friendly to the Mufes. The temple of Apollo founded by Pittheus exceeded in age any temple known to Paufanias. The temple of Minerva at Phocæa and that of Apollo Pythius at Samos were by far more modern. The ftoa or portico of the market-place was adorned with ftatues, reprefenting fome of the Athenian matrons and their children, who were fent to this city for fafety before the battle of Salamis. Near the Theatre was a temple of Diana erected by Hippolytus. This hero had a facred portion with a temple and image, and was honoured with yearly facrifices. The priefthood was for life, and it was the cuftom for virgins before their nuptials to cut off one of the treffes of their hair, and to carry it as an offering to the temple. Within the inclofure was a temple of Apollo dedicated by Diomed on his efcape from the ftorm which happened on his return from Troy. Againft the inclofure was part of the ftadium of Hippolytus, as it was called; and above, a temple of Venus *the Spectator*, where Phædra beheld him at his exercifes. A myrtle, which grew there, produced leaves full of holes, as they afferted, from the time of her diftraction, when fhe perforated the foliage with the clafp of her hair. Her tomb was not far from the barrow of Hippolytus, which was near the myrtle, but not acknowleged by the Trœzenians. They denied that he was dragged by horfes and killed; fuppofing him to have been changed into the conftellation called *the Charioteer*. The temple of Neptune was without the city-wall. They ftyled him *Plant-falter*, becaufe, in his anger, he had permitted the feawater to penetrate to the roots and feeds; rendering the land barren. They claimed the god Orus as a native, and, if any people, were given to embellifh their city with local ftories. Its territory included the peninfula of Methana, and the promontory Scyllæum. A road between the mountains led to Hermione,

Hermione, which city was diſtant about eighty ſtadia or ten miles from Scyllæum. Our mariners called it Caſtri, and had been employed in tranſporting materials from it to the monaſtery building at Hydre.

THE ruins of Trœzen are moſtly in the plain at the foot of a lofty range of mountains croſſing from the Saronian lake or bay to the gulf of Epidauria. The ſite, with the whole iſthmus, is overrun with buſhes, but ſome ſpots produce corn and cotton. Many rills of water deſcend from the mountains, and are conducted and diſtributed as the crops and ſoil require. The ſcattered churches are numerous, and occupy, it is likely, the places of the temples. In ſeveral are inſcribed pedeſtals. The veſtiges, with pieces of wall and remnants of brick buildings, ſpread to a conſiderable extent; the ſpace diſpoſed in terraces, the areas clear, with rubbiſh lying along the edges. The principal ruin ſeems to have been the ſubſtruction or baſement of the temple of Venus, and on three ſides is of the maſonry termed Incertum. It ſtands on an eminence, overlooking the cavity of the ſtadium, and has on it ſome remnants of a later ſtructure. Theodore, the general who preſerved Greece in the time of Theodoſius the firſt, was a great benefactor to this place. Beſides ſaving the city by the wiſdom of his councils, he bequeathed a large ſum of money to the public. He was rewarded, as uſual, with ſtatues; and in one of the inſcriptions the people are diſtinguiſhed by their old name Pittheidæ.

THE acropolis or citadel of Trœzen was on the top of one of the mountains, which tower high above the plain. There was antiently a temple of Minerva. We had been told at Damalá that many ruins remained, and I was unwilling to defer the examination, as our recent ſufferings and the reputed unhealthineſs of this tract had rendered us all eager to be gone. It was near noon, and the ſun reigned in a cloudleſs ſky, when I began to aſcend. The rock was heated ſo much that it could not be handled in climbing without pain; and the way was impeded

peded with loose stones and low dry shrubs and parched herbage, which crackled, and blinded me in passing with dust and down. After frequent pauses to obtain refreshment from scanty shade and water, I attained to the summit, with the assistance of a Greek servant and a sailor; and found only the rubbish of some churches, with two fragments of marble inscribed. We tarried awhile to recover from our fatigue, and to enjoy a most extensive prospect; and then descended by a better track toward Damalá. A gentle breeze, which had sprung up, was of signal service to us, the air in the lee of the rocks feeling almost as fire.

IN our way down from the summit, or on the eastern side, we crossed a torrent-bed; and on the other is a stream more considerable, with a mill at the mountain-foot, by which a man was treading milk in a skin to make butter. One of these was called Chrysorrhoas, *the Golden*, because it had continued to flow after a drought of nine years, when the other springs failed. The fountain of Hercules in the city, and one named Hippocrene, was supplied from these hills. But it was remarked, that the waters of Trœzen rising from sources like the Athenian partook of the same bad properties, affecting the nerves and feet; nor could better be procured by digging wells.

I WAS directed at Damalá to the house of a Greek priest, to which my companions had repaired from the ruins. The town is small and situated on the mountain-side. It inherits the stinking atmosphere as well as the bad water of Trœzen. The inhabitants are of a sallow complexion, and August is commonly a month of great mortality. It is the see of a bishop, and noted for being frequently vacant, as it then was; the occupier seldom long surviving his new dignity.

A PROVERBIAL saying, *the bishop of Damalá*, is current in these parts, and applied to persons who suffer by their own indiscretion. The story is simple enough. He was presented with some fishes, offended at their size, and, being told that such only could be procured, resolved to attend the trial. The boat was surprized by a Barbary cruiser. He was carried into slavery, and employed to grind wheat, and at the same time to rock a child; until he moved the compassion of his owner by singing some words, which he composed, void of poetry, but expressive of his folly and its consequences. I shall insert them from a copy written by the priest, as a specimen of the versification and language of modern Greece.

ωίσκοωες. Ἰὰ δαμαλά.
μὴ Ἰε νὰ. μήἰεμηαλὰ—
Ἰαλινά. δενίθελες.
Ἰὰ μεγάλα. γιρέβες.
Ἰράξα Ἰὸ χερόμηλο.
κύνα. Ἰαραωόωκλο.

A Bishop without brain or sense,
Deserving such a recompense!
With smaller fishes not content---
Author of thine own punishment!
Turn, turn the mill, a fit employ,
And lull to sleep the Arab-boy.

CHAP. LI.

The gulf of Epidauria --- Of Methana --- An antient charm --- A hot spring --- The islets --- Of Epidaurus --- The harbour.

WE returned to the shore in the evening from Damalá, and before night landed on the island Calaurea. The next day we sent some men in the boat for provisions to the town of Poro. They came back at noon. We sailed, and landed again on the peninsula of Methana, on the side toward Attica. Here was a
ruined

ruined church, with a well. The mountain was bare and black, a fire having lately confumed the wood. We lay among huge fingle rocks, fome poifed, as it were, on a point. In the morning we embarked haftily with a fair breeze; which failing, we continued for fome hours on a fmooth fea, expofed to the intenfe heat of a cloudlefs fun. We paffed between fome iflets, and entered a gulf or deep bay, in which is Methana; with Epidaurus oppofite, but nearer the mouth.

METHANA or Methone was a fmall city on the weftern fide of the peninfula. The name is ftill retained. The acropolis or citadel was on a mountain moderately high; rough, and partly inacceffible. The wall was of excellent mafonry, and has been repaired, but is again in ruins. I faw an imperfect infcription by the entrance of a church, on the fite perhaps of the temple of Ifis, but without a roof. Round about the rock were many fences of piled ftones, inclofing in April, when I was there, ploughed fields and neglected churches. The face of the country was then brown and difmal. A femicircular range of mountains rifes behind.

PAUSANIAS relates, that he wondered moft at a device ufed at Methana to avert Libs or the fouth-weft wind, which, coming from the Saronic gulf, withered the vines, when in bud. A couple of men, while it was blowing, divided a cock with white feathers into two parts, and running in a contrary direction encompaffed the vineyards, each bearing a portion. They buried the cock on their arrival at the place, from whence they had ftarted.

THE hot baths were computed about thirty ftadia or three miles and three quarters from Methana. The fpring appeared firft when Antigonus fon of Demetrius reigned in Macedonia, after a fiery eruption from a volcano, which raifed in a level plain a mountain feven ftadia or near a mile high; for fome time inacceffible by day on account of the heat and the ftrong fulphureous odour;

odour; but at night, fmelling agreeably, fhining at a great diftance, and affording warmth. The fea, which boiled with the lava as far out as five ftadia or above half a mile, was difturbed twenty ftadia or two miles and a half; and rocks were extant in it, not lefs than towers. The flame dying away, a current, warm and exceedingly falt, fucceeded; but no cold water was found there, and fwimming in the bay was dangerous, it abounding with other monfters, and with dog-fifh. This fpring is on the fide of the mountain, by a village, which is in view; and tinges the foil near it with the colour of ochre. Ovid has defcribed the alteration of this fpot in a fpeech of Pythagoras to Numa.

THE rocks before Methana, in the mouth of the bay, were called *the iflets of Pelops*. They were nine in number; produced, it is likely, by the volcano, and once bare. Some fhrubs grow on them, and we found water to fill our cafks, with a ruined church or two. It was antiently affirmed, that on one no rain ever fell. Our author knew not whether this were true; but relates, that he had feen men by facrifices and incantations turn away hail. An ifland named Sphæra, and afterwards Hiera, was perhaps more within the bay. There was a monument, it was faid, of Sphærus, who drove the chariot of Pelops, and a temple of Minerva, in which the virgins of Trœzen confecrated their zones, before marriage. The fame offering is ftill feen in the churches at Athens, with towels richly embroidered, and various other articles. The water was fordable, and it may be fufpected that this ifland, which was near, is now joined to the main land.

EPIDAURUS was no obfcure city. It ftood in a recefs of the Saronic gulf, fronting the eaft, and was fortified by nature, being inclofed by high mountains reaching to the fea, and rendering it difficult of accefs. It had temples, and in the acropolis or citadel was a remarkable ftatue of Minerva. The fite is now called Epi-thavro. The traces are indiftinct, and it has

probably

probably been long deserted. In April it was sown with corn, or over-run with bushes, flowering shrubs, cedars, and almond-trees; the aspect fresh and pleasing. We found plenty of wild asparagus; a maimed statue of bad workmanship, the posture recumbent; some masses of stone, brick, and rubbish; a few pieces of marble and a sepulchral inscription, ΑΛΕΞΑΝΔΡΕΑ ΧΑΙΡΕ *Alexandrea farewell.*

The harbour of Epidaurus is long. Its periplus or circuit was fifteen stadia or near two miles. The entrance is between mountains, and on a small rocky peninsula on the left hand are ruins of a modern fortress. This, it seems, was the point on which a temple of Juno stood. It is frequented by vessels for wood or corn; and near the upper end is a beautiful young palm-tree, flourishing by the sea-side.

CHAP. LII.

Land in Epidauria --- Set out on foot for the grove of Æsculapius --- At Ligurió --- The evening --- Remains by Ligurió.

WE landed in the Morea, about half an hour from Epi-ya-tha, a village on a high mountain, by a large fortress, in view; about two hours from Epidaurus, which is more within the bay; intending to visit the grove of Æsculapius and his temple, which was five miles from that city. We sent to Epi-yatha, but the people were engaged in harvest-work, and their beasts could not be spared. The locusts were very numerous. Night approached. We lay on the shore, not far from a small lake running into the sea, the stream full of fish, and supplied by cold and clear water rushing in, very copiously, from beneath a rock. We made fires of cow-dung, hoping the smoke would drive away the gnats, but were still tormented by them exceedingly.

Our

Our meffengers returned again from Epi-yatha, early in the morning, and informed us, that no beafts could be procured. We were impatient to change our quarters. Our fleep had been much difturbed; the air was reputed very unhealthy; and the wine, being impregnated with lime, was deemed as ruinous to the ftomach and as intoxicating as pleafant to the eye and tafte. I now determined to tarry there no longer, and taking an umbrella fet out on foot, attended by our janizary, a fervant, and two failors, armed and carrying provifions and other neceffaries. We paffed by the fortrefs of Epi-yatha, over hills, and through dales and ripe corn. The ftreams and fountains, which occurred on the way, with the myrtles and ever-greens in the water-courfes, afforded us refrefhment; or the exceffive heat of the fun would have been infupportable. It was mid-day when we arrived greatly fatigued at Ligurió.

Ligurió is the name of four feparate villages, or of a diftrict. The place, where we ftopped, is clean and enjoys a good air. It is pleafantly feated on the fide of a hill, the plain beneath it overfpread with vines producing a ftrong red wine, which is defervedly in great repute. They infufe refin inftead of lime. The people were abroad in the fields, and we tarried under a fhady tree fome time, until we were better accommodated by an Albanian woman. The houfe was neat though mean, and much recommended afterwards by the honeft heartinefs of its owner her hufband, and of his family.

I had expected to find at Ligurió the facred poffeffion of Æfculapius, but was told, that the ruins were at Gérao about an hour diftant. In the evening an Albanian peafant with a caloyer or monk offered to conduct me to the fpot; and the janizary with the failors defired to accompany me. On our return, the villagers, who had been employed in their harveft-work, readily furnifhed as many beafts as were required, and offered to proceed with them by moonlight to Epi-yatha. After

fupping

TRAVELS IN GREECE. 223

supping on the ground before the house; a violin was procured. The janizary played, and the Albanians and Greeks began singing and dancing, with their usual alacrity. When they had finished, we lay dispersed, in the open air, in the area of the court. The next day about noon, my companions arrived, greatly fatigued, and one of them ill; their attendants also complaining of their sufferings by the sea-side and on the road.

ON a summit near Ligurio are some vestiges, it is supposed, of Lessa, once a village with a temple and statue of Minerva, near the confines of Epidauria and Argolis or the territory of Argos. Below, at the foot of the opposite mountain, is the ruin of a quadrangular structure; the masonry of the species styled Incertum, the sides inclining as in a pyramid. Lessa fronted the road leading by the temple of Æsculapius to Epidaurus; and a track beneath Liguriò now passes through the plain by Gerao to that port.

CHAP. LIII.

The grove of Æsculapius --- His statue and temple --- Inscriptions --- The Stadium --- The Theatre --- Mount Cynortium --- Water, &c. --- Serpents.

THE grove of Æsculapius was inclosed by mountains, within which all the sacrifices as well of the Epidaurians as of strangers were consumed. One was called Titthion, and on this the god when an infant was said to have been exposed, and to have been suckled by a she-goat. He was a great physician, and his temple was always crouded with sick persons. Beyond it was the dormitory of the suppliants; and near it, a circular edifice called the Tholus, built by Polycletus, of white marble, worth seeing. The grove besides other temples, was adorned with a

portico,

portico, and a fountain remarkable for its roof and decorations. The bath of Æsculapius was one of the benefactions of Antoninus Pius, while a Roman Senator; as was also a house for the reception of pregnant women and dying persons, who before were removed out of the inclosure, to be delivered or to expire in the open air. The remains are heaps of stones, pieces of brick wall, and scattered fragments of marble; besides some churches or rather piles of rubbish mis-called, being destitute of doors, roofs, or any kind of ornament.

THE statue of Æsculapius was half as big as that of Jupiter Olympius at Athens. It was made of ivory and gold, and, as the inscription proved, by Thrasymedes son of Arignotus of Paros. He was represented sitting, holding his staff, with one hand on the head of a serpent, and a dog lying by him. Two Argive heroes, Bellerophon combating with the monster Chimæra and Perseus severing the head of Medusa, were carved on the throne. Many tablets described the cures performed by the deity, yet he had not escaped contumely and robbery. Dionysius deprived him of his golden beard, affirming it was very unseemly in him to appear in that manner when his father Apollo was always seen with his face smooth. Sylla amassed the pretious offerings belonging to him and to Apollo and Jupiter at Delphi and Olympia, to pay his army before Athens. The marks in the walls testified that a great number had been plucked down. A few fragments of white marble exquisitely carved occur in the heap of the temple.

THE inclosure of the temple once abounded in inscriptions. In the second century six marbles remained, on which were written in the Doric dialect the names of men and women, who had been patients of the god, with the distemper each had laboured under and the remedies he had directed. We found only a couple of votive inscriptions, and two pedestals of statues, one of which represented a Roman and was erected by the city of the Epidaurians. The divine prescriptions have perished or are buried

in

in the ruin, but a specimen is extant[1] from similar records, once preserved in his temple in the isle of Tiber near Rome. The complaint was spitting of blood, and the person deemed incurable; but Æsculapius prevailed. He was restored, and returned thanks publicly before the people.

The Stadium was near the temple. It was of earth, as most in Greece were. At the upper end are seats of stone, but these were continued along the sides only a few yards. A vaulted passage leading underneath into the area, now choked up, was a private way by which the Agonothetæ or presidents with the priests and persons of distinction entered.

Two large cisterns or reservoirs remain, made by Antoninus for the reception of rain-water. One measured ninety nine feet long, and thirty seven wide. Beyond them is a dry water-course, and in the mountain-side on the right-hand are the marble seats of the Theatre, overgrown with bushes. We regretted that the Proscenium or front was vanished, as this fabric also was the work of Polycletus and much admired. The Roman theatres, as Pausanias observes, far exceeded all in ornament, and in size that of Megalopolis in Arcadia; but, he subjoins, what architect can compare with Polycletus in harmony and beauty?

Going up the water-course, between the mountains, is a church, where, besides fragments, we found a short inscription. " Diogenes the hierophant to far-darting Apollo, on account " of a vision in his sleep." Apollo had a temple on mount Cynortium, probably on this spot; and on a summit beyond are other traces, it is likely, of a temple of Diana.

The springs and wells by the ruins are now supposed to possess many excellent properties. To these and a good air,

[1] See Comment on Strabo, p. 164. or Gruter Inscript. p. 72.

with

with the recreations of the Theatre and of the Stadium, and to the medicinal knowlege and experience of the priefts, may be attributed both the recovery of the fick and the reputation of Æfculapius. The renown and worfhip of this god began in Epidauria, and continued for many centuries. Since he failed, fome faints have fucceeded to the bufinefs; and I have feen patients lying in beds in their churches at Athens. The whole neighbourhood has for ages plundered the grove. The Ligurians remembered the removal of a marble chair from the Theatre, and of ftatues and infcriptions, which, among other materials, were ufed in repairing the fortifications of Nauplia, now called Napoli, or in building a new Mofque at Argos.

THE tortoifes of mount Cithæron were facred to Pan; the ferpents of Epidauria to Æfculapius. One fpecies, yellower than common, was peculiar to this region, and tame, perhaps, like the cranes, from being never molefted. Thefe reptiles ftill abound. Some, as the Ligurians relate, are very large, not venomous, and, if attacked, fight with their tails.

CHAP. LIV.

Leave Ligurió --- Nauplia --- Tiryns --- The river Inachus --- Old Argos --- The prefent town.

OUR fick companion was able to travel after refting two days. The failors left us at night, with orders to proceed in the felucca to the port of Corinth, and wait our arrival by land. The Janizary and Swifs went for horfes to Napoli, and, not fucceeding there, to Argos. They returned at midnight much fatigued, with eight only and a couple of Argives. The next evening we defcended from Ligurió into the plain, and crofling with the pyramidal ruin on our right entered between two

ridges

ridges of mountains. The track was ſtony, among buſhes, by ſlender ſtreams, and over dry water-courſes. After three hours we diſmounted at a place called *The Gardens.* We had here figs ripe and large. We reſolved to continue our journey by moonlight, to avoid the heat of the ſun and alſo the flies, which had terribly tormented our horſes. We ſupped and lay in an orchard, chiefly of pomgranate and mulberry trees; among which was the plant called Opuntia, then in flower. We ſet out again at two in the morning, and by a rough track entered the plain of Argos. This paſs has been ſtrongly guarded. Several ſummits of the mountains on each ſide are crowned with large neglected caſtles. The road led us through olive groves, near to Nauplia, now Napoli of Romania.

NAUPLIA, the port of Argos, was ſituated at the bottom of a deep gulf. The people were ſuppoſed to have accompanied Danaus from Egypt. They were expelled by the Argives for rebellion. In the ſecond century the town was deſolate; but ruins of the walls remained, with a temple of Neptune, and a fountain, which ſtill flows, called Canathus. The Argives were accuſtomed to waſh at it a ſtatue of Juno, yearly, on her feſtival. The harbour is the moſt ſecure and beſt defended in the Morea. The houſes are on a tongue of land running out into the ſea, and overlooked by a high and abrupt mountain. It is a place of a good appearance, and is ſtrongly fortified both by nature and art. It was taken, with the caſtle of Argos, by the Venetians in 1686. We could ſee two ſhips at anchor, and were told that a couple of French frigates had ſailed the night before to chaſtiſe the Dulciniotes, who had been recently guilty of piracies. We left Nauplia behind us, and travelled toward Argos.

OUR guides led us out of the direct road to an abandoned fortreſs on a rocky eminence in the plain. The wall has large ſtones toward the bottom; the ſuperſtructure chiefly modern, and mere patch-work. This was once Tiryns, the citadel of Prœtus, the ruins of which were extant on the right-hand of the road from Argos to Epidauria. The Cyclopes, who came from Lycia, were said to have erected the wall, which only remained in the second century. It confifted of rough ftones, the fmalleft of which could not have been moved at firft by a yoke of mules; with leffer ftones fitted to fill the vacant fpaces. Farther on, by the fea and Nauplia, were caverns called Cyclopia, with labyrinths, or, as they were named, the chambers of the daughters of Prœtus; probably quarries. The inhabitants of Tiryns, and alfo of Midéa, a place of which the fite was vifible on the left of that road, had been transferred to Argos.

WE continued our journey over a level plain, of fine impalpable foil, and by cotton-grounds, gardens, and the ftubble of wheat. We approached Argos, and croffed a fhallow ftream once called Charadrus, and alfo the bed of the Inachus. The Argives related, that this was one of the river-gods who adjudged the country to Juno, when fhe contended for it with Neptune, which deity in return made their water to vanifh; the reafon why the Inachus flowed only after rain, and was dry in fummer. The fource was a fpring, not copious, on a mountain in Arcadia, and the river ferved there as a boundary between the Argives and Mantineans.

ANTIENT Argos ftood chiefly on a flat. The fprings were near the furface, and it abounded in wells, which were faid to have been invented by the daughters of Danaus. This early perfonage probably introduced the pyramidal monuments. He lived in the acropolis or citadel, which was named Lariffa and accounted moderately ftrong. On the afcent was a temple of *Apollo on the ridge*, which in the fecond century continued the feat of an Oracle. The woman, who prophefied, was debarred from commerce with the male fex. A lamb was facrificed in the night, monthly; when, on tafting of the blood, fhe became poffeffed with the divinity. Farther on was a Stadium, where the Argives celebrated games in honour of Neméan Jupiter and of Juno. On the top was a temple of Jupiter, without a

roof,

roof, the statue off the pedestal. In the temple of Minerva there, among other curious articles, was a wooden Jupiter, with an eye more than common, having one in the forehead. This statue, it was said, was once placed in a court of the palace of Priam, who fled as a suppliant to the altar before it, when Troy was sacked.

Argos retains its original name and situation, standing near the mountains which are the boundary of the plain, with Napoli and the sea in view before it. The shining houses are whitened with lime or plaster. Churches, mud-built cottages and walls, with gardens and open areas, are interspersed, and the town is of considerable extent. Above the other buildings towers a very handsome mosque shaded with solemn cypresses; and behind, is a lofty hill, brown and naked, of a conical form, the summit crowned with a neglected castle. The devastations of time and war have effaced the old city. We enquired in vain for vestiges of its numerous edifices, the Theatre, the Gymnasium, the temples, and monuments, which it once boasted, contending even with Athens in antiquity and in favours conferred by the gods. We tarried in a miserable khan during the heat of noon, and toward evening set out, with an additional baggage-horse, for a place called *The Columns*.

CHAP. LV.

Mycenæ near Argos --- Agamemnon slain at Mycenæ --- The city ruined --- The temple of Juno --- We miss the site.

THE kingdom of the Argives was divided into two portions by Acrisius and his brother Prœtus. Argos and Mycenæ were their capitals. These, as belonging to the same family and distant only about fifty stadia or six miles and a quarter from

each

TRAVELS IN GREECE.

each other, had one tutelary deity, Juno; and were jointly proprietors of her temple, the Heræum, which was near Mycenæ.

AGAMEMNON enlarged his dominions by his valour and good fortune. He poffeffed Mycenæ with the region about Corinth and Sicyon, and that called afterwards Achæa. On his return from Troy, he was flain with his companions at a banquet. Mycenæ then declined; and, under the Heraclidæ, was made fubject to Argos.

THE Mycenæans, fending eighty men, partook with the Lacedæmonians in the glory acquired at Thermopylæ. The jealoufy of the Argives produced the deftruction of their city; which was abandoned after a fiege and laid wafte in the firft year of the feventy-eighth Olympiad [1]. The wall was faid to have been a work of the architects, who conftructed that of Tiryns, and was fo ftrong, it could not be forced by the Argives. Some part of it remained in the fecond century, with a gate, on which were lions; a fountain; the fubterraneous edifices, where Atreus and his fons had depofited their treafures; and, among other fepulchral monuments, one of Agamemnon, and one of his fellow foldiers and fufferers.

ARGOS was forty ftadia or five miles, and Mycenæ ten or fifteen ftadia, about a mile and a half, from the Heræum. This renowned temple was adorned with curious fculpture, and numerous ftatues. The image was very large, made by Polycletus, of gold and ivory, fitting on a throne. Among the offerings was a fhield taken by Menelaus from Euphorbus at Ilium; an altar of filver, on which the marriage of Hebe with Hercules was reprefented; a golden crown and purple robe given by Nero; and a peacock of gold fet with pretious ftones dedicated by Hadrian. Near it were the remains of a more antient temple,

[1] In the year before Chrift, 466.

which had been burned; a taper fetting fome garlands on fire, while the prieftefs was afleep.

THE ruin called *The Columns*, we had been informed, was near the direct road to Corinth. We fuppofed the building to have been the temple of Jupiter at Nemea, and it was expected that on the way to it we fhould difcover Mycenæ and the temple of Juno. " Having re-afcended Tretus, fays Paufanias, on the " left hand of the road to Argos are the ruins of Mycenæ." We croffed the wide bed of the torrent-river, and the Inachus, and then travelled in a dufty road in the plain, and about funfet arrived at Tretus. On reviewing our journey, I found with regret, that Mycenæ was at no great diftance on our right, when we entered between the mountains.

CHAP. LVI.

We arrive at Nemea --- Of the temple of Jupiter --- The Nemean games --- Ruin of the temple --- Mount Apefas, &c. --- A village, and monaftery.

THE pafs of Tretus is narrow, the mountains rifing on each fide. The track is by a deep-worn water-courfe, which was filled with thickets of oleander, myrtle, and ever-greens; the ftream clear and fhallow. Some Turks keep guard on it to apprehend fugitives and fufpected perfons, living under a fhed covered with boughs. Three of them, on feeing us, came to the way-fide with water, which civility we requited with a few peraus. Soon after we turned out of the road to the left, and, by a path impeded with fhrubs afcended a brow of the mountain, in which are caves, ranging in the rock, the abode of fhepherds in winter. One was perhaps the den of the Nemean lion, which continued to be fhown in the fecond century. From the

ridge

ridge above them may be seen Nauplia, Argos, and the citadel of Corinth. We defcended on the oppofite fide into a long valley, and had in view before us *The Columns* or the ruin of the temple, by which the village called Nemea antiently ftood.

The temple of Jupiter Nemeus is mentioned by Paufanias as worth feeing. The roof was then fallen, and the image had been removed. Round it was a grove of cyprefs-trees. The prieft was chofen by the Argives, who facrificed in the temple, and at the winter congrefs propofed a race for men in armour; joining this deity in their folemn invocations with Juno. One Bito, it was related, feeing them leading the victim, which was a bull, toward Nemea, took it up and carried it thither on his fhoulders. A ftatue at Argos reprefented him performing this feat.

The Nemean games were triennial and celebrated in the grove, in memory of Opheltes or Archemorus, a child, whom his nurfe, while fhe conducted the Achæan captains going againft Thebes to a fountain, placed on the grafs, and on her return found with a ferpent folded about his neck. His tomb was inclofed by a ftone fence, within which were altars; and a heap of earth marked the burial-place of his father Lycurgus. The horfe-race for boys, which had been dropped, was reftored to this and to the Ifthmian feftival by the emperor Hadrian. The Agonothetæ or prefidents were elected from the neighbouring cities Argos, Corinth, and Cleonæ. Their apparel was black. The reward of victory was a crown of parfley, which herb was fabled to have fprung from the blood of Archemorus.

The temple of Jupiter was of the Doric order, and had fix columns in front. The remains are two columns fupporting their architrave, with fome fragments. The ruin is naked, and the foil round about it had been recently ploughed. We pitched our tent within the cell, on the clean and level area. The roof it is likely was removed foon after its fall. A wild pear-
tree

tree grows among the stones on one side, but our cook found it necessary to shelter his fire with bushes of mastic to prevent its being extinguished by the sun. We were supplied with milk and lambs from a mandra or fold in the valley, and with water from a fountain, once named the Adrastéan, at a little distance on the slope of the hill.

BEYOND the temple is a remarkable summit, the top flat and visible in the gulf of Corinth. This was probably the mountain above Nemea called Apesas, on which Perseus was said to have sacrificed to Jupiter. On one side is a ruinous church, with some rubbish, perhaps where Opheltes and his father were said to have been interred. Near is a very large spreading fig-tree. To this a most simple goatherd repaired daily before noon with his flock, which huddled together in the shade until the extreme heat was over, and then proceeded orderly to feed in the cool upon the mountain.

BETWEEN the temple and the church is a road, which, branching from that on Tretus, crosses the valley, and passing through the opposite ridge turns to the right to a village called Hagio Georgio or St. George, from whence we procured tools to dig, and wine, with other necessaries. Near are vestiges, perhaps of Bembina; a village, from which as well as from Nemea the region was sometimes named. On the left hand, at a distance from the road, is a small romantic monastery, fixed as it were against the side of a steep mountain, high up. It possesses a most transparent water and an old picture of the Panagia or Virgin Mary, which performs miracles and is covered, except the face and hands, with silver. The priest showed me in the wall a Greek sepulchral inscription, ΛΕΟΝΤΙΣ ΧΑΙΡΕ, *Leontis farewell.*

CHAP. LVII.

To Cleonæ --- Arrive at Corinth --- The situation --- The ports --- The city destroyed and re-peopled --- Described by Strabo --- By Pausanias --- Taken by Alaric and the Turks --- Its present state --- A ruin.

WE passed by the fountain at Nemea to regain the direct road from Argos to Corinth, re-ascending Tretus. We then travelled over a mountainous tract among low shrubs; the hills with their tops washed bare, some shining, and with chanels worn in their sides; the way crossed by very deep water-courses and shallow streams. We came to a small plain, in which are some vestiges of Cleonæ; a city once overspreading a knoll or rising rock, and handsomely walled about; deserving in the opinion of Strabo the epithet *well-built* bestowed on it by Homer. It is mentioned by Pausanias as a place not large, with a temple of Minerva. It was eighty stadia or ten miles from Corinth, and fifteen stadia or near two miles from Nemea. Two ways led to Argos, which was an hundred and twenty stadia or fifteen miles distant; one fit for couriers and short; the other that on Tretus, likewise narrow, being inclosed by mountains, but more proper for carriages.

WE continued our journey, and, coming in view of the gulf of Corinth, had on our left a plain covered with vines and olive-groves. The fertility of this region was alluded to by the witty oracle, which answered a person who enquired what he should do to become rich, that he needed only to get all the land between Corinth and Sicyon. We arrived on the Isthmus, and about evening entered the town. We were hospitably received at the house of a Greek named Gorgonda Notara, a baratary

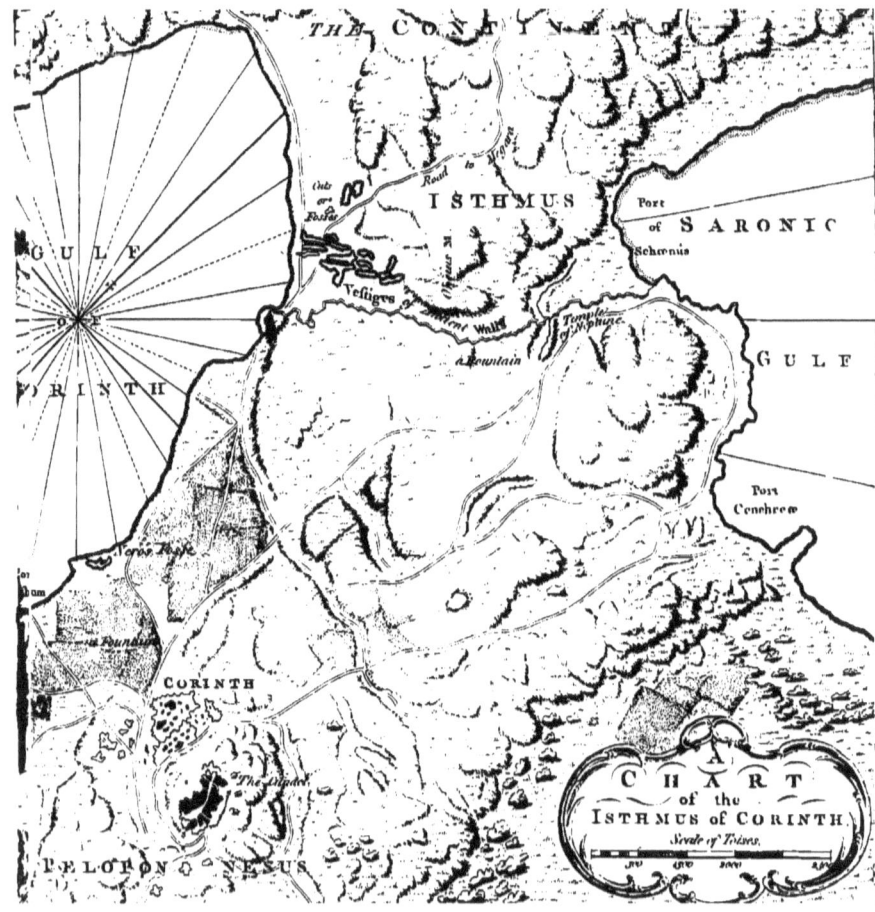

baratary, or perſon under the protection of the Engliſh embaſ-
ſador at Conſtantinople. In the morning we were viſited by
the archons or principal Greeks in a body as at Athens, and
by Mr. Robart a Frenchman, agent of Mr. Keyrac who had
engroſſed the trade of the Morea.

THE city of Corinth ſtands in the Iſthmus on the ſide of the
Peloponneſus, a ſituation once peculiarly happy, from which
alſo its antient proſperity was derived. Its ports were com-
modiouſly diſpoſed by nature, to receive the ſhips of Europe,
and of Aſia, and to render it the centre of their commerce.
The circumnavigation of the Peloponneſus was tedious and
uncertain to a proverb; while at the Iſthmus not only their
cargoes, but, if requiſite, the ſmaller veſſels were eaſily tranſported from ſea to ſea. Moreover, it held the keys of the
peninſula, and taxed both the ingreſs and egreſs. The Iſthmian games likewiſe by the concourſe of people at their
celebration contributed to its opulence, which was immenſe.
The temple of Venus poſſeſſed above a thouſand female ſlaves
conſecrated as courtezans. The prodigality of the merchants
made the place ſo expenſive, it was a ſaying, *that not every
man could go to Corinth*. Amid this luxury it produced many
able ſtateſmen as well as capital maſters in painting, ſculpture,
and the fine arts in general, all which were principally nurtured
there and at Sicyon. The Acrocorinthus or citadel was one of
the horns, on which Philip was adviſed to lay hold, in order
to ſecure the heifer or the Peloponneſus. It has been alſo
ſtyled one of the fetters of Greece.

THE port of Corinth on the ſide of Aſia was named Cenchreæ,
and diſtant as much as ſeventy ſtadia or eight miles and three
quarters. It was forty five ſtadia or above five miles and a half
by ſea from the port of Schœnus. The port toward Italy was
called Lechæum. It lay beneath the city, the road to it between *long walls* reaching twelve ſtadia or a mile and a half.

When Xerxes had defeated the party, which guarded the ſtrait of Thermopylæ, the Peloponneſians firſt deſtroyed the Scironian way, and then erected a wall acroſs the Iſthmus from the ſea of Cenchreæ to that of Lechæum.

A DISPUTE in which the Roman ſenate interpoſed produced a war equally fatal to Grecian liberty and to Corinth. The general of the Achæans was defeated, and flying into Arcadia abandoned this city. Lucius Mummius, who commanded the Roman army, apprehenſive of ſome ſtratagem, did not enter until the third day, though the gates ſtood open. The Corinthians were put to the ſword or ſold as captives, and the city pillaged and ſubverted. The hiſtorian Polybius, who was preſent, laments, among other articles, the unworthy treatment of the offerings, and works of art; relating, that he ſaw exquiſite and famous pictures thrown neglectfully on the ground, and the ſoldiers playing on them with dice. The pretious ſpoil was among the prime ornaments of Rome, and of the places, in which it was diſperſed. The town lay deſolate until Julius Cæſar ſettled there a Roman colony, when, in moving the rubbiſh and digging, many vaſes were found, of braſs or earth finely emboſſed. The price given for theſe curioſities excited induſtry in the new inhabitants. They left no burying-place unexamined, and Rome, it is ſaid, was filled with the furniture of the ſepulchres of Corinth.

STRABO was at Corinth ſoon after its reſtoration by the Romans. He deſcribes the ſite, as follows. " A lofty moun-
" tain, in perpendicular height as much as three ſtadia and a
" half[1], the aſcent thirty ſtadia[2], ends in a pointed ſummit
" called Acrocorinthus. Of this the portion to the north is
" the moſt ſteep, beneath which lies the city on a level area,
" at the foot of the Acrocorinthus. The circuit of the city

[1] Near half a mile.   [2] Three miles and three quarters.

" alone

" alone has been forty ftadia¹, and as much of it as was un-
" sheltered by the mountain has been walled about. Within
" the inclofure was comprehended alfo the Acrocorinthus,
" where the mountain was capable of receiving a wall; and,
" as we afcended, the veftiges were plain; fo that the whole
" circumference exceeded eighty five ftadia². On the other
" fides, the mountain is lefs fteep, but rifes very high, and is
" vifible all around. Upon the fummit is a fmall temple of
" Venus; and below it, the fpring Pirene, which does not
" overflow, but is always full of pellucid and potable water.
" They fay, it unites with fome other hidden veins and forms
" the fpring at the mountain foot, running into the city and
" affording a fufficient fupply for the ufe of the inhabitants.
" In the city is plenty of wells, and in the Acrocorinthus,
" as they fay, for we did not fee any.---There, they relate, the
" winged horfe Pegafus was taken, as he was drinking, by
" Bellerophon.---Below Pirene is the Sifyphéum, fome temple
" or palace of white ftone, the remains not inconfiderable.
" From the fummit is beheld to the north Parnaffus and
" Helicon, lofty mountains covered with fnow; and below
" both, to the weft, the Criffæan gulf bounded by Phocis, by
" Bœotia and the Megaris, and by Corinthia and Sicyonia
" oppofite to Phocis. Beyond all thefe are the mountains
" called the Oneian, ftretching as far as Bœotia and Cithæron
" from the Scironian rocks on the road to Attica." Strabo faw
likewife Cleonæ from thence. Cenchreæ was then a village,
Lechæum had fome inhabitants.

New Corinth had flourifhed two hundred and feventeen
years when it was vifited by Paufanias. It had then a few
antiquities, many temples and ftatues, efpecially about the
Agora or market-place, and feveral baths. The emperor
Hadrian introduced water from a famous fpring at Stymphalus
in Arcadia; and it had various fountains alike copious and

¹ Five miles. ² More than ten miles and a half.

ornamental

ornamental. The ſtream of one iſſued from a dolphin, on which was a brazen Neptune; of another, from the hoof of Pegaſus, on whom Bellerophon was mounted. On the right-hand coming along the road leading from the market-place toward Sicyon was the Odéum, and the Theatre, by which was a temple of Minerva. The old Gymnaſium was at a diſtance. Going from the market-place toward Lechæum was a gate, on which were placed Phaeton and the Sun in gilded chariots. Pirene entered a fountain of white marble, from which the current paſſed in an open chanel. They ſuppoſed the metal called Corinthian braſs to have been immerged, while red-hot, in this water. On the way up to the Acrocorinthus were temples, ſtatues, and altars; and the gate next Tenea, a village with a temple of Apollo ſixty ſtadia or ſeven miles and a half diſtant, on the road to Mycenæ. At Lechæum was a temple and a brazen image of Neptune. At Cenchreæ were temples; and by the way from the city, a grove of cypreſs-trees, ſepulchres and monuments. Oppoſite was *The bath of Helen*, water tepid and ſalt, flowing plentifully from a rock into the ſea. Mummius had ruined the Theatre of Corinth, and the munificence of the great Athenian Atticus Herodes was diſplayed in an edifice with a roof, inferior to few of the moſt celebrated ſtructures in Greece.

THE Roman colony was reſerved to ſuffer the ſame calamity as the Greek city, and from a conqueror more terrible than Mummius, Alaric, the ſavage deſtroyer of Athens and univerſal Greece. In a country harraſſed with frequent wars, as the Peloponneſus has ſince been, the Acrocorinthus was a poſt too conſequential to be neglected. It was beſieged and taken in 1459 by Mahomet the ſecond; the deſpots or lords of the Morea, brothers of the Greek emperor who was killed in defending Conſtantinople, refuſing payment of the arrears of the tribute, which had been impoſed by Sultan Morat in 1447. The country became ſubject to the Turks, except ſuch maritime places as were in the poſſeſſion of the Venetians; and many

of

of the principal inhabitants were carried away to Conftantinople. Corinth, with the Morea, was yielded to the republic at the conclufion of the war in 1698, and again by it to the Turks in 1715.

CORINTH retains its old name, and is of confiderable extent; ftanding on high ground, beneath the Acrocorinthus, with an eafy defcent toward the gulf of Lepanto; the houfes fcattered or in parcels, except in the Bazar or market-place. Cypreffes, among which tower the domes of mofques, with corn-fields, and gardens of lemon and orange-trees, are interfperfed. The air is reputed bad in fummer, and in autumn exceedingly unhealthy. The principal Corinthians retire into the country, from whence our hoft, who had been apprized of our coming, was recently arrived. We vifited the archbifhop, his fon, a young man with a thick black beard; and faw the church, which is decorated, as ufual, with portraits of faints. The extreme heat, with fome other circumftances, rendered us impatient to get away; and prevented us from afcending to the Acrocorinthus, in which are a few inhabitants, as in the citadel of Athens. Wheler relates, that from the top he enjoyed one of the moft agreeable profpects, which this world can afford. He gueffed the walls to be about two miles in compafs, inclofing mofques, with houfes and churches moftly in ruins. An hour was confumed in going up on horfeback. It was a mile to the foot of the hill; and from thence the way was very fteep, with many traverfes. The families living below were much infefted by corfairs, and on every alarm flocked up to the caftle. Our felucca was at anchor in the port ftill called Cenchreæ, now as little frequented as the Piræus. I was affured, that nothing remained there, but a ftatue found in digging and much mutilated.

CORINTH has preferved but few monuments of its Greek or Roman citizens. The chief remains are at the fouthweft corner of the town, and above the Bazar or market; eleven columns fupporting their architraves, of the Doric order, fluted,

and

and wanting in height near half the common proportion to the diameter. Within them, toward the weſtern end, is one taller, though not entire, which, it is likely, contributed to fuſtain the roof. They have been found to be ſtone, not marble; and appear brown, perhaps from a cruſt formed on the outſide. The ruin is probably of very remote antiquity, and a portion of a fabric erected not only before the Greek city was deſtroyed, but before the Doric order had attained to maturity. I fuſpect it to have been the Siſyphéum mentioned by Strabo. North of the Bazar ſtands a large maſs of brick-work, a remnant, it may be conjectured, of a bath or of the Gymnaſium.

CHAP. LVIII.

Of the Iſthmus---The place where veſſels were drawn over--- Attempts to unite the two ſeas---A wall erected acroſs---The temple of Iſthmian Neptune---The ſite.

THE Corinthians related that Neptune and the Sun had contended for their country; that the latter obtained the Acrocorinthus and yielded the poſſeſſion of it to Venus; and that Neptune had continued proprietor of the Iſthmus, which divided the Corinthian from the Saronic gulf, and united the Peloponneſus with the Continent.

THE root of mount Oneius extending along the Iſthmus rendered the Corinthian territory, which was not rich in ſoil, browy and uneven, with hollows. On the ſide of the Corinthian gulf the beach receded toward that of Schœnus, which was oppoſite. There the neck was moſt narrow, the interval between the two ſeas being only forty ſtadia or five miles; and there was the Diolcos or drawing-place, at which it was uſual

to

to convey light veffels acrofs on machines. The fame practice prevailed in the wars of the Turks and Venetians.

VARIOUS attempts have been made to open a communication between the Ionian and the Ægæan fea by a navigable cut through the Ifthmus. The project was adopted by Demetrius Poliorcetes, but his furveyors found the water in the Corinthian gulf much higher than before Cenchreæ, and were of opinion, that Ægina and the neighbouring iflands would be flooded and the canal unferviceable. It was revived by Julius Cæfar, and by Caligula. Nero commenced a foffe from Lechæum, and advanced about four ftadia or half a mile. Atticus Herodes was ambitious of engaging in it, but, as Nero had failed, was afraid of offending the emperor by afking his permiffion. " All thofe, " fays Paufanias, who have endeavoured to render the Pelo- " ponnefus an ifland, have been prevented while labouring to " divide the Ifthmus. It is manifeft where they began digging, " and the rock is untouched. As it was made originally it " remains, and is now Continent.---So difficult is it for man to " force nature." The veftiges of thefe fruitlefs efforts, which he faw, are ftill extant.

THE wall erected by the Peloponnefians from fea to fea, reaching forty ftadia or five miles, croffed the Ifthmus where moft narrow. It was reftored, or another was built, to prevent hoftile incurfions, under the Greek emperors. Conftantine, defpot or lord of Lacedæmon, repaired this wall, which, with a town within it, was called Hexmillia, becaufe the Ifthmus there was fix miles over. Sultan Morat advanced againft it in the year 1447, and the defpot affembled all the people of the Morea for its defence. The Turkifh army ranged in equal extent on the fide of the foffe, and, after mutual cannonading, made a general affault on the feventh day, which fucceeded. Mahomet the fecond in 1451 ordered that the wall fhould be demolifhed. In the war of the Turks and Venetians in 1463 the firft care of the Greeks and Albanians of the Morea was to render it again tenable, and the Venetians affifted, conveying ftone and materials to the fpot by fea, but on the approach of the enemy it was abandoned. Bajazet in 1500 entered the country unobftructed at the Ifthmus. In 1697 the Venetians, who had fubdued the whole Peninfula, were bufied in repairing the fence, to fecure their conquefts by land. The peace concluded in the following year made Hexmillia their boundary. A village on the weftern gulf is ftill called by that name. Pococke mentions great remains of a large fquare caftle at the end of the wall by the fea. The paffes of the mountains to the fouth of Corinth have alfo been fecured with ftrong walls, which run high up the acclivities and are of great extent.

THE temple of the Ifthmian Neptune was fituated near the port of Schœnus. On one fide of the approach was a grove of pine-trees regularly planted; and on the other, ftatues of perfons who had been victorious in the Games. Tritons of brafs were placed on the cell, which was not of the greater fize; and at the entrance were two ftatues of Neptune, and an image of Amphitrite with the fea, likewife of brafs. Among the offerings in the temple was one prefented by Atticus Herodes; Neptune and Amphitrite in a chariot, and the boy Palæmon on a dolphin, all of ivory and gold; the four horfes gilded, with ivory hoofs; and by them two golden Tritons, the lower parts ivory. The fculpture on the bafement beneath the chariot reprefented the Sea producing Venus attended by the Nereids. On the pedeftal of the ftatue of Neptune were carved Caftor and Pollux, deities propitious to veffels and mariners. On the left hand within the inclofure was a temple of Palæmon, in which was his image, and alfo Neptune and Leucothea. Another had a fubterraneous paffage, where, they faid, Palæmon was hid, and if any perfon, whether a Corinthian or ftranger, fwore falfely, it was impoffible for him to efcape punifhment. They facrificed on an antient altar to the Cyclopes. There was alfo a Theatre, and a Stadium of white ftone, worth feeing. The

TRAVELS IN GREECE. 243

care of the Games, which had been committed to the Sicyonians, was reftored to the Roman city.

I VISITED the fite of the Ifthmian temple from the port of Schœnus. It is a large level area, nearly fquare, about half an hour from the fea. Some pieces of pillars, with a Doric capital and other fragments much injured, lie on the fpot. A ruinous church ftanding there had in it a pedeftal and the bafe of a column for the facred table. I obferved the veftiges of a thick wall of maffive ftones, which had defcended from the rock on the fide of the Saronic gulf, and, taking a fweep, had formed two fides of the inclofure; beyond which it was continued on the margin of a wide and very deep water-courfe, but difappears on the brow. At the angle toward the fea is a femi-circular bafement. Wheler faw remains of a town and of the theatre, with feveral old churches. The building and the repairing of the numerous fortreffes, with the wall acrofs the Ifthmus and that behind Corinth, has occafioned a great removal of antient materials from all quarters. I enquired of the goatherds, and they conducted me to various places, but neither the Theatre nor the Stadium were vifible. A marble half-buried in the ground, by a fmall ruined church, was copied here in 1676. The infcription records the munificence of a high-prieft, in erecting new ftructures and in reftoring and decorating thofe which had fuffered from time and earthquakes[1]. I fearched for it unfuccefsfully; and have fince found, that it has been tranfported into Italy, and is now preferved in the Mufeum at Verona.

[1] Wheler, p. 438. See Mufeum Veronenfe, p. xxxix.

CHAP. LIX.

The Archbishop of Athens restored---We leave Corinth---Embark---Of Anticyra---The site.

WE were informed at Corinth, that soon after our departure from Athens the Archbishop had arrived there from Constantinople and been re-instated in his See by officers commissioned for that purpose; that the Bey or Vaiwode had received him kindly, and ordered his musicians to attend him at his palace; and that a complete revolution had happened in his favour. Lombardi was greatly distressed and embarrassed, his intrigues defeated, disappointed in his views of revenge, unincluded in the general amnesty, fearing to return and not knowing whither to fly.

WE hired a bark belonging to the island of Zante. The sailors assisted in transporting the marbles and our baggage across the Isthmus on horses and mules. Our weather-beaten captain left us, well satisfied. We took leave of our host and of Lombardi, whose services we requited with a handsome gratuity in money, besides various presents, some of which he requested. We descended to the sea, the plain on each side of the way covered with caper-bushes in flower. On the shore were several huts and sheds or ware-houses; and near it were barks and small vessels lying at anchor.

WHILE our felucca waited at Epi-yatha, the Corfiote, to whom we had given a passage from Athens, seized an opportunity, which offered, to proceed to Corinth, where he re-joined us. We expected to find him again at the sea-side, but he was gone by land to Patræ, and we saw him no more. On embarking, we were saluted with a discharge of pop-guns or chambres.

Our

Our Janizary and one of our Greeks left us with many friendly wiſhes of proſperity and a happy voyage, intending to return to Athens. In the evening we ſailed, but had little wind, and the following day after noon we put into a bay in Phocis, on the north ſide of the gulf.

The Phocéans ſeizing the temple of Apollo at Delphi, a war, called *the ſacred*, commenced, and laſted ten years; when Philip, father of Alexander the great, avenged the god by deſtroying many of the cities of the pillagers. Anticyra, one of the number, was ſituated in this bay, not far from the ruins of Medeon, which, with Ambryſſus and Stiris ſuffered the ſame puniſhment. This place was again taken and ſubverted by Atilius a Roman general in the war with the Macedonians. It afterwards became famous for its hellebore. That drug was the root of a plant, the chief produce of the rocky mountains above the city, and of two kinds; the black, which had a purgative quality; and the white, which was an emetic. Sick perſons reſorted to Anticyra to take the medicine, which was prepared there by a peculiar and very excellent recipe. By the port in the ſecond century was a temple of Neptune, not large, built with ſelected ſtones, and the inſide white-waſhed; the ſtatue of braſs. The agora or market-place was adorned with images of the ſame metal; and above it was a well with a ſpring, ſheltered from the ſun by a roof ſupported by columns. A little higher was a monument formed with ſuch ſtones as occurred, and deſigned, it was ſaid, for the ſons of Iphitus. One of theſe, Schedius, was killed by Hector, while fighting for the body of Patroclus, but his bones were tranſported to Anticyra; where his brother died after his return from Troy. About two ſtadia or a quarter of a mile diſtant was a high rock, a portion of the mountain, on which a temple of Diana ſtood, the image bigger than a large woman, and made by Praxiteles.

The walls and other edifices at Anticyra were probably erected, like the temple of Neptune, with ſtones or pebbles.

The fite is now called Afprofpitia or *The White Houfes*; and fome traces of the buildings, from which it was fo named, remain. The port is land-locked, and frequented by veffels for corn. Some paces up from the fea is a fountain. At night it blew hard, but we could get no fhelter from the wind on fhore. Our carpets and coverlets were fpread on the poop of our bark, and the men lay on the deck. From that time we began to be fickly; the gulf, with the coafts of the Morea, being infamous for a bad air, efpecially at this feafon or toward autumn.

CHAP. LX.

At Dyftomo --- An infcription --- Ambryffus --- The road to Anticyra.

ON our arrival at Afprofpitia we difpatched men to Dyftomo, a village two hours diftant, to hire fuch beafts as the place afforded, to carry us to the monaftery of St. Luke, and to Caftri or Delphi. The people were bufy at harveft, and declined fending any before the next morning, when a train of affes and mules came early down to the fea-fide with peafants to guide and attend them on foot. Our bark was ordered to wait in the port of Salona. The captain, with two or three failors, accompanied us. We beftrode our beafts, and foon after began to afcend a lofty mountain by a fteep road partly paved. We gained the fummit, beyond which is Dyftomo, where we refrefhed at the houfe of an Albanian.

WE purfued our journey to the monaftery of St. Luke, and returned to Dyftomo in the evening; when we were told, that an infcription had been difcovered in one of the cottages. I was pleafed in copying it, by candle-light, to find it preferved the name of the antient inhabitants. It is on a pedeftal of rough ftone, which has fupported a ftatue of the emperor Marcus

Marcus Aurelius Commodus Antoninus, decreed by the senate, and erected by the city of Ambryssus.

The Athenians and Thebans restored Ambryssus and Stiris, with other cities of Phocis, which Philip had destroyed. The latter people, when the war distinguished by the fatal battle of Chæronea commenced, surrounded Ambryssus with a double wall of the stone of the country, which was dark coloured and exceedingly hard; each circle wanting a little of an orgyia or of six feet in width, the space between them one orgyia, and their height two and a half, when entire; without battlements, towers, and the accustomed ornaments, as constructed for immediate defence. This fortification ranked, in the second century, among the most noted for strength and solidity. Many of the statues of stone in the market-place, which was not large, were then broken. Remnants of the wall may still be seen without the village, which is situated, as the city was, under mount Parnassus.

The road from Ambryssus to Anticyra is described as at first up hill, but, after ascending about two stadia or a quarter of a mile, the ground became level. On the right was a temple of Diana with an image of black stone much reverenced by the Ambryssensians. The way from thence was down a declivity.

CHAP. LXI.

Way from Ambryssus to Stiris --- Of Stiris --- Inscriptions.

WE turned eastward from Dystomo, and in an hour and a half reached the monastery of St. Luke, beneath which in a valley is the site of Stiris now called Palæo-Stiri. This city was about sixty stadia or seven miles and a half from Ambryssus, the

the way in a plain lying between mountains, the part belonging to Ambryſſus planted chiefly with vines, and with a ſhrub by ſome called Coccus, diſpoſed in rows, and producing a ſcarlet dye. The colour was the blood of a ſhort inſect bred in the berries, which were gathered before they were ripe, becauſe it then took wing, reſembling a gnat. The level is now without vines or ſhrubs, but cultivated. It is high above the ſea, and encompaſſed with mountains reaching to the ſky.

STIRIS derived its name from a town in Attica, and the people, it was believed, were originally Athenians expelled by Ægeus. It was ſubject from its ſituation to ſcarcity of water in ſummer; the wells, which were few, furniſhing only ſuch as would ſerve for waſhing, and for cattle. The inhabitants were ſupplied by a fountain hewn in the rock, about four ſtadia or half a mile diſtant. They had a temple of Ceres, of unbaked brick; the image of Pentelic marble. The place is now deſolate, but not without ſome veſtiges.

THE monaſtery of St. Luke was raiſed with the materials of Stiris. Several inſcriptions were fixed in the walls; ſome ſo high as not to be legible. One, copied by Wheler, records the perſons, who defrayed the expenſe of making the chanel for water and of building the fountain; from which it was probably removed. We found a ſtone of the ſepulchral claſs, inſcribed only with the name of the deceaſed, *Pyrrhicus*. Stiris was one hundred and twenty ſtadia or fifteen miles from Chæronea in Bœotia, the way moſtly rough and mountainous.

CHAP.

CHAP. LXII.

Summary of the Life of St. Luke of Stiris.

ST. LUKE of Stiris flourished in the tenth century. He is commemorated by the Greek church on the seventh of February, and styled in the Menology, *The Glory of Hellas* or Greece; but the history given of him is superficial and unsatisfactory. The learned Combefis in 1648 published extracts of his life from a manuscript in the library of the French king. The *holy father* and *wonder-worker* was before so much forgotten, that he is unnoticed by Baronius. A translation of the whole record may be found in the Latin Acts of the Saints. The author was a disciple of St. Luke, is diffuse, and inclines to the marvellous. The following summary will display the wretchedness of Greece after the decline of the Roman empire, and, like a mirror, reflect a portrait of the times, to which it refers.

ST. LUKE Junior was so named to distinguish him from another saint who lived under the same emperors. He was descended of a family, which had fled from Ægina, that island being harrassed by the Saracens in possession of Crete, and settled first by the mountain of St. John in Phocis, but, pirates infesting the seas and coast, removed to a port called Bathys, where Stephen the father of Luke was born; and from thence to a village named Castorium. Luke was seized at an early age with the frenzy of the times, and resolving to be a hermit retired about the year 908, when he was eighteen years old, to the above mountain, commonly called Johanitza; his mother Euphrosyne consenting with reluctance. He was invested with the divine and apostolical habit, as it was termed, by two aged monks on their way to Rome. In the seventh year of his abode in that solitude, the Bulgarians under Symeon made an irruption into the empire. Eubœa and the Peloponnefus were filled with fugitives, and Luke with a multitude paffed over to the neighbouring iflands. He efcaped his purfuers by fwimming, and arrived at Corinth, where, as he was illiterate, he went to fchool. At Patræ was one of the living ftatues, then not infrequent; a madman ftanding on a column. To this Stylites did Luke minifter for ten years, fifhing, getting wood, and dreffing victuals; preventing him from ftarving, and enabling him to preferve his footing on his pedeftal.

PETER, who fucceeded Symeon, making peace with the Romans in 927, Luke returned to Johanitza. From thence, for greater privacy, he withdrew to Calabium. In 934, fome of the Turkifh race overrunning the country, he took refuge in an iflet named Ampelon; and refided three years on that dry and barren rock, often diftreffed for food and water, when the winds were rough and the feas impaffable. He removed next to the fpot, which, fays the biographer, faw him die, and is now enriched by his facred reliques [1]. The companions of his late danger reprefented to him, that he was continually difturbed on the iflet by boats and paffengers. They prevailed on him to leave it, and conducted him to a place delectable indeed, cool and filent, with plenty of limpid water to allay his thirft, or to promote vegetation; and fcarcely acceffible to man. Luke cleared the wood, planted a variety of herbs and trees, was hourly employed in improving and adorning his garden, and in rendering it a terreftrial Paradife. He erected his cell afar off from it and the fountain, for concealment, among fome thickets.

[1] Many names of places in Greece were corrupted or changed in this century. Criffa, it is likely, is intended by the author, where he mentions Ἰν Χρυσῦ επαρχιαν---τα ἰν Χρυσυ μιεν. Bathys, it is fuppofed, was oppofite to Eubœa, and, with Caftorium, in Theffaly; Calabium, in Attica; Ampelon, one of the iflets of the Saronic gulf. Luke retired finally, it is faid, to Σωτηριν χυρον. The editor of *Aɛta S. S.* fuppofes this name derived from the cures effected by the dead faint, and afterwards contracted into Στηριον; but the true reading is, Στηρις χωρον. Thus in the lives of the Saints, Luke, we read, γινομενος αυτω ρησις (fc. σωτηριας)---φασιν εις Ἰον Ἰοπιν Ἰν Στηρις. The place was Stiris.

LUKE

LUKE was now in high reputation, admired for his aufterities, revered for the fanctity of his deportment, and regarded as a prophet. After feven years he called together his friends and neighbours, and taking an affectionate farewel defired their prayers, for it was uncertain whether they fhould meet again. He returned to his cell, and lingered fome months, when his fever increafing he died, much lamented; the people flocking to attend his fick-bed, though it was winter, the weather extremely fevere, and the ways after an immenfe fall of fnow almoft impaffable.

LUKE had directed Gregory, a Prefbyter, to dig beneath where he lay, and bury him; adding, that God would glorify the fpot, and occafion it to be vifited by multitudes of the faithful. He obeyed, and depofiting the facred body publickly, as a common treafure, with the ufual ceremonies, replaced the brick-pavement. After fix months, a monk and eunuch named Cofmas, ftopping on his paffage to Italy, was conducted as by a divine hand to the hermitage and cell of Luke, which pleafed him fo much, that he vowed never to leave it; and feeing his grave neglected, he raifed the holy coffin above the ground, and inclofed it in a tomb, encompaffed with rails to prevent any from touching it, but thofe who were difpofed to approach with devotion.

THE pious care of Cofmas was not unrewarded. Two years after, fome of his followers perceived a fragrant oil flowing plentifully from the holy coffin. This incited them to erect cells; to decorate, as well as they were able, the rude church of St. Barbara; and to provide fmall houfes for the accommodation of ftrangers; believing, it may be prefumed, with the editor of the life, that this property, for which feveral fanctified carcaffes have been renowned, was not beftowed by God but as a teftimony that the body fhould prove an invaluable

fountain

fountain of medicine. Many miraculous cures were performed. The fame of the faint was propagated. His cell was converted into a handfome oratory in the fhape of a crofs; and numbers repaired to his tomb, as to another Siloe.

CHAP. LXIII.

The monaftery of St. Luke --- The founder --- The church --- The reliques of St. Luke --- The tombs of the emperor Romanus and his queen --- The hermitage.

THE monaftery of St. Luke is a barbarous edifice, and of an ordinary appearance. Near it by the road-fide is erected a wooden crofs. It is reckoned two hours from the fea, and four weft of Lebadea. The apartments or cells are very mean. The number of monks was then an hundred and twenty, moft of them abfent, keeping flocks or employed in agriculture. We were entertained by the hegumenos or abbot, who told us that the convent was greatly in debt, and that they fuffered much from exactions, befides paying to the amount of an hundred and feventy-five pounds fterling yearly tribute to the Turks. The air is bad, and water diftant. It is likely they go to the fountain, which fupplied the inhabitants of Stiris.

IN the church is a copy of Iambic verfes in two columns, in an antiquated hand, hung up in a frame, and containing a panegyric on the monaftery written foon after it was built. I copied them from a tranfcript produced by the abbot, which had a profe-expofition in more modern Greek, placed oppofite. The author informs us, that Romanus Porphyrogennetus was the founder. This emperor was the fon of Conftantine Porphyrogennetus, who was defcended from Fla-

vius

vius Bafilius a Macedonian of Armenian origin, and of the race of the Arfacidæ. He was crowned in 945, or about the time when Luke died, by his father, and, at the inftigation of his wife, endeavoured to deftroy him by poifon, but he furvived until 960. Romanus died in 963, about two years after the taking of Crete. Theophano was made regent for her fons, and lived feveral years. A firm attachment to Romanus is recommended in the Iambics. St. Luke was faid to have foretold, that Crete would be fubdued under an emperor of that name. His biographer obferves, that this prophefy had been fulfilled; but, it is remarkable, does not mention the regard fhown by Romanus to his favourite faint.

The monaftery of St. Luke is ftyled by its panegyrift the glory of Hellas and the queen of all monafteries on account of its church, which for magnificence and the grandeur of its proportions is not equalled perhaps in all Greece. This fumptuous fabric within retains the fhape of the oratory, into which the cell of Luke was changed. It has fuffered greatly, as might be expected, from age and earthquakes; and the outfide is much encumbered and deformed by the addition of huge buttreffes to fupport the walls, and by the ftopping up of feveral windows,. particularly thofe of the principal dome. The infide is lined with polifhed marble, impannelled; but fome of the chapels have been ftripped. The pavement is inlaid with various colours artfully difpofed. The domes are decorated with painting and gilding in Mofaic, well executed; reprefenting holy perfonages and fcriptural ftories. The gallery is illuminated with pieces of the tranfparent marble called Phengites, fixed in the wall in fquare compartments, and fhedding a yellow light; but without, refembling common ftone and rudely carved. A fabric thus fplendid in decay, muft have been, when recently finifhed,. exceedingly glorious. The encomiaft extols it as the rival of St. Sophia at Conftantinople, and the crown of the beauties of Hellas.

The

The pretious reliques of the thrice-bleſſed Luke were the important treaſure, which once ennobled this church. Among the cures effected by them and recorded by his biographer, one is of a Dæmoniac. In a diſtich in the Menology, it is affirmed, he had filled Hellas with miracles, and continued them, though dead. In the ſervice of the day, to omit other eulogiums, he is addreſſed as repelling evil affections; as healing lepers and all diſeaſes; as giving ſight to the blind; reſtoring the uſe of limbs; and diſpenſing an univerſal panacéum. The abbot ſhowed us a ſmall ſarcophagus or coffin, with a wooden lid, and a cover before it, in a chapel or receſs. This was the caſket, but he could not inform us what portion of the ſaint it had contained, or by whom or whither removed. He related, that the marble pannel on each ſide formerly exſuded an ointment of prodigious virtue; a tale received by ſome of our company with much reverence and croſſing. The entire body, it is probable, was deemed early too rich a jewel to be poſſeſſed by one ſpot; for in a catalogue of the reliques, which belonged to the great church of the monaſtery of St. Laura at mount Athos, is mentioned a part of St. Luke Stiriotes. He produced likewiſe ſome old pictures of the Panagia or Virgin Mary painted on wood, with a fine portrait of St. Luke the evangeliſt, which had been procured from Muſcovy.

Beneath the church is an extenſive vault, in which maſs is celebrated on certain feſtivals. There is the cœmetery of the monks. The body is incloſed in an horizontal niche on a bier, which is taken out when wanted. The bones, are waſhed with wine, and thrown on a heap. In the area are two flat tombs raiſed above the floor. The marble ſlab on the top of one of them is plain, except a Greek croſs engraved on the right ſide. In the other a plate of braſs or metal has been fixed, with an inſcription. They were erected, as the abbot informed us, over the founder Romanus and the empreſs his wife.

THE

The ſpot cultivated by Luke was poſſeſſed in 1676 by a hermit, whom Wheler viſited. The way from the monaſtery was down the hill to the ſouth; acroſs a ſmall river in a pleaſant plain, planted with vines and olive-trees; and then up a ſteep rock, cut wide enough for two carts to paſs, the aſcent eaſy. On the top were ruins of a town and caſtle; and beneath, a metochi or farm near a port, in which the caloyers or monks fiſh, and veſſels load with corn. He turned to the left over a craggy ridge and arrived at the hermitage, ſituated on the ſouth-eaſt ſide of a rock, and diſtant a mile and a half from the monaſtery. The garden was large, with a cell and a pretty oratory at the upper end. Below was a fountain of good water; and beyond it, a river, which deſcended in a caſcade from the high cliffs of mount Zagara or Helicon, and paſſed by, murmuring among the vaſt rocks and ſtones in its chanel. The hoary head of the hermit, who was clothed in a long brown garment, reſembled the ſnowy ſummits. He carved ſcriptural ſtories on croſſes with admirable art, and was eſteemed a ſaint. An humble companion miniſtered to him, as Luke to Stylites. Two caloyers or monks, who lived in a hut beneath, produced bread and olives, white honeycomb, and excellent wine, for the refreſhment of our traveller; who was ſo charmed with the harmony of birds and the natural beauties of the place, and ſo ſoothed with the idea of enjoying perfect peace and innocence, that, as he relates, he was near reſolving to bid adieu to a vain world, and, like another Coſmas, to fix his abode there.

CHAP.

CHAP. LXIV.

Of Bulis --- Places on the coast between Bulis and the Isthmus --- The bay of Livadostro --- Ascra --- Mount Helicon --- The grove of the Muses --- Of the site, &c.

ANTICYRA had on the east or the side next to the Isthmus the town of Bulis. The mountains, which intervened, were scarcely passable. The port was one hundred stadia or twelve miles and a half on the way to Lechæum. The town was seated on high, at the distance of about seven stadia or near a mile. By the track, ascending to it, was a torrent river, called Heraclius, running into the sea. A fountain was called Saunium. The inhabitants were mostly employed in procuring the shell-fish, which yielded a purple colour. Bulis as well as Stiris was abandoned in the tenth century, and both the cell and garden of Luke had ruin and desolation in their vicinity.

BULIS was on the confines of Bœotia and Phocis. Mychus, the last harbour of Phocis, was in a bay or recess, the deepest of any in the gulf. Beyond it was mount Helicon, and Ascra, and Thespiæ, with its port Creusa: and more within, Pagæ and Oenoe, one bounding the Megaris, the other Corinthia. Pagæ and the port of Schœnus were nearly equi-distant from the Piræus. Between Pagæ and Lechæum was Olmiæ, a promontory opposite to Sicyon, making the recess; once the seat of an oracle of Juno. From thence the passage over to Corinth was about seven miles and a half.

THE course of vessels crossing from the Peloponnesus to the port of Thespiæ was crooked, with a rough sea broken by capes and liable to violent gusts and eddies of wind from the mountains. Sailing from thence, not up the bay, but along the coast

or

or toward Phocis, you came to the port of Thisbe; and, crossing a mountain by the sea, entered a plain, beyond which was another mountain with the city at its feet, on the borders of Thespiæ and Coronea. The plain would have been a lake, but a strong mound was made across it, and, by confining the waters, rescued a portion, which was cultivated. Thisbe was eighty stadia or ten miles from Bulis, and its port one hundred and sixty stadia or twenty miles from Sicyon. The rocks near it abounded in doves. Sailing on as before, you came to Tipha, a small town by the sea.

The gulf or recess within Olmiæ is now called the bay of Livadostro. It is overlooked on the north by mount Elatea or Cithæron, which ends by the harbour of St. Basilio, once Creusa. Beyond a ridge, which commences there, is the harbour of Livadostro or of Thisbe. Farther on, westward, a very high rock runs into the sea; after which is a port and town called Cacos, once Typha. Helicon begins there to soar aloft, until its head reaches above the clouds. By the promontory, which lies west-south-west from St. Basilio, are four islands called Calanesia or *The good Islands*. From St. Basilio Wheler arrived in about an hour at the town of that name, which had been recently ruined by pirates. The remains of antiquity, and the situation, as connected with the port, render it probable that was Thespiæ. He descended from a lofty village named Rimocastri to Castri or the ruins of Thisbe, near a large plain and a stagnant lake. At Livadostro was an old tower and a church frequented by mariners[1].

Ascra, the birth-place of Hesiod, was in the territory of Thespiæ, on the right side of Helicon, distant from the city

---

[1] Wheler found ruins, as he supposes, of Thespiæ, on a hill about four miles from Rimocastri westward, and five or six from Cacos; but this site cannot be reconciled with the geographers. It seems to have been Coronea. See Strabo, p. 411.

The ruins beyond St. Basilio called Palæocastro, on the way to Thebes, were, it is likely, Haliartus. See Pausanias, p. 306.

about forty ſtadia or five miles. It ſtood on a high and rough ſpot, and is characterized by the poet as a wretched village, not pleaſant in any part of the year; but the ſoil produced corn. A tower only remained there in the ſecond century.

HELICON was one of the moſt fertile and woody mountains in Greece. On it the fruit of the adrachnus, a ſpecies of arbutus, or of the ſtrawberry-tree, was uncommonly ſweet; and the inhabitants affirmed, that the plants and roots were all friendly to man; and, that even the ſerpents had their poiſon weakened by the innoxious qualities of their food. It approached Parnaſſus on the north, where it touched on Phocis; and reſembled that mountain in loftineſs, extent, and magnitude.

THE Muſes were the proprietors of Helicon. There was their ſhady grove, and their images; with ſtatues of Apollo and Bacchus, and Linus and Orpheus, and the illuſtrious poets, who had recited their verſes to the harp. Among the tripods, in the ſecond century, was that conſecrated by Heſiod. On the left hand going to the grove was the fountain Aganippe; and about twenty ſtadia or two miles and a half higher up, the violet-coloured Hippocrene. Round the grove were houſes. A feſtival was celebrated there by the Theſpiéans, with Games called Muſéa. The vallies of Helicon are deſcribed by Wheler as green and flowery in the ſpring; and enlivened by pleaſing caſcades and ſtreams, and by fountains and wells of clear water.

THE Bœotian cities in general, two or three excepted, were reduced to inconſiderable villages in the time of Strabo. The grove of the Muſes was plundered under the auſpices of Conſtantine the great. The Heliconian goddeſſes were afterwards conſumed in a fire at Conſtantinople, to which city they had been removed. Their antient ſeat on the mountain, Aganippe and Hippocrene, are unaſcertained. Narciſſus too is forgotten. The limpid baſin, in which he gazed, was ſhown in the Theſpian territory, and the flower, into which he was changed,

continues

continues to love and to adorn its native foil. It abounded in that region, and was very fragrant, in the month of April.

CHAP. LXV.

We leave Dyſtomo --- The way called Schiſte --- The road into Phocis from Bœotia --- Of Orchomenus and Chæronea --- We arrive at Delphi.

WE ſet out from Dyſtomo early in the morning for Caſtri or Delphi. This city was on the ſouth ſide of Parnaſſus, with an abrupt mountain named Cirphis before it; and a river called the Pleiſtus running through a grove beneath.

WE travelled ſome time with the ſea behind us, and afterwards, turning to the left, came on the road antiently called Schiſte or *The rent*, lying between the lofty mountains Cirphis and Parnaſſus, and once deemed to be polluted with the blood of Laius, who was killed there by Œdipus; a principal event in his renowned and tragical ſtory.

A ROAD led into Phocis and to Delphi from Bœotia. On this ſtood Chæronea, near which were the cities of Orchomenus and Lebadea. Panopeus was diſtant twenty ſtadia or two miles and a half from Chæronea, and Daulis ſeven ſtadia more, or near a mile; after which was Schiſte. The bodies of Laius and his ſervant were buried where three ways met, or where the road from Dyſtomo branches off to Daulis and to Delphi. Their graves were marked with heaps of ſtones, perhaps ſtill to be ſeen.

THE treaſury of Minyas, a fabric of remote antiquity, remained entire at Orchomenus in the ſecond century. It is deſcribed as a circular edifice of ſtone with a roof artfully constructed, and as a wonder not inferior to any in Greece or elsewhere. By Chæronea was a barrow with a lion on the top, beneath which the Thebans were interred, who perished in the battle with Philip. A traveller into these countries, under the guidance of Pausanias, will discover classical monuments, natural and artificial curiosities, and vestiges of remarkable buildings and places not hitherto explored.

It was now the beginning of July, but the summits of the mountains were white with snow. Many rills descend, and fertilize a few spots bearing grain, vines, and the cotton-plant. We saw snakes near the water by the road-side, and peasants reaping with green wreaths to defend their heads from the sun. At length, leaving Schiste, we turned to the right and began to ascend an acclivity of Parnassus, the track stony and rough, difficult even to a person on foot. We passed the stream of the Pleistus, which turns an over-shot mill, and, after a wearisome ride of about five hours, alighted at a monastery of the Panagia or Virgin Mary. We found there a caloyer or monk and an old woman, who supplied us with good wine. Our lodging was in the portico of the church, which is supported by broken and ill-matched columns.

CHAP. LXVI.

Sanctity of Delphi --- The Amphictyonic assembly --- The oracle --- The temple --- Its riches --- Its decline.

DELPHI was the chief and most illustrious city in Phocis. Its sanctity was deduced through a long succession of ages from a period involved in fable and obscurity. The influence of its god has controlled the councils of states, directed the course of armies, and decided the fate of kingdoms. The antient

antient hiftory of Greece is full of his energy, and an early regifter of his authority.

The circumjacent cities were the ftewards and guardians of the god. Their deputies compofed the famous Amphictyonic affembly, which once guided Greece. It was convened in fpring and autumn at Delphi or Thermopylæ. The Romans abolifhed that and the Achæan congrefs, but both were revived. Paufanias, who wrote about the year of the Chriftian æra one hundred and feventy five, mentions the former as then confifting of thirty perfons. They prefided at the Pythian games, which were celebrated every fifth year at Delphi, and beftowed the reward of victory, a crown of laurel.

The oracular power was fuppofed to refide in a deep cavern, with a fmall and narrow mouth, faid to have been difcovered by goatherds, who were infpired by the vapour, which arofe out of it, and prophefied as from Apollo. A lofty tripod, decked with laurel, was placed over the aperture. The Pythia or prieftefs, after wafhing her body and efpecially her hair in the cold water of Caftalia, mounted on it, to receive the divine effluvia. She wore a crown of laurel, and fhook a facred tree, which grew by. Sometimes fhe chewed the leaves; and the frenzy, which followed, may with probability be attributed to this ufage, and the gentler or more violent fymptoms to the quantity taken. In one inftance the paroxyfm was fo terrible, that the priefts and fuppliants ran away, and left her alone to expire, it was believed, of the god. Her part was unpleafant, but, if fhe declined acting, they dragged her by force to the tripod. The habit of her order was that of virgins. The rules enjoined temperance and chaftity, and prohibited luxury in apparel. The feafon of enquiry was in the fpring, during the month called Bufius; after which Apollo was fuppofed to vifit the altars of the Hyperboreans. Delphi was conveniently fituated for the conflux of votaries, lying in the centre of Greece, and, as was then imagined, of the Univerfe. The god profpered in his bufinefs.

His

His servants and priests feasted on the numerous victims, which were sacrificed to him; and the riches of his temple were proverbial even before the war of Troy.

The temple of Apollo, it is related, was at first a kind of cottage covered with boughs of laurel; but he was early provided with a better habitation. An edifice of stone was erected by Trophonius and Agamedes, which subsisted about seven hundred years and was burned in the year six hundred and thirty six after the taking of Troy, and five hundred forty-eight before Christ. It is mentioned in the hymn to Apollo, ascribed to Homer. An opulent and illustrious family, called Alcmæonidæ, which had fled from Athens and the tyrant Hippias, contracted with the deputies for the building of a new temple, and exceeded their agreement. The front was raised with Parian marble, instead of the stone called Porus; which resembled it in whiteness, but was not so heavy. A Corinthian was the architect. This temple is described by Pausanias. The pediments were adorned with Diana, and Latona, and Apollo, and the Muses; the setting of Phœbus or the Sun; with Bacchus, and the women called Thyades. The architraves were decorated with golden armour; bucklers suspended by the Athenians after the battle of Marathon, and shields taken from the Gauls under Brennus. In the portico were inscribed the celebrated maxims of the seven sages of Greece. There was an image of Homer, and in the cell was an altar of Neptune, with statues of the Fates, and of Jupiter and Apollo, who were surnamed *Leaders of the Fates*. Near the hearth before the altar, at which Neoptolemus the son of Achilles was slain by a priest, stood the iron chair of Pindar. In the sanctuary was an image of Apollo gilded. The inclosure was of great extent, and filled with Treasuries, in which many cities had consecrated tenths of spoil taken in war, and with the public donations of renowned states in various ages. It was the grand repository of antient Greece, in which the labours of the sculptor and statuary, gods, heroes, and illustrious persons, were

seen

TRAVELS IN GREECE. 263

feen collected and arranged; the inequalities of the area or acclivity contributing to a full difplay of the noble affemblage.

IT is obferved by Strabo that great riches, though the property of a god, are not eafily fecured. Several attempts to rob Apollo are on record. Neoptolemus was flain, while facrificing, on fufpicion. Xerxes divided his army at Panopeus, and proceeded with the main body through Bœotia into Attica, while a party, keeping Parnaffus on the right, advanced along Schifte to Delphi, but was taken with a panic, as near Ilium, and fled. This monarch, it is related, was as well apprized of the contents of the temple and the fumptuous offerings of Halyattes and Crœfus as of the effects which he had left behind in his own palace. The divine hoard was feized by the Phocenfians under Philomelus, and diffipated in a long war with the Amphictyons. The Gauls experienced a reception like that of the Perfians, and manifefted fimilar difmay and fuperftition. Sylla, wanting money to pay his army, fent to borrow from the holy treafury, and when his meffenger would have frightened him, by reporting a prodigy, that the found of a harp had been heard from within the fanctuary, replied, it was a fign that the god was happy to oblige him.

THE trade of Apollo, after it had flourifhed for a long period, was affected by the male practices of fome concerned in the partnerfhip, who were convicted of bribery and corruption, and ruined the character of their principal. The temple in the time of Strabo was reduced to extreme poverty, but the offerings, which remained, were very numerous. Apollo was filent, except fome efforts at intervals to regain his loft credit. Nero attempted to drive him, as it were by violence, from the cavern; killing men at the mouth and polluting it with blood; but he lingered on and would not entirely forfake it. Anfwers were reported as given by him afterwards, but not without fufpicion of forgery. An oracle of Apollo at another place informed the
confulters,

consulters, that he should no more recover utterance at Delphi, but enjoined the continuance of the accustomed offerings.

CHAP LXVII.

Site of Delphi---The court of the temple---Extinction of Apollo--- Vestiges---An inscription---Other inscriptions---Castalia.

THE city of Delphi was seated on a high rock, with the oracle above it; and was in circuit sixteen stadia or two miles. The natural strength of the place excited admiration as much as the majesty of the god. It was free under the Romans. Pausanias has described it. Near the entrance from Schiste was a temple in ruins; with one empty. A third contained a few images of Roman emperors. Beyond these was the temple of Minerva styled Pronæa, because after it was the principal temple, that of Apollo. There the god interposed to repel the Persians. By the temple of Minerva was the portion of Phylacus, an heroum or monument. His spectre, it was believed, had appeared to the Persians and to the Gauls, in armour, huge and tall. A court of the Gymnasium was said to have been the birth-place of the wild sow, which wounded Ulysses. Turning from it to the left and going down not more than three stadia, less than half a mile, you came to the stream of the Pleistus. Proceeding up to the temple of Apollo, on the right hand was the water of Castalia, sweet to drink. The houses, with the sacred inclosure of the temple, which overlooked the city, stood on an acclivity. The area or court within the wall was large, and many ways were cut, leading out of it. A Sibyl was said to have chanted her oracles from a prominent rock above the Athenian portico. Coming out of the temple, the wall was on the left, and also the tomb of Neoptolemus, to whom the Delphians made yearly oblations. Higher up was a stone, not big, on which they poured oil daily, and upon festivals put white wool. On the

the way back to the temple was the fountain Caſſotis, and a wall with a paſſage up to it. The water was ſaid to run underground, and in the ſanctuary of the temple to render women prophetical. Above Caſſotis was a building called Leſche, in which the ſtory of Troy was painted by Polygnotus with equal ſkill and labour. In the ſacred incloſure was a Theatre worthy of notice. Without it and above all, was a Stadium, conſtructed originally with the ſtone of Parnaſſus, which had been changed for Pentelic marble at the expenſe of Atticus Herodes.

APOLLO, though frequently pillaged and poor in money and plate, was ſtill poſſeſſed of an invaluable treaſure in the offerings, which remained within the court of his temple. The number, variety, and beauty of theſe monuments was prodigious. Some were venerable for their antiquity, and the occaſions on which they had been dedicated. The inſcriptions were authentic records, pregnant with information. The Greek was here deeply intereſted, peruſing the national ſtory, and viewing his famous countrymen or illuſtrious anceſtors. The ſtore appeared inexhauſtible, and the robbery of Nero, who removed five hundred brazen images, was rather regretted than perceived. The holy Treaſuries, though empty, ſerved as memorials of the piety and glory of the cities, which erected them. The Athenian portico preſerved the beaks of ſhips and the brazen ſhields; trophies won in the Peloponneſian war. A multitude of curioſities was untouched. The account given of them by Pauſanias may convey ſome idea of the opulence of the ſpot, which indeed was amazing even after repeated diminution.

CONSTANTINE the Great proved a more fatal enemy to Apollo and Delphi than either Sylla or Nero. He removed the ſacred tripods to adorn the Hippodrome of his new city; where theſe, with the Apollo, the ſtatues of the Heliconian Muſes, and the celebrated Pan dedicated by the Greek cities after the war with the Medes, were extant, when Sozomen wrote his hiſtory. Afterwards Julian ſent Oribaſius to reſtore the temple, but he was admonifhed by an oracle to reprefent to the emperor the deplorable condition of the place. " Tell him the well- " built court is fallen to the ground. Phœbus has not a " cottage, nor the prophetic laurel, nor the fpeaking fountain " (Caffotis); but even the beautiful water is extinct."

WE paffed by many broken farcophagi or ftone coffins, when we approached the monaftery. Higher up on the right hand was a fquare ruin with a fmall door-way, perhaps the bafement of the monument of Phylacus. The mafonry is of the fpecies termed Incertum. Some veftiges of temples are vifible; and above them, in the mountain-fide, are fepulchres, niches with horizontal cavities for the body, fome covered with flabs. Farther on is a niche cut in the rock with a feat, intended, it feems, for the accommodation of travellers wearied with the rugged track and the long afcent. On a part fmoothed is engraved a large crofs. The monaftery is on the fite of the Gymnafium. Strong terrace walls and other traces of a large edifice remain. In the wall of the church was a marble in- cribed, ΑΙΑΚΙΔΑΧΑΙΡΕ *Æacides farewel*; and on another, within an olive crown,

Ο ΔΗΜΟΣ Ο ΑΘΗΝΑΙΟΣ
ΠΥΘΙΟΙΣ

In the pavement within was a long infcription, the letters effaced. We found alfo feveral architectural fragments. The village is at a diftance. Caftalia is on the right hand as you afcend to it, the water coming from on high and croffing the road; a fteep precipice, above which the mountain ftill rifes immenfely, continuing on in that direction. The village con- fifts of a few poor cottages of Albanians covering the fite of the temple and oracle. Beneath it to the fouth is a church of St. Elias, with areas, terrace walls, arches, and veftiges of the buildings once within the court. The concavity of the rock in this part gave to the fite the refemblance of a theatre. Turning to the left hand, as it were toward the extremity of one of the wings, you come again to fepulchres hewn in the rock,

rock, and to a femicircular recefs or niche with a feat as on the other fide. Higher up than the village is the hollow of the Stadium, in which were fome feats and fcattered fragments.

At the village we fearched for a piece of wall, of the mafonry termed Incertum, from which Mr. Wood had copied feveral infcriptions. We difcovered a ftone of it containing, befides fome other lines, a decree in honour of an Athenian living in Ætolia, the facred herald of the Amphictyons; giving him from the god a crown of laurel, with various privileges, one of which is precedence at the games. The letters were fair, but with gaps between them, the furface appearing as eaten by time, and refembling honey comb, of a white colour. This, it is likely, was the ftone called Porus. A fpecimen of it may be feen in the collection of marbles at Oxford. The remnant of wall was probably a portion of the cell of the temple, which fronted the road from Caftalia.

Higher up, within the village, is a piece of antient wall concealed from view by a fhed, which it fupports. The ftone is brown, rough, and ordinary, probably that of Parnaffus. On the fouth fide are many infcriptions, with wide gaps between the letters, which are negligently and faintly cut; all nearly of the fame tenor, and very difficult to copy. They regifter the purchafe of flaves, who had entrufted the price of their freedom to the god; containing the contract between Apollo and their owners, witneffed by his priefts and by fome of the archons. This remnant feems to be part of the wall before Caffotis; as above it is ftill a fountain, which fupplies the village with excellent water, it is likely, from the antient fource.

The water of Caftalia, from which the Pythia and the poets, who verfified her anfwers, were believed to derive a large fhare of their infpiration, defcends through a cleft of Parnaffus; the rock on each fide high and fteep, ending in two fummits;

of which, one was called Hyampeia, and had beneath it the sacred portion of Autonoüs, a local hero as diftinguifhed as Phylacus. From this precipice the Delphians threw down the famous Æfop. By the ftream, within the cleft, are fmall broken ftairs leading to a cavity, in which is water, and once perhaps up to the top. Grooves have been cut, and the marks of tools are vifible on the rock; but the current, inftead of fupplying a fountain, now paffes over its native bed, and haftens down a courfe deep-worn, to join the Pleiftus. Clofe by, at the foot of the eaftern precipice, is a bafin with fteps on the margin, once, it is likely, the bath ufed by the Pythia. Above, in the fide of the mountain, is a petty church dedicated to St. John, within which are excavations refembling niches, partly concealed from view by a tree. The water is limpid, and exceedingly cold. Returning from the village in the evening, I began to wafh my hands in it, but was inftantly chilled, and feized with a tremor, which rendered me unable to ftand or walk without fupport. On reaching the monaftery, I was wrapped in a garment lined with warm fur, and, drinking freely of wine, fell into a moft profufe perfpiration. This incident, when Apollo was dreaded, might have been embellifhed with a fuperftitious interpretation. Perhaps the Pythia, who bathed in this icy fluid, miftook her fhivering for the god.

C H A P. LXVIII.

Of mount Parnaffus --- The Corycian cave --- Wheler's journey on mount Parnaffus --- Remarks --- Some Albanians arrive at the monaftery.

PARNASSUS was the weftern boundary of Phocis, and ftretching northward from about Delphi toward the Œtæan mountains feparated the weftern Locri from thofe who poffeffed the

the fea-coaft before Eubœa. It was a place of refuge to the Delphians in times of danger. In the deluge, which happened under Deucalion, the natives were faved on it by following the cry of wolves. On the invafion by Xerxes fome tranf-ported their families over to Achaia, but many concealed them in the mountain and in Corycium, a grotto of the Nymphs.

ALL Parnaffus was renowned for fanctity, but Corycium was the moft noted among the hallowed caves and places. " On the
" way to the fummits of Parnaffus, fays Paufanias, as much as
" fixty ftadia ¹ beyond Delphi, is a brazen image; and from
" thence the afcent to Corycium is eafier for a man on foot and
" for mules and horfes.---Of all the caves, in which I have
" been, this appeared to me the beft worth feeing. On the
" coafts and by the fea-fide are more than can be numbered;
" but fome are very famous both in Greece and in other coun-
" tries.---The Corycian cave exceeds in magnitude thofe I have
" mentioned, and for the moft part may be paffed through
" without a light. It is fufficiently high; and has water,
" fome fpringing up, and yet more from the roof, which petri-
" fies; fo that the bottom of the whole cave is covered with
" fparry icicles. The inhabitants of Parnaffus efteem it facred
" to the Corycian Nymphs and particularly to Pan. From the
" cave to reach the fummits of the mountain is difficult even
" to a man on foot. The fummits are above the clouds, and
" the women called Thyades madden on them in the rites of
" Bacchus and Apollo." Their frantic orgies were performed yearly.

WHELER and his company afcended Parnaffus from Delphi, fome on horfes, by a track between the Stadium and the clefts of the mountain. Stairs were cut in the rock, with a ftrait chanel, perhaps a water-duct. In a long hour, after many traverfes, they gained the top, and entering a plain turned to

¹ Seven miles and a half.

the right, toward the fummits of Caftalia, which are divided by deep precipices. From this eminence, they had a fine profpect of the gulf of Corinth and of the coaft; mount Cirphis appearing beneath them as a plain, bounded on the eaft by the bay of Afprofpitia and on the weft by that of Salona. A few fhepherds had huts there. They returned to the way, which they had quitted, and croffed a hill covered with pines and fnow. On their left was a lake, and beyond it a pike, exceedingly high, white with fnow. They travelled to the foot of it through a valley four or five miles in compafs; and refted by a plentiful fountain called Drofonigo, the ftream boiling up, a foot in diameter, and nearly as much above the furface of the ground. It runs into the lake, which is about a quarter of a mile diftant to the fouth-eaft. They did not difcover Corycium, or proceed farther on, but keeping the lake on their right came again to the brink of the mountain, and defcended by a fteep and dangerous track to Racovi, a village four or five miles eaftward from Delphi.

IT was the opinion of Wheler that no mountain in Greece was higher than Parnaffus; that it was not inferior to mount Cenis among the Alps; and that, if detached, it would be feen at a greater diftance than even mount Athos. The fummits are perpetually increafing, every new fall of fnow adding to the perennial heap, while the fun has power only to thaw the fuperficies. Caftalis, Pleiftus, and innumerable fprings are fed, fome invifibly, from the lakes and refervoirs; which, without thefe drains and fubterraneous vents would fwell, efpecially after heavy rain and the melting of fnow, fo as to fill the vallies and run over the tops of the rocks down upon Delphi, fpreading wide an inundation, fimilar, as has been furmifed, to the Deucalionéan deluge.

WE purpofed to afcend Parnaffus, hoping to find the Corycian cave, but before we had finifhed at Delphi, feventeen Albanians arrived at the monaftery. Thefe belonged to a guard, which

which patroled on the roads. They were robuſt dirty ſavages, wearing their hair in ſmall plaits hanging down their ſhoulders. In the evening they roaſted a ſheep, and the captain invited us to partake, and, on our making ſome excuſe, preſented us with a portion of the meat. After eating in groups, they continued their wild ſinging and dancing to a late hour. They ſlept on the ground, each with his arms by him, and ſome much nearer to us than was agreeable. Sultan Morat in 1447 forced many of their nation to change their religion, and converted the churches of Albania into moſques. This ſet were Mahometans, deſcended from Chriſtian proſelytes. They were repreſented to us as drunken and quarrelſome, given to deteſtable vices, and as dangerous as the banditti, againſt whom they were employed. We diſliked their company, and dropped our intended excurſion in queſt of the cave; it appearing more prudent to depart ſuddenly for the port of Salona, in which, as a ſailor informed us, our bark was then at anchor.

CHAP. LXIX.

Of Cirrha---Of Amphiſſa---The port of Delphi---We leave Delphi ---Embark.

DELPHI was diſtant ſixty ſtadia, or ſeven miles and a half from the ſea at Cirrha. This city was the Criſſa of Homer, from which the Criſſæan bay had its name. The port was called Chalæon, and frequented by veſſels from Sicily and Italy. The people were enriched by the cuſtoms, but, beſides other impieties, they impoſed heavy taxes on the votaries of Apollo, who arrived there; and encroached on his boundary. War was declared and the oracle conſulted by the deputies, when the Pythia replied, that the ſea muſt waſh the domain of Apollo before the city, which was beſieged, could be taken. The

Cirrhæan

Cirrhæan territory was immediately confecrated by the advice of Solon, one of their generals. The town was fupplied by a duct with water from the Pleiftus. He intercepted the current, and infufing roots of hellebore it produced a general flux. Cirrha was demolifhed, and dire execrations were pronounced againft any perfon or power prefuming to moleft the god in the enjoyment of his new poffeffions.

THE port of Cirrha was convenient for Amphiffa, a principal city of the Locri Ozolæ, diftant from Delphi one hundred and twenty ftadia or fifteen miles. The people feized it, recultivated the plain, and exacted from ftrangers even more than the Criffæans, but not with impunity. The *facred war* followed and Amphiffa was deftroyed.

CIRRHA continued to be the port of Delphi in the time of Paufanias. It had then a temple of Apollo. On the way to it was the Hippodrome, or courfe for the Pythian horfe-races. This was in the plain, then naked. No one would plant, either fearing the curfe, or knowing the foil to be unfit for trees.

WE left the monaftery early in the morning, and going back to the mill, defcended into the vale between the Cirphis and Parnaffus. Here, as we travelled along, we had frefh occafion to regard with wonder the rough and romantic fituation of Delphi; the rock rifing prodigioufly high with precipices, fome perpendicular, between us and the village, and ftill towering up behind; the fummits intruding into the blue fky. The fmall ftream of the Pleiftus, inftead of purfuing its way to Cirrha and the fea, was abforbed among the olive-trees, vineyards, and plantations.

THE rich vale ending, we croffed the Cirrhæan or Criffæan plain, which, as antiently, was bare. We faw the town of Salona on our right, at a diftance, on a knoll or eminence.

We

We paſſed over a root of mount Cirphis, and came, after about three hours, in view of our bark, lying at anchor, with ſome ſmall-craft. By the water-ſide was a magazine or two, and a mean cuſtom-houſe, at which we waited for a boat, to convey us on board. The property of the ſoil is again changed, and Cirrha belongs, not to Delphi and Apollo, but to Amphiſſa or as it is now called Salŏna.

CHAP. LXX.

At Gallixithium---At Thithavra---A plane-tree on the ſhore of the Morea---Site of Boſtitza---Ægium----The mouth of the gulf---Lepanto---The Caſtles---Arrive at Patræ.

WE ſet ſail without delay, and, after clearing the bay of Salona, the wind blowing hard and contrary, got to Gallixithium, a mean town, of mud-built houſes, with traces of antient wall by the ſea-ſide. It is ſuppoſed Œanthéa, a town of the Locri Ozolæ.

WE were detained in port until the morning, when we tacked often, and the gale increaſing, put in for ſhelter at Thithavra, where we found other ſmall-craft. We had in view the Acro-corinthus, and the flat ſummit by Nemea.

EARLY in the morning we croſſed over to the Morea, and anchored by ſome ſmall-craft and a French veſſel, which had ſailed with us from Corinth. A plane-tree by the ſhore is remarkable for its vaſt ſize and height. It is ſound and flouriſhing, with huge limbs, affording a moſt capacious and thick ſhade. A company of armed Albanians, like that at Delphi, was ſleeping beneath it, and prevented us from meaſuring the trunk. We were told that an earthquake and a mighty inundation

dation of the sea happened not many years ago; that the water thrice mounted above this tree, and the tall cliff behind it; that some of the branches were torn off by its violence; and that the people fled to the mountains.

ABOVE the sea is a town called Boſtitza, which ſtands on or near the ſite of Ægium; for by the plane-tree is a plentiful ſource of excellent water, ſtreaming copiouſly from ten or more mouths of ſtone; and many tranſparent ſprings riſe on the beach. Ægium is deſcribed as retired from the ſhore, which afforded plenty of water agreeable to drink from the fountain and pleaſing to the eye.

ÆGIUM was a city of no mean note, in the region called Ægialos and afterwards Achaia. It had a theatre and temples, ſome near the ſea. One was of Jupiter ſtyled Homagyrius, becauſe Agamemnon aſſembled there the principal chieftains of Greece before the expedition to Troy. It was for many ages the ſeat of the Achæan congreſs. The Turks burned Ægium in 1536, and put the inhabitants to the ſword, or carried them away into ſlavery.

IT continued to blow until it was dark, when a calm enſued. We proceeded, before the dawn of day, about two miles toward the mouth of the gulf, which is formed by the promontories once called Rhium and Antirhium. The wind, ſetting in again, met us, and we tarried near a point of land named antiently Drepanum, becauſe the curve between it and Rhium reſembled a Sicle. We ſailed in the evening, and tacked from ſhore to ſhore, but made little way all night.

AT day-break we had a diſtinct view of Lepanto, a city often attacked, taken, and recovered in the wars of the Turks and Venetians. It is ſeated on the acclivity of a ſteep hill, and has been likened to the Papal crown, the lateral walls being croſſed

by

by four other ranges, and afcending to a point or fummit, on which is a caftle terminating the fortification. The wall next to the fea is indented with an oval harbour, of which the entrance is narrow and capable of admitting only barks and fmall gallies. The valley on each fide of the town was dufky with trees. The gulf is named from it; but by the Greeks the place is called Epactos, as antiently Naupactos. It belonged to the Locri Ozolæ; whofe fea-coaft, beginning from Cirrha and Phocis, extended a little more than two hundred ftadia or twenty five miles.

Passing Lepanto, we came between the promontories Rhium and Antirhium, diftant from each other feven ftadia, or lefs than a mile. The ftrait, which divides them, was five ftadia wide. The Chriftians often invading the Ottoman dominions on this fide, Bajazet in 1482 erected caftles at the mouth of the gulf. One is called the caftle of Romelia, the other of the Morea. Both were taken by the Venetian admiral in 1536. The Turkifh governors in 1687 blowed up their walls, which were afterwards reftored. We failed clofe by the latter, a mean fortrefs, on a low point of land, much out of repair, with the lion of St. Mark over the gate-ways.

We doubled cape Rhium, and before noon anchored in the road of Patræ. Between this place and Lepanto the Chriftians in 1571 obtained a victory from the Turks in one of the moft confiderable battles, which ever happened at fea. The gulf of Corinth was reckoned eighty five miles long.

CHAP. LXXI.

Of Patræ --- The city --- Feaſt of Diana --- The preſent town --- The ſouth ſide of the gulf of Corinth --- Neglect of travellers.

PATRÆ aſſiſted the Ætolians, when invaded by the Gauls under Brennus; but afterwards was unfortunate, reduced to extreme poverty, and almoſt abandoned. Auguſtus Cæſar reunited the ſcattered citizens, and made it a Roman colony, ſettling a portion of the troops, which obtained the victory of Actium, with other inhabitants from the adjacent places. Patræ reflouriſhed, and enjoyed dominion over Naupactus, Œanthéa, and ſeveral cities of Achaia.

In the time of Pauſanias, Patræ was adorned with temples and porticoes, a Theatre, and an Odéum which was ſuperior to any in Greece but that of Atticus Herodes at Athens. In the lower part of the city was a temple of Bacchus Æſymnetes, in which was an image preſerved in a cheſt, and conveyed, it was ſaid, from Troy by Eurypylus; who, on opening it, became diſordered in his ſenſes. By the port were temples; and by the ſea, one of Ceres, with a pleaſant grove and a prophetic fountain of unerring veracity in determining the event of any illneſs. After ſupplicating the goddeſs, with incenſe, the ſick perſon appeared, dead or living, in a mirror ſuſpended ſo as to touch the ſurface of the water.

In the citadel of Patræ was a temple of Diana Laphria, with her ſtatue in the habit of a huntreſs, of ivory and gold, given by Auguſtus Cæſar, when he laid waſte Calydon and the cities of Ætolia to people Nicopolis. The Patrenſians honoured her with a yearly feſtival, which is deſcribed by Pauſanias, who was a ſpectator. They formed a circle round the altar with pieces

of

of green wood, each sixteen cubits long; and within heaped dry fewel. The folemnity began with a moft magnificent proceffion, which was clofed by the Virgin-Prieftefs in a chariot drawn by ftags. On the following day, the city and private perfons offered at the altar; fruits, and birds, and all kinds of victims, wild boars, ftags, deer, young wolves, and beafts full grown; after which the fire was kindled. He relates, that a bear and another animal forced a way through the fence, but were re-conducted to the pile. It was not remembered that any wound had ever been received at this ceremony, though the fpectacle and facrifice were as dangerous as favage. The number of women at Patræ was double that of the men. They were employed chiefly in a manufacture of flax, which grew in Elis, weaving garments and attire for the head.

PATRÆ has been often attacked by enemies, taken, and pillaged. It is a confiderable town, at a diftance from the fea, fituated on the fide of a hill, which has its fummit crowned with a ruinous caftle. This made a brave defence in 1447 againft Sultan Morat, and held out until the peace was concluded, which firft rendered the Morea tributary to the Turks. A dry flat before it was once the port, which has been choked with mud. It has now, as in the time of Strabo, only an indifferent road for veffels. The houfe of Nicholas Paul Efquire, the Englifh conful, ftood on part of the wall either of the Theatre or the Odéum. By a fountain was a fragment of a Latin infcription. We faw alfo a large marble buft, much defaced; and the French conful fhowed us a collection of medals. We found nothing remarkable in the citadel. It is a place of fome trade, and is inhabited by Jews, as well as by Turks and Greeks. The latter have feveral churches. One is dedicated to St. Andrew the Apoftle, who fuffered martyrdom there, and is of great fanctity. It had been recently repaired. The fite, by the fea, is fuppofed that of the temple of Ceres. By it is a fountain. The air is bad, and the country round about overrun with the low fhrub called Glycyrrhiza or Licorice.

SICYON,

SICYON, with several cities of Achaia, stood on the south side of the gulf of Corinth. Wheler visited the former, now called Basilico. Pococke mentions a ruin on a high hill, about six miles nearer to Patræ, and supposes it Ægira. About seven miles beyond, he saw a piece of thick wall on the sea-shore, where perhaps was Helice. At Vostitza, was a ruin of a small antient building, at the west end of the town; and in the front of an old church, a fine relief, of a lion seizing a horse. A river, the Selinus, falls into the sea to the east of the town, and has over it a large bridge. In a beautiful little plain, a league to the south, is another river, either the Phœnix or Meganitas. From Corinth to the castle of the Morea is reckoned a journey of twenty two hours.

THE places between Sicyon and Patræ, their order, their situation, their distances from the sea and from each other, are so exactly marked by Strabo and Pausanias, as not easily to be mistaken [1]. It is matter of regret, that travellers too commonly hasten along in the beaten road, uninformed of the objects on the way; when by consulting and following those invaluable guides, they might increase their own pleasure, and at the same time greatly advance the general knowlege of antient geography.

C H A P.

[1] From Patræ to the promontory Rhium the distance was fifty stadia. Then to port Panormus, fifteen. To the wall of Minerva, fifteen. To port Erineus, now, it is supposed, Lambirio, ninety. To Ægium, sixty. In the whole, two hundred and thirty stadia or twenty eight miles and three quarters. Strabo reckons Rhium and Antirhium forty stadia from Patræ. This city was forty stadia nearer to Ægium by land than by sea. After some rivers was cape Drepanum. A little above the road were remains of Rypes, about thirty stadia from Ægium. Forty stadia beyond Ægium was Helice. From this city the worship of Jupiter Heliconius was transferred to Ionia. The inundation attending the earthquake, which destroyed it, was so great that only the tops of the trees in the grove of Neptune were visible. The town, though twelve stadia or a mile and a half from the shore, was absorbed. Remnants of the buildings were discernible under the water in the time of Pausanias. Beyond Helice on the right of the road was Cerunéa on a mountain. Proceeding, not a great way, you turned aside

CHAP LXXII.

We leave Patræ --- On the coast of Ætolia --- Flats --- The river Achelous --- The islands called Echinades --- The Fishery --- A monoxylo or skiff --- Towns --- Cause of the bad air in the gulf --- Encroachments of the river.

WE enquired at Patræ for ruins of the antient cities of the Peloponnesus, but unsuccessfully. The vestiges of the former inhabitants overspread the country, but have not awakened curiosity or reflection in the present race. Finding we could obtain no intelligence, we resolved to proceed in our bark to Chiarenza, or, as it was once called, Cyllene. This place was the port of Elis, and lay in our course to Zante, whither, if we tarried in the Morea, we purposed to send our baggage, retaining only necessaries for the journey. On the second evening after our arrival at Patræ, we bade adieu to the worthy consul, by whom we had been politely entertained, and descended to the sea, at a late hour, accompanied by his son; our servants lighting us with long paper lanthorns.

WE passed over to the level coast opposite to Patræ, antiently called Ætolia, now Romelia. In the afternoon I went ashore in the boat with the captain, and the men gathered tall strong bull-rushes to tie the sails. Some peasants were dividing the carcase of a cow, which they had killed, among the thickets at

aside to Bura, likewise on a mountain, forty stadia from the sea. The more antient city had been absorbed with Helice. On the way from Bura toward the shore, was a river called Buraicus and a small Hercules in a cave, which was distant on the direct road thirty stadia from Helice, and seventy two from the port of Ægira, crossing the river Crathis, by which Ægæ once stood. Ægira was twelve stadia above its port, which was an hundred and twenty from that of Pellene. This was a strong fortress sixty stadia above the sea, and the place next Sicyon.

a distance,

a diſtance, and wanted to ſell part of it; but, ſeeing me in the long dreſs with a white towel round my head, the meſſenger miſtook me for a Turk, and ran away. He was prevailed on to return, and we went with him.

THE water was weedy, and ſo ſhallow, that our bark anchored afar off from the ſhore. In the evening the air ſtunk abominably; and frogs croaked in chorus without ceaſing. We anchored again, the following afternoon, near a very large tract of low land overſpread by the ſea and encompaſſed with reed-fences. Theſe flats have been formed chiefly by the mud of the river Achelous, which was deſcribed to us as of great ſize, and as flooding the country in winter.

THE Achelous is ſtyled by Homer the prince of rivers. The ſtream deſcended from the north and mount Pindus into the plain of Acarnania, and, dividing that country from Ætolia, entered the ſea by the city Œniadæ, creating continually new land. Alcmæon ſettled near it, when directed by the Delphic oracle to fly from the Fury, which haunted him as the murderer of his mother, to ſome ſpot manifeſted by the ſea after his pollution. The two nations, their boundaries ſhifting, engaged in many bloody conflicts for the region about the mouth, called the Parachelöitis.

BEFORE the Achelous lay the iſlets named Echinades, many in number, barren and rugged. Several of theſe had been added very early to the continent, and, in the opinion of an antient hiſtorian, it was eaſy to foretell the fate of the remainder. In the time of Strabo, the water ſtagnated in a large lake about Œniadæ; and, he obſerves, ſome of the Ætolian promontories had been iſlands. Auguſtus Cæſar removing the inhabitants into Nicopolis, the city which he founded near Actium, the country was unſown, and the quantity of ſlime decreaſed. This is aſſigned by Pauſanias as the reaſon why the

junction

TRAVELS IN GREECE.

junction of the Echinades with the main land had not been completed. Depopulation has alfo fince retarded its progrefs.

THE Achelous was among the rivers moft noted for fhoals of fifh, which entered from the fea, efpecially in fpring. It was particularly frequented by mullet, which delight in foul and muddy water. The multitudes now taken yearly at that feafon on the fhallows furpafs belief. The rows are made into Bottarga and Caviaro; a fpecies of food, which the antients efteemed as a delicacy. The fmall fheds, erected each on a fingle poft, extended as far as we could fee, and appeared innumerable. They are defigned for watchmen, who obferve the finny fquadrons, and by clofing the avenues of the fences, fecure them in prifon.

ON a knoll within the inclofures was a fmall thatched hut, which we endeavoured to reach in our boat, but we grounded at the diftance of half a mile. A man waded to it, and procured for us a monoxylo or tray, the trunk of a tree made hollow. This is the common vehicle over the flats; capable of containing a very few perfons; long, narrow, and unfteady; but refpectable for its antiquity, being on record among the veffels in primitive ufe; fuiting the fhallows, on which navigation received its firft rudiments. A boy, who efpied us, fled in extreme confternation, punting with all his might toward the hut, jumping into the water, and pufhing his fkiff before him, when impeded by the weeds, which fpring up from the bottom. We purchafed fome dried fifh, and returned in the monoxylo to our boat.

WE could fee many veffels lying at a diftance off Meffa-longia and Nathaligo, two towns inhabited chiefly by Greeks, on little iflands amid the flats. The monoxyla or fkiffs carry every thing to and fro, and in calm weather are employed in lading them, principally with fifh, fpreading over the fhining furface of the water, innumerable.

THE wind in Autumn commonly sets toward the Morea and into the gulf of Corinth, before which the Echinades with Cephallenia lie. It becomes impregnated with salts from putrefying weeds in its passage over these extensive flats; wafting noisome vapours and disease. In the creeks, where we stopped, we had seen sick persons, removed for ease and quiet from the vessels, lying on the rocks. The complaints, which prevailed among us, may be imputed partly to fatigue. Our servants had been all ill at different times; and one, with a sailor, who attended us to Delphi, was now unable to stand on the deck.

THE changes effected by the Achelous deserve to be attentively examined. The low land on the south side of the Corinthian gulf, and on the western coast of the Morea, is perhaps its offspring; and Lechæum as well as the port of Patræ may have been choked by the river. The traveller, who shall trace the past encroachments, will be enabled to prognosticate with certainty many future alterations. Perhaps in some distant age the growing soil may unite with the opposite shore of the Morea, and the entrance of the Corinthian gulf be closed up; when that water will be seen removed from the sea in the same manner by the Achelous, as the bay of Myus has been by the Mæander.

CHAP. LXXIII.

We sail---In the bay of Chiarenza---Cyllene---At Gastouni---At Elis---Its territory sacred---The city---Vestiges.

WE sailed at night with a strong wind and a high sea, which beating on the side of the vessel rolled us along toward Chiarenza. We passed cape Papa, called antiently Araxus, a promontory, which belonged to Elis, and was one thousand stadia or an hundred

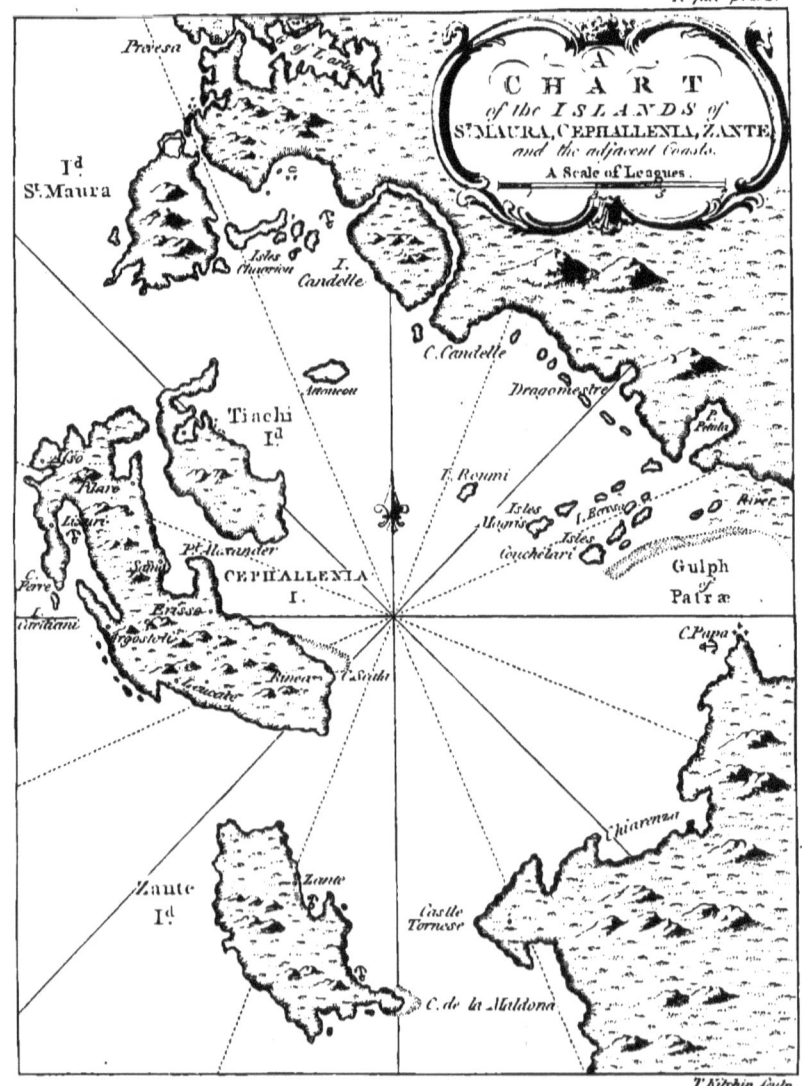

hundred and twenty five miles from the Isthmus. Dyme, a city without a port, the last of Achaia to the west, was sixty stadia or seven miles and a half from the cape. Olenus, a deserted city, was forty stadia or five miles from Dyme, and eighty stadia from Patræ.

WE anchored soon after day-break in the bay of Chiarenza, which is frequented by small-craft from Zante and the places adjacent, chiefly for passengers and provisions. On the beach was a low cart, the only one we had seen since we left Sigeum, the form and wheels antique, drawn by two horses abreast. The buildings are a custom-house and a few sheds or magazines.

CYLLENE stood on a rough tongue of land on the south side of the bay, an hundred and twenty stadia or fifteen miles from Elis. It was a middling village, and possessed two or three temples. In one was an ivory statue of Æsculapius, wonderful to behold. The site under the Venetians was occupied by Chiarenza, a flourishing town. Sultan Morat in 1447 laid waste the Morea as far as this place, and carried off sixty thousand people. Some masses of wall and other vestiges remain. The port is choked up. Cyllene which gave its name to Mercury was a very high mountain in Arcadia celebrated for his temple. Zante is opposite to the region of Elis.

WE were informed here of a place called Palæopolis, which we agreed to visit, hoping to find ruins of the city of Elis. Horses, and men to attend them on foot, with an agoiatis or guide to Gastouni were procured without difficulty. We dined at a Greek monastery, half an hour from the shore, and then proceeded through a plain. On our right hand was a town named Clemontzi or Clemouzzi, beyond which on a hill distinctly visible from Zante, and about six miles from the shore, is a fortress commonly called *Castle-Tornese*. The Venetians under Morosini appeared before it in 1687, after their victory at Patræ, and it surrendered. A barrow occurred on our left, and afterwards two near each other. We then croſſed the river Peneus, a ſhallow ſtream in a wide and deep bed. In about three hours we arrived at Gaſtouni, which is a large town.

Our captain conducted us to the houſe of a Zantiote, who admitted us into his garden, in which we paſſed the night. We were detained, waiting for horſes, until the following evening, when in four hours we reached Callivia, a ſmall village near Palæopolis. By the way was a barrow. We ſaw large tracts of land overrun with tall thiſtles and the licorice-ſhrub; cotton-grounds and vineyards interſperſed. The garden of a peaſant was our lodging.

The city of Elis owed its origin to an union of ſmall towns, after the Perſian war. It was not encompaſſed immediately with a wall; for it had the care of the temple at Olympia, and its territory was ſolemnly conſecrated to Jupiter. To invade or not protect it was deemed impiety; and armies, if marching through, delivered up their weapons, which, on their quitting it, were reſtored. Amid warring ſtates the city enjoyed repoſe, was reſorted to by ſtrangers, and flouriſhed. The region round about it was called Cœle or *Hollow*, from the inequalities. The country was reckoned fertile, and particularly fit for the raiſing of flax. This, which grew no where elſe in Greece, equalled the produce of Judæa in fineneſs, but was not ſo yellow.

Elis was a ſchool, as it were, for Olympia. The Athletic exerciſes were performed there, before the more ſolemn trial, in a Gymnaſium, by which the Peneus ran. The Hellanodics or Præfects of the games paired the rival combatants by lot, in an area called Plethrium or *The Acre.* Within the wall grew lofty plane-trees; and in the court, which was called the Xyſtus, were ſeparate courſes marked for the foot-races. A ſmaller court was called the quadrangle. The Præfects, when choſen, reſided for ten months in a building erected for their uſe, to be inſtructed in the duties of their office. They attended before

ſun-fun-rife, to prefide at the races; and again at noon, the time appointed for the Pentathlum or *Five Sports*. The horfes were trained in the Agora or market-place, which was called the Hippodrome. In the Gymnafium were altars, and a cenotaph of Achilles. The women, befides other rites, beat their bofoms in honour of this hero, on a fixed day toward funfet. There alfo was the town-hall, in which extemporary harangues were fpoken, and compofitions recited. It was hung round with bucklers for ornaments. A way led from it to the baths through the *Street of Silence*; and another to the market-place, which was planned with ftreets between porticoes of the Doric order adorned with altars and images. Among the temples one had a circular periftyle or colonnade, but the image had been removed and the roof was fallen, in the time of Paufanias. The Theatre was antient, and was alfo a temple of Bacchus, one of the deities principally adored at Elis. Minerva had a temple in the citadel, with an image of ivory and gold made, it was faid, by Phidias. At the gate leading to Olympia was the monument of a perfon, who was buried, as an Oracle had commanded, neither within nor without the city.

THE ftructures of Elis feem to have been raifed with materials far lefs elegant and durable than the produce of the Ionian and Attic quarries. The ruins are of brick, and not confiderable, confifting of pieces of ordinary wall, and an octagon building with niches, which, it is fuppofed, was the temple with a circular periftyle. Thefe ftand detached from each other, ranging in a vale fouthward from the wide bed of the river Peneus, which, by the margin has feveral large ftones, perhaps reliques of the Gymnafium. The citadel was on a hill, which has on the top fome remnants of wall. Olympia was diftant about three hundred ftadia or thirty feven miles and a half.

CHAP.

CHAP. LXXIV.

Set out for Olympia --- Arrangement of the coast --- At a monastery --- The night --- A tree-frog --- At Pyrgo --- Pitch our tent by a ruin --- Gnats.

WE had been visited in the garden at Gastouni by a Turkish Aga called Muláh or *The Virtuoso* Solyman, a person of some knowlege, uncommonly polite, and of a graceful deportment. He informed us, that he had seen ruins by Miraca, near the Rophia a very large river. The site and distance agreeing with Olympia, it was hoped, that spot would prove more important than Palæ-opolis. We left Callivia in the evening, and passing by some barrows, which probably were not far from the gate next Olympia, and afterwards by one in the plain, travelled with Gastouni behind us toward the sea.

THE arrangement of the coast to the south of Cyllene was as follows. After the mouth of the Peneus was Chelonatas, the most westerly promontory of the Peloponnesus, distant two miles from Cyllene; near which was a mountainous point called Hormina or Hyrmina. Next was Point Pheia, with an inconsiderable river of the same name near it; and before it an islet; and a port, distant one hundred and twenty stadia or fifteen miles from Olympia, going the nearest way from the sea. A cape succeeded, called Icthys, extending far out westward. This was one hundred and twenty stadia from the island Cephallenia, which was eighty stadia or ten miles from Cyllene. After Icthys was the mouth of the river Alpheus, distant two hundred and eighty stadia or thirty miles from Chelonatas, with a temple near it and a grove of Diana, eighty stadia or ten miles from Olympia. The whole region abounded in places sacred to Venus and to Diana; and, being well watered, in caves of the Nymphs.

Nymphs. By the roads were frequent ſtatues of Mercury; and on the capes, of Neptune. The iſlands called Strophades were thirty five miles from Zante.

We came to the ſea-ſide below Chelonatas, and travelled ſouthward to a monaſtery of the Panagia Scaphidia or *Virgin of the Skiffs*, ſituated on an eminence not far from Point Pheia, on the north; the beach ſo inſecure, that it is cuſtomary to load the boats on ſhore and then puſh them into the water. Near it is a lake fed by a ſmall ſtream, probably the ſtagnant water mentioned by Pauſanias, meaſuring about three ſtadia, on the road from Olympia to Elis by the plain. The ſupper-bell rung as we approached. We rode into the court, and ſaw the prieſts and monks ſeated at their reſpective tables, or in companies on the ground. We diſmounted, wondering that nobody ſtirred, or took any notice of us. We were informed afterwards, that they had miſtaken us for Frenchmen, and that their uſual courteſy had been witheld from national prejudices. The ſociety was in a flouriſhing ſtate, and had partly completed their deſign of rebuilding the monaſtery.

We were conducted to a good apartment, in which we ſupped. Afterwards ſome preferred ſleeping in the court, hoping to find the air cooler, and to be leſs moleſted by vermin; but innumerable gnats, which ariſe from the lake, diſturbed us with their continual buzzing, and preyed on us exceedingly. The poultry, which roofted cloſe by in a mulberry-tree, at dawn of day fluttered down from the branches in long ſucceſſion; and at our next ſtage we diſcovered that myriads of large fleas had taken poſſeſſion of the folds of our garments.

In the morning we made our early repaſt, as uſual, on fruit, bread and coffee. We were ready to depart, when one of my companions found a tree-frog in the garden. The back ſo exactly reſembled in colour the green leaf of a lemon-tree, on which it was ſitting, that the reptile was not eaſily to be diſtinguiſhed, tinguifhed, except by its lively eyes. It was fmall, and in fhape like a toad; the belly of an ugly pale, fpeckled, the hinder legs long. The toes, which are clammy, enable it to raife or let down its body, as it occafionally does, fometimes hanging by one foot, and to travel without danger over the bending foliage. It was unwieldy and inactive. On our fhaking the bough to put it in motion, it fell to the ground, tired perhaps with a former exertion; and lay as dead. Its chirping or filence are faid to be among the prognoftics of changes in the weather. The Greeks call it Spordaca. The fpecies is mentioned by Pliny.

In two hours we came to a village named Pyrgo, from a houfe in it with a tower. Upon a mount on the right hand was a caftle called Katacoli, near which veffels of burthen are laden; at the port, it is likely, mentioned as fifteen miles from Olympia. The whole plain from Elis affords but fcanty fhade. Sheds, covered with boughs, are the fhelter of the cattle at noon. The peafants were bufy at their harveft-work. The wheat-fheaves were collected about the floors; and horfes, running abreaft round a ftake, were treading out the grain. The habitations were very mean, chiefly low mud-built huts, many of an oval form, with a fence before them. We tarried at Pyrgo in a garden, while our men procured bread and other neceffaries, it being expected that our next *Conac* or refting-place would be deftitute of every thing.

When the heat of noon was over, we croffed a hilly country, and had frequent views of the Rophia or Alpheus, at a diftance. This portion of the road to Olympia was called *The mountainous*, to diftinguifh it from that nearer Elis, which was in the plain. The track by the bank of the river was deep-worn in a ridge of the mountain. From it we turned to the left up a valley, which there becomes more contracted; and in about four hours were near a ruin. The fun was fet, and we pitched our tent in a field, which had been fown with corn.

HERE

HERE gnats fwarmed around us innumerable, infefting us, if poffible, more terribly, than ever before. We endeavoured to fleep, in vain. Our Greeks too called on their Panagia, but were not relieved. It is related, Jupiter on a like petition from Hercules, whom they molefted while facrificing at Olympia, drove them all beyond the river; from which exploit he acquired the title of Apomuius or the *Fly-expeller:* and the Eleans, at the feafon of the Games, invoked him, facrificing a bull; when, it is faid, the gnats all perifhed; or, which is recorded as extraordinary, no infect being lefs docile and intelligent, retired in clouds out of the Olympic territory.

CHAP. LXXV.

Of Pifa --- Of Olympia --- Of the temple of Jupiter --- The ftatue --- The great altar --- Other altars --- Riches of Olympia --- Solemnity of the games --- Herodes a benefactor --- Ruin of Olympia.

OLYMPIA was in a region named Pifatis from a city which had been fubdued by the Eleans. The fite of Pifa was on an eminence between two mountains called Offa and Olympus; but in the time of Paufanias no wall or building remained, and it was planted with vines. This place had been rendered excefively illuftrious by the power and reputation of its antient princes, among whom were Œnomaus and Pelops; by the Oracle and temple of the Olympian Jupiter; by the celebrity of the grand Panegyris or general affembly held at it; and by the renown of the Agon or Games, in which to be victorious was deemed the very fummit of human felicity.

THE glory of Olympia was not diminifhed by the ruin of Pifa. The Altis or Sacred Grove was furrounded with a wall. Within

TRAVELS IN GREECE.

Within was the temple of Jupiter; and alfo a temple of Juno, fixty three feet long, with columns round it, of the Doric order; and a Metroum or temple of the mother of the gods, a large Doric edifice; with holy Treafuries, as at Delphi. Thefe, and the Porticoes, a Gymnafium, Prytanéum, and many more buildings, chiefly in the inclofure, with the houfes of the priefts and other inhabitants, made Olympia no inconfiderable place. The Stadium was in the grove of wild olive-trees, before the great temple; and near it was the Hippodrome or courfe for the races of horfes and chariots. The Alpheus flowed by from Arcadia with a copious and very pleafant ftream, which was received on the coaft by the Sicilian fea.

THE temple of Jupiter was of the Doric order, fixty eight feet high to the pediment, ninety five wide, and two hundred and thirty long; the cell encompaffed with columns. It was erected with the country-ftone; the roof, not of earth baked, but of Pentelic marble, the flabs difpofed as tiles; the way to it up a winding ftaircafe. The two pediments were enriched with fculpture, and one had over the centre a ftatue of Victory gilded; and underneath, a votive buckler of gold. At each corner was a gilded vafe. Above the columns were fixed twenty one gilded bucklers offered at the conclufion of the Achæan war by the Roman general Mummius. The gates in the two fronts were of brafs, and over them were carved the labours of Hercules. Within the cell, as in the Parthenon at Athens, were double colonnades, between which was the approach to the image.

THE Jupiter of Olympia was accounted alone fufficient to immortalize its maker, Phidias. It was of ivory and gold, the head crowned with olive. In the right hand was a ftatue of Victory; in the left, a flowered fceptre, compofed of various metals, on which was an eagle. The fandals were of gold, as alfo the veftment, which was curioufly emboffed with lilies and animals. The throne was gold inlaid with ebony and ivory,

and

and ſtudded with jewels, intermixed with paintings and exquiſite figures in relievo. The pillars between the feet contributed to its ſupport. Before it were walls, ſerving as a fence, decorated principally with the exploits of Hercules; the portion oppoſite to the door of a blue colour. It was the office of a family deſcended from Phidias, called Phædruntæ or *The Poliſhers*, to keep the work bright and clean. The veil or curtain was cloth rich with the purple dye of Phœnicia and with Aſſyrian embroidery, an offering of king Antiochus; and was not drawn up as in the temple of Diana at Epheſus, but was let down from above by looſing the ſtrings. The image impreſſed on the ſpectator an opinion that it was higher and wider than it meaſured. Its magnitude was ſuch, that though the temple was very large, the artiſt ſeemed to have erred in the proportions. The god, ſitting, nearly touched the ceiling with his head; ſuggeſting an idea, that if he were to riſe up, he would deſtroy the roof. A part of the pavement before it was of black marble, incloſed in a rim of Parian or white, where they poured oil to preſerve the ivory. Pauſanias has remarked, that the dry air and lofty ſituation of the citadel at Athens rendered water more proper for the Minerva in the Parthenon. He enquired why neither was uſed at Epidaurus, and was informed that the image and throne of Æſculapius ſtood over a well.

The altar of Jupiter Olympius was of great antiquity, and compoſed of aſhes from the thighs of the victims, which were carried up and·conſumed on the top with wood of the white poplar-tree. The aſhes alſo of the Prytanéum, in which a perpetual fire was kept on a hearth, were removed annually on a fixed day, and ſpread on it, being firſt mingled with water from the Alpheus. The cement, it was affirmed, could be made with that fluid only, and therefore this river was much reſpected, and eſteemed the moſt friendly of any to the god. On each ſide of the altar were ſtone ſteps. Its height was twenty two feet. Girls and women, when allowed to be at Olympia, were ſuffered to aſcend the baſement, which was an hundred and twenty five feet in circumference. The people of Elis facrificed daily, and private perfons as often as they chofe.

RELIGION flourifhed at Olympia, and many deities were worfhipped befides Jupiter. Paufanias has enumerated above fixty altars of various fhapes and kinds. One, of the *Unknown Gods*, ftood by the great altar. The people of Elis offered on all thefe, monthly; laying on them boughs of olive; burning incenfe, and wheat mixed with honey; and pouring libations of fuch liquors as the ritual prefcribed. At the latter ceremony fometimes a form of prayer was ufed, and they fung hymns compofed in the Doric dialect.

OLYMPIA preferved much longer than Delphi, and with lefs diminution, the facred property, of which it was a fimilar repofitory. Some images were removed by Tiberius Nero. His fucceffor Caius Caligula, who honoured Jupiter with the familiar appellation of brother, commanded that his image fhould be tranfported to Rome, but the architects declared it was impoffible without deftroying the work; and his commiffioner, Memmius Regulus, terrified by prodigies, ventured to apologize for a difobedience, which endangered his life. The God in the time of Paufanias retained his original fplendor. The votive offerings of crowns, and chariots, and of charioteers, and horfes, and oxen, in brafs, the pretious images of gold, ivory or amber, and the curiofities confecrated in the temples, the treafuries, and other edifices, could not be viewed without aftonifhment. The number of ftatues within the Altis or grove was itfelf an amazing fpectacle. Many were the works of Myron, Lyfippus, and the prime artifts of Greece. There kings and emperors were affembled; and Jupiter towered in brafs, of coloffal proportions, from twelve to near thirty feet high. The clafs of men and boys, conquerors in the games, in brafs, which was the largeft, continually increafed. The ftatue of a Roman fenator, who had been victorious, was

erecting,

TRAVELS IN GREECE. 293

erecting, when the collection was viewed by Paufanias. Let the reader perufe the detail given by that traveller, and imagine, if he can, the entertainment, which Olympia muft then have afforded to the conoiffeur, to the hiftorian, and the antiquary.

PAUSANIAS declares, that a perfon might fee many things wonderful to tell of, among the Greeks; but that the Olympic Agon or Games, with the Eleufinian Myfteries, partook in an efpecial manner of the deity. The former grand exhibition was conducted with prodigious folemnity. The order of the exercifes and the ceremonial were controlled by the Præfects, who were commonly ten or twelve in number, elected, one from each tribe of the Eleans. Thefe, and the competitors, were required to qualify by taking an oath, with dire imprecations, in the prefence of Jupiter Horcius. The terrible image ftood in the council-chamber, bearing in either hand avenging thunder; and a boar was the victim. The fpectators affembled in the Stadium, which was of earth, like that of Epidaurus, and had feats for the Præfects, who entered with the candidates by a private way. Oppofite to them was an altar of white marble, on which the prieftefs of Ceres fate; and before them on a table were laid crowns of oleafter or wild olive, made from a tree growing near the back front of the temple of Jupiter.

FROM the filence of Homer it has been argued, that the four great fpectacles of Games in Greece either did not exift, when he wrote, or were in no repute. That of Olympia, however, deduced its origin from remote antiquity, and continued to a late period, undergoing feveral alterations. Among its kindeft benefactors is reckoned Herodes, who was afterwards king of Judæa. Seeing on his way to Rome this relique of old Greece fubfifting in a manner unworthy of its former renown, and dwindling from poverty, he difplayed vaft munificence as Prefident, and provided an ample revenue for its future fupport and dignity; extending, it is faid, his liberality through the Eleans

to

to the whole world, which was interested in the prosperity of Olympia.

The computation of time by Olympiads, which began about four hundred years after the destruction of Troy, was used until the reign of Theodosius the Great; when a new mode of reckoning, by Indictions or from the victory of Augustus Cæsar at Actium, was introduced; the Olympic Games, with general assembly, were abolished; and the image made by Phidias was removed to Constantinople. Jupiter and Pelops were banished from the seat, which they had possessed for ages. Olympia has since been forgotten in its vicinity, but the name will be ever respected as venerable for its pretious æra by the chronologer and historian.

CHAP. LXXVI.

Vestiges of Olympia---Miráca---The river Alpheus.

EARLY in the morning we crossed a shallow brook, and commenced our survey of the spot before us with a degree of expectation from which our disappointment on finding it almost naked received a considerable addition. The ruin, which we had seen in the evening, we found to be the walls of the cell of a very large temple, standing many feet high and well-built, the stones all injured, and manifesting the labour of persons, who have endeavoured by boring to get at the metal, with which they weer cemented. From a massive capital remaining it was collected that the edifice had been of the Doric order. At a distance before it was a deep hollow, with stagnant water and brick-work, where, it is imagined, was the Stadium. Round about are scattered remnants of brick-buildings, and vestiges of stone-walls. The site is by the road-side, in a green valley, between two ranges of even summits pleasantly wooded. The mountain

TRAVELS IN GREECE. 295

mountain once called Cronium is on the north, and on the south the river Alpheus.

As Miráca was not far off we refolved to enquire there for other ruins. It was a fmall village on a hill, perhaps that of Pifa. Sheaves of wheat were collected about an area or two, and a few men with women and children were employed in harveft-work. Our approach occafioned fome alarm, and they appeared fhy, until we informed them of our bufinefs. We defcended again into the valley, and travelled up it for two hours. We then returned, and our men with difficulty procured fome fowls, on which we dined by the fhallow brook.

The Alpheus had now a majeftic ftream, which in winter is greatly increafed by torrents rufhing from the mountains. The wide bed on each fide was dry. It is accounted the largeft river in the country, and affords plenty of fifh. We faw a weir of ftakes made acrofs it, on which a man was watching, fitting under a fhed roofed with boughs, over the middle of the current.

C H A P. LXXVII

Journey of Mr. Bocher---Ruin of a temple---Near Phigalia.

Mr. JOACHIM Bocher, architect, a native of Paris, vifited us in the Lazaretto at Zante, which ifland he had adorned with feveral elegant villas. This gentleman in November, 1765, from Pyrgo croffed the Alpheus, and paffing by Agolinizza traverfed a wood of pines to Efidero, where is a Turkifh Khan. An hour beyond, leaving the plain by the fea, he began to afcend the mountains, and paffing by fome villages arrived at Vervizza at night. This was a long journey. His defign was to examine an antient building near Caritena. He was ftill

remote

remote from that place, when he perceived a ruin, two hours from Vervizza, which prevented his going any farther.

THE ruin called *the Columns* ſtands on an eminence ſheltered by lofty mountains. The temple, it is ſuppoſed, was that of Apollo Epicurius, near Phigalia, a city of Arcadia. It was of the Doric order, and had ſix columns in front. The number, which ranged round the cell, was thirty eight. Two at the angles are fallen; the reſt are entire, in good preſervation, and ſupport their architraves. Within them lies a confuſed heap. The ſtone inclines to gray with reddiſh veins. To its beauty is added great preciſion of execution in the workmanſhip. Theſe remains had their effect, ſtriking equally the mind and the eyes of the beholder.

PAUSANIAS deſcribes Phigalia as ſurrounded by mountains, of which one, named Cotylium, was diſtant about forty ſtadia or five miles. The temple of Apollo ſtood on this, at a place called Baſſæ. It was planned by the ſame architect as the Parthenon at Athens, and had a roof of ſtone. The Peloponneſians had no temple, one at Tegea excepted, ſo much celebrated for the beauty of the materials and the harmony of the proportions. The god was ſtyled Epicurius, from the aid he was ſuppoſed to have given in a peſtilence. The ſtatue, which was of braſs, and twelve feet high, had been removed, and was then in the agora or market-place of Megalopolis. This city, now called Leontari, was fifty ſtadia or ſix miles and a quarter in circuit. The river Heliſſon ran through it into the Alpheus.

CHAP.

CHAP. LXXVIII.

Our ſituation --- We return to Chiarenza --- Arrive at Zante --- Perform quarantine---Remove from the Lazaretto.

WE had experienced ſince our leaving Athens frequent and alarming indiſpoſition. We had ſuffered from fruits, not eaſily eaten with moderation; from fatigue; from the violent heat of the ſun by day, and from damps and the torments inflicted by a variety of vermin at night; beſides the badneſs of the air, which was now almoſt peſtilential on this ſide of the Morea. My companions complained. Our ſervants were ill; and the captain, whoſe brown complexion was changed to ſallow, had grown mutinous, and declared he would go away with his veſſel, as he muſt perform a long quarantine at Zante, if his return were delayed; the annual unhealthineſs of the Morea toward the end of harveſt requiring increaſe of caution, and the magiſtrates of the iſland reſtraining the intercourſe with the continent at that ſeaſon.

IN the afternoon we mounted for Pyrgo. We paſſed the night in the garden, in which we had ſtopped before; the gnats again moleſting us exceedingly. Irritated on finding our faces, hands, and legs carefully covered, the terrible inſect buzzed about us with a droning noiſe, which ſounded in the ear ſcarcely leſs loud than a trumpet. The following day we dined under a ſpreading tree near a clear ſpring among thickets; probably that called antiently Piera, in the way through the plain to Elis. There the Præfects of Olympia and the matrons choſen to preſide at the games in honour of Juno killed a pig and were purified with holy water, before they entered on their offices. We reſted in the garden at Gaſtouni, and ſet out early in the morning for Chiarenza; both my companions, with

ſome

some of our men, much indisposed. We found the Athenian lad, whom we had left behind ill of a tertian fever, mended. The sick sailor had embraced an opportunity, which offered, and was gone home to Zante.

WE sailed from Chiarenza on Sunday the twentieth of July, 1766; and the same evening entered the harbour of Zante, in which a squadron of Venetian ships of war under admiral Emo lay at anchor, waiting, as we were informed, for orders to proceed against the Dey of Algiers. We were hailed from the land, and the boat going ashore, the British consul John Sargint Esquire acquainted us that we must attend in the morning at the *Health-Office*. We were then ordered to the Lazaretto to perform a quarantine of fourteen days.

THE Lazaretto is by the sea-side at a distance from the town. We were lodged over our servants and baggage in a chamber without any furniture, the walls white-washed. The customary precautions were explained to us. In the evening our ward was regularly locked; and no body was permitted to see us but in the presence of our keeper. The Consul and English merchants visited us, and with the former came a physician; my companions and two of our servants being ill of a fever, which was ascribed to the bad air of the Morea. We continued to supply him with patients, until we left the island.

THE civility of the prior of the Lazaretto, and of the good fathers of the Latin convent adjoining, with the attention of our countrymen, rendered our confinement very tolerable. When the term was nearly expired, a small gratuity to the chancellor of the Health-Office obtained us a release. We paid our fees, as directed by the consul, and gave money to the guard of soldiers. In the evening we crossed in a boat to the town, where a lodging was provided. A capacious harbour filled, besides other vessels, with large ships and glittering gallies, a flourishing city with steeples and noble edifices, the sound of

bells,

bells, the drefs and manners of Italy, were all articles to which we had been long difufed. The ˌtranfition from mifery and defolation was as ftriking as it had been fudden. We drew a moft favourable contraft, and rejoiced on our fafe arrival in the happier regions of Chriftendom.

CHAP. LXXIX.

Of the ifland of Zante---The city---The Corinth-grape---Currants ---Extract from Herodotus---The tar-fprings---Remarks--- Earthquakes---Not able to proceed---Occurrences at Zante--- Embark for England.

ZANTE is a fmall ifland [1] belonging to the Venetians, full of villages and people; called by the Greeks Zákynthos. It confifts of two or three not very ample vallies, fheltered by high bare mountains, well cultivated, and rich in their produce as well as pleafant to the eye; the foil fuiting the vine and the olive, orange, lemon and citron-trees. Its wines and oil are defervedly extolled. Its melons and peaches are of uncommon fize and exquifite flavour. It has been ftyled not hyberbolically, *The Golden Ifland.* But room is wanting, and a confiderable portion of the profits arifing from currants, the ftaple commodity, is refunded for corn and cattle. They import live ftock daily from the Morea; and in tempeftuous weather a temporary famine not rarely enfues. The governor is appointed by the republic, and is fubject to the fuperior jurifdiction of a general, who refides alternately at the places under his command. We were introduced to this officer, who was then in the city, by

---

[1] In circuit more than one hundred and fixty ftadia or twenty miles, and fixty ftadia or feven miles and a half from Cephallenia. *Strabo.* In circuit thirty fix miles. *Pliny.*

the conful. The inhabitants are chiefly Greeks, but wear the Italian drefs, and are much latinized in their religious tenets and ceremonies. They are divided by internal feuds, and are exceedingly addicted to revenge, perpetrating affaffinations even in their churches. The Morea ferves them as it were for a fanctuary, and abounds in fugitives for murder and mifdemeanours.

The city of Zante extends along the fhore, and is adorned with feveral handfome ftructures. The Roman Catholics have their churches, nunneries, and convents, with various orders of friars ; and the Greeks, whom we had feen humble and depreffed, here rivalled the fplendid pomp of their worfhip. High above the town is a fteep round hill, crowned with a caftle ; the antient citadel, called Pfophis. The governor now lives below, but the fummit is inhabited, and fome religious houfes ftand on it. The reflexion of the fun renders the town extremely hot in fummer, but the inflamed air is then ufually tempered in the day-time by the fea-breeze. The harbour is open to the northeaft. One fide is formed by a lofty promontory, on which is the church and miraculous picture of *the glorious* Madonna di Scoppo, from whofe power and efficacious interceffion many fignal benefits, as they affirm, have been derived on the people. At the oppofite extremity, by the fea-fide, is a copious fountain of excellent water, fuppofed to come from the Morea, the ftream bringing leaves of trees and plants not growing in the ifland. The maidens are carefully concealed as in Turkey. I faw a woman in a houfe, with the door open, bewailing her little fon, whofe dead body lay by her, dreffed, the hair powdered, the face painted and bedecked with leaf gold.

The Corinth-grape, for which the ifland is now noted, was the produce chiefly of the country near the Ifthmus, when it began to be particularly efteemed. We were prefented with bunches newly ripened, while in the Lazaretto, and afterwards eat of them daily with much pleafure. It is a fmall fpecies, the clufters large, the colour black or a deep purple. The ftocks, as ufual, are planted in rows, and the leaf is bigger than in the common vine. As a good feafon for the harveft is of great confequence to the people, they generally implore the interceffion of their faints; folemnly vifiting their churches, the priefts and magiftrates and perfons of rank, both Italians and Greeks, walking in proceffion, in pairs, with lighted tapers in their hands. If thefe difappoint them, and the emergency require it, the glorious and miraculous picture of the Madonna di Scoppo is expofed, and fails not to influence the weather to their wifhes.

The grapes intended to be preferved as currants are fpread, when gathered, in beds on the ground. When dried by the fun and air, they are tranfported to the city on horfes and mules guarded by armed peafants; and poured down a hole into magazines, in which they cake together. When the price is fixed and the duties are paid, the fruit is dug out with iron-crows, and ftamped into cafks by men with legs and feet bare. In the fhips it fweats, and, as we experienced, often fills the veffel with a ftench fcarcely tolerable. The Englifh, who have two or three merchants refident there, are the principal confumers. The Dutch partake, and fupply the other northern nations. The iflanders believe it is purchafed to be ufed in dying, and in general are ignorant of the many difhes in which currants are an ingredient. Our cook made a pudding, which was equally a fubject of wonder and applaufe in the family where we lived.

The tar-fprings of Zante are a natural curiofity deferving notice. " I myfelf, fays the venerable hiftorian and traveller
" Herodotus, have feen tar brought up out of a lake and water
" in Zacynthus. And indeed the lakes are feveral, but the
" biggeft is feventy feet wide every way, and twelve deep.
" Into this they let down a pole with a myrtle-bough tied to
" it, and then bring up tar on the myrtle-bough, in fmell like
" to Afphaltus, in other refpects fuperior to the tar of Pieria.
" They then pour it down into a pit dug near the lake; and, when
" enough

"enough is collected, in like manner from the pit into earthen "veſſels. All that falls back into the lake, going under ground, "appears again in the ſea, which is diſtant about four ſtadia." The Pierian tar was reckoned the beſt made in Greece.

The tar is produced in a ſmall valley, about two hours from the town, by the ſea, and encompaſſed with mountains, except toward the bay; in which are a couple of rocky iſlets. The ſpring, which is moſt diſtinct and apt for inſpection, riſes on the farther ſide, near the foot of the hill. The well is circular, and four or five feet in diameter. A ſhining film, like oil, mixed with ſcum, ſwims on the top. You remove this with a bough, and ſee the tar at the bottom, three or four feet beneath the ſurface, working up, it is ſaid out of a fiſſure in the rock; the bubbles ſwelling gradually to the ſize of a large cannon-ball, when they burſt, and the ſides leiſurely ſinking, new ones ſucceed, increaſe, and in turn ſubſide. The water is limpid, and runs off with a ſmart current. After drinking of it, I was much heated. The ground near is quaggy, and will ſhake beneath the feet, but is cultivated. The grapes, of which we eat, were exquiſite. At ſome diſtance, oppoſite, are the other wells, ſo nearly contiguous as not eaſily to be counted, or indeed examined, the ſpot being mariſhy. Theſe have leſs waſte water, are deeper, of a ſtronger taſte, a blacker dye, and more ſullen aſpect. We filled ſome veſſels with tar, by letting it trickle into them from the boughs which we immerſed; and this is the method uſed to gather it from time to time into pits, where it is hardened by the ſun, to be barreled, when the quantity is ſufficient, and taxed as an article of the revenue. The odour reaches a conſiderable way. We were told that a ſpring exiſts likewiſe in the ſea, near the ſhore; and that the film floats on the ſmooth ſurface in calm weather.

Tar-furnaces are numerous in Turkey. They are formed in a bank, the bottom narrow; and filled with ſappy wood of pines, cleaved into pieces. A fire is kindled at the top, and, burning

burning downward, the juice, which diſtils, finds a paſſage out at a vent below. It has been conjectured, that the thick fluid ſubſtance emerging with the water is generated by a proceſs analogous to this ; ſubterraneous fire feeding on ſulphureous matter, of which a portion is diſcharged at theſe apertures. Our thermometer roſe in the air from ſeventy five to eighty degrees as the heat of the ſun increaſed during our ſtay, and in the different wells from ſixty four to ſeventy. A communication, it is ſuppoſed, may ſubſiſt between theſe and ſprings of a ſimilar nature by Dyrrachium and Apollonia, cities on the coaſt of Illyria ; and their common fountain may be ſome diſtant Volcano.

The tar is ſaid to be emitted moſt abundantly when the wind is weſterly, and when earthquakes happen. Theſe are frequent. Soon after our arrival in the Lazaretto, we felt a very ſmart ſhock, which did much damage in the neighbouring iſland of Cephallenia ; and was repeated, but with leſs violence, ſix times in the ſpace of about twenty four hours. The Zantiotes had been familiarized to this ſource of calamity, and the terror of it was then in a manner ſwallowed up in their apprehenſions for the approaching vintage.

On leaving Athens it was our purpoſe, after refreſhing at Zante, to proceed to Ithaca, Cephallenia, and Corfu, the countries of Ulyſſes and Alcinous; and from the latter iſland to Brindiſi and Naples. We were compelled to abandon that plan by the difficulty of procuring from Leghorn ſo large a ſum of money as was neceſſary, and, beſides other conſiderations, by the infirm ſtate of health, under which we laboured. The conſul accepted our bills for three hundred Venetian zechins; of which near one hundred and thirty were remitted to Mr. Paul the conſul at Patræ, who had moſt readily and obligingly ſupplied us to that amount. Our return to England was reſolved on, and we waited impatiently for the ſhips expected from Venice;

Venice; whither it is required that all veffels go before they lade with currants at Zante.

During our refidence in the city, the houfe of a perfon who had fled from juftice was razed to the ground by a party of foldiers; and the body of a ftate-prifoner, one Balfamachi of Cephallenia, who had been fent in irons from Conftantinople, was expofed for a day on a gallows. He fucceeded us in our apartments in the Lazaretto, and, when his quarantine expired, was privately ftrangled there, conveyed in a boat acrofs the harbour, and fufpended in the morning early; a paper hanging on his breaft, infcribed with his name, his country, and crime in capital letters.

Some fmaller veffels, which arrived, brought us intelligence that the Roman Emperor, Capt. Lad, and the Sea-horfe, Capt. James for London, were preparing to fail from Venice. We agreed for a paffage, and put our baggage and provifions on board the Roman Emperor, but were induced to remand them; and then fixed our hopes on the Sea-horfe. That fhip tarrying elfewhere, we embarked in the evening, on Sunday September the firft, New Stile, 1766, in the brig Diligence, Captain Long, carrying five men and two boys, bound for Briftol. After a ftormy and perilous voyage we anchored in King-road on the fecond of November; but the Sea-horfe was loft at Scilly on the eleventh of the following month.

www.ingramcontent.com/pod-product-compliance
Lightning Source LLC
Chambersburg PA
CBHW031859220426
43663CB00006B/693